The Hidden War: PTSD on the Front Lines

Memoirs of a Psychologist Treating Warriors at a Forward Operating Base in Afghanistan

by Constance Louie-Handelman, PhD

Clinical Psychologist

(former) Captain/Medical Service/US Army Reserve

Energy Psychology Press
Fulton, CA 95439
www.EnergyPsychologyPress.com
Cataloging-in-Publication Data

Name: Louie-Handelman, Constance, PhD
Title: The Hidden War: PTSD on the Front Lines – Memoirs of a Psychologist
Treating Warriors at a Forward Operating Base in Afghanistan /
by Constance Louie-Handelman, PhD
Description: First editon. | Fulton, CA: Energy Psychology Press, 2018.
Identifiers: ISBN 978-1-60415-268-5 | ISBN 978-1-60415-269-2 (ebook)
Subjects: 1. Afghanistan War, 2001 – Personal narrative, American. 2. Louie-
Handelman, Constance. 3. Officers-United States-Biography. I. Title.

DS371.413.E87 2018
958.104/740973-dc23

© 2018 Constance Louie-Handelman, PhD

Cover design by Victoria Valentine
Editing by Stephanie Marohn • Typesetting by Karin Kinsey
Typeset in ITC Galliard and Franklin Gothic Medium
First Edition • Printed in Canada by Marquis Book Printing
10 9 8 7 6 5 4 3 2 1

Author's Note

The events and people in this book are real. However, to respect the privacy of all clients and certain individuals whose lives have touched mine, the names, ranks, and identifying details of the people mentioned in the book have been changed.

Although I kept a daily journal to move along the days, the many monotonous days, this book highlights certain events and counseling sessions while omitting others.

All photographs are courtesy of the author, except where noted.

*This book is dedicated to all veterans who were willing
to wear the uniform to bear the responsibility of our national defense.
Your service will never be forgotten.*

*Preventing war is much better than protesting against the war.
Protesting the war is too late.*

—Thich Nhat Hanh, *Being Peace*

Contents

Prologue

The helicopter blades swirled the summer's hot dusty air against my face. I climbed up the ramp and stepped inside the copter cabin. My rucksack, body armor, and weapon seemed heavier than ever. I dropped into the nearest seat, adjusted my helmet and rifle, and cinched my seat belt tight. At last, after 16 months of preparing for this day, I was flying over southern Afghanistan to my assigned forward operating base. Only minutes after taking off, the helicopter's two door gunners were rapidly firing rounds from their machine guns. My breath caught in my throat. Glancing around uneasily at the edgy faces of the other passengers, I wondered if I'd even get to fulfill the duty I'd signed up for—I could get killed before I had a chance to land in country!

Enlisting

Two years earlier, in 2009, I had read a disturbing article about the increasing number of suicides among active and reserve military personnel. The reported veteran suicide rate was 29.5 per 100,000, roughly 50% higher than the rate among the civilian population. The article said 22 veterans take their own lives each day. It cited possible reasons as two questionable wars, lengthy and multiple deployments, physical and mental injuries, depression, substance abuse, family stress, and financial strain. The article ended with a call for psychologists.

I discovered that the US Army Reserve was recruiting and had a program called the Officer Accession Pilot Program, which offered qualified medical professionals between the ages of 42 and 60 an initial appointment as an Army Medical Department officer, with a two-year military service obligation. At 56 years old, I was apprehensive, but I needed to follow my gut and my strong desire to help. I called and arranged an appointment with an army health care recruiter, and on March 5, 2009, I walked into her small office.

This was the beginning of a long application process that included a background check; lengthy questioning; verification of my education, training, and previous employment; character references; proof of my mother's citizenship; and, finally, a physical examination. I wrote the following as part of my application:

My motivation for serving with the United States Army Reserve Health Care Team is to provide vital mental health services to soldiers and their families. Learning about the Army's 2008 suicide rates, I was saddened by the distressing statistics. I would like to offer my 13 years of experience as a licensed clinical psychologist. I have worked in the community, a university counseling center, and hospitals as a member of a professional team assisting the seriously mentally ill, and with young adults adjusting to life challenges. I was also a clinical director with a staff of 30 overseeing the care of 600 outpatients. Lastly, as a former police officer, I understand the reluctance of people in uniform asking for help. I hope that this trend is changing and quality and compassionate care are available to those seeking it.

At this period of my life, I cannot think of anything I would rather do than to be a part of something as important as the Army Reserve Health Care Team: healing soldiers' lives.

Being a member of the military is in my blood. I come from a family of Chinese-Americans who have a history of serving in the armed forces. My father, born and raised in San Francisco, volunteered and served as a gunner's mate in the US Navy in the Pacific during WWII. My nephew, a Marine Corps reservist, was deployed to Iraq in 2009. As the first female in our family to join the military, I was continuing the trend. (A year later, my niece joined the US Army Reserve Dental Corps.)

Author's father circa 1942.

Niece, nephew, and author.

The army recruiter made it clear that there was a strong probability I would be deployed to Iraq or Afghanistan. I was excited about the idea, and yet there was a side of me that didn't want to deploy. Was I willing to risk my life? Could I endure the hardships of war? Could I do it at my age?

My husband, Rob, was supportive, although I think he quietly hoped that I wouldn't be selected. In 29 years of marriage, he had repeatedly witnessed my extremely independent nature and my determination and ambition in all things in life. When I set goals, I achieved them.

And at that point in my life, I was ready for another challenge. From 1979 to 1991, I had worked as a police officer in San Francisco. After a patrol injury—I tripped on a curb (ouch) chasing a robbery suspect at night and had to get surgery on my left ankle—I was assigned light duty. I spent five years in the police academy as a recruit training officer for the newly hired police officers. During this time, I trained as a peer counselor in order to offer guidance when officers came to me with their concerns. This led me to night classes at the University of San Francisco on marriage and family counseling. After graduating with a master's degree, I had a hunger to learn even more. So I resigned my position at the SFPD and earned my doctoral degree in clinical psychology.

After I received my psychology license in 1996, I worked as a clinical supervisor and, later, clinical director for a community-based agency in Oakland, California. The clients we served were mainly Asians with chronically severe mental illnesses. As clinicians, our job was to educate the client and family members about the illness, how to deal with the stigma, and the importance of medication compliance so that the client could continue to live in the community. Feeling burned out, I walked away from my job in 2005. After being a police officer and a clinical director—equally demanding and challenging jobs—I was ready for another adventure. When I was officially accepted into the Army Reserves, a good friend of mine observed, "You just combined your last two jobs into one!"

On March 12, 2010, one year and seven days after I started the process, I proudly raised my right hand for my oath of office and was sworn in as a captain in the US Army Reserve. My army recruiter had provided guidance and support throughout the past year. She drove me to Travis Air Force Base in Solano County, California, and helped me select the required Army Combat Uniform (ACU), boots, PT (physical training) uniform, beret, and cap. My orders soon arrived: I was to report to the 2D (Second) Medical Brigade in San Pablo, California. This was my first battle assembly weekend.

Fortunately, I had the right schooling and training as a psychologist. In 1993, prior to the last year of my doctoral clinical psychology program, I had applied for an American Psychological Association internship. These internships are accredited training programs in professional psychology. They are highly sought after and extremely competitive throughout the country. There were three APA internships in the Bay

Area. I applied to two of them and was accepted to the Richmond Area Multi-Services in San Francisco. The agency offered comprehensive, culturally competent mental health services in psychotherapy, testing, and assessment. The training also included a rotation to the SF General Hospital psychiatric inpatient ward. Little did I know that 17 years later my APA accredited graduate program and internship gave me entrée to the US Army. Even with a current license to practice, I couldn't have joined without the APA requirements. Lucky I was competitive and had pursued the best training.

On May 1, 2010, at 0730 hours, standing erect and watching the raising of the US flag, I was in formation with 70 soldiers, filled with pride at wearing my new uniform. Though it was a comfortably warm morning, I had goose bumps on my arms from excitement. I was in partial disbelief that, at 57 years old, I was now a member of the US Army Reserve. How could I be member of the army? This seemed surreal.

I was surprised when the brigade colonel called my name and asked me to stand next to him in front of the formation. As he introduced me to the unit, he proclaimed that freedom isn't free, that sacrifices are made so that Americans can enjoy freedom. In that moment, my mind embraced those words. I thought I understood them, but I couldn't yet know the extent of the sacrifices my husband and I would make over the following years.

Training, Training, Training

What is it like to be a reservist, working one weekend a month? Well, there were times I would sit and leisurely read magazines, and there were other times I could barely keep up with the weekend activities. There were required briefings, training, issuing of equipment, firearms qualification, and paperwork. Besides that, I had to learn a whole new language. The army uses so many acronyms, from TA-50 and RFO to RST and PHA to BLS and APFT. There are different names for the same item; for example, the standard-issue helmet is called a Kevlar or K-pod, brain bucket, or ACH (advanced combat helmet).

I discovered that I wasn't assigned to do any clinical work with soldiers during the weekends. Instead, being a reservist meant being on standby for deployment overseas or mobilization stateside. A psychologist—a lieutenant colonel—served as my mentor, but a few months later he resigned his commission because his name was on an upcoming deployment list. After that, there was a clinical social worker I could go to with questions, but I was disappointed that I wasn't called upon to counsel any soldiers.

As a trained psychologist, the army didn't have to teach me how to do my job, but they did need to teach me how to be a soldier. I had to attend BOLC (Basic Officer Leader Course), a 26-day in-residence training at Fort Sam Houston, Texas. Before I could attend the training, however, I had to complete another round of physical exams, vision tests, hearing tests, inoculations, dental X-rays and exams, and verification of my credentials. This was time-consuming and frustrating. My health hadn't changed since I had started this process, nor had my credentials, yet the army is a large bureaucracy and soldiers must do what they are told.

BOLC classes were always full, so it required a year to enroll in one. The medical command reserved me a spot in the February 25 to March 21, 2011 class. The command wanted me to complete my basic training so that I could deploy to Iraq with the 113th CSC (Combat Stress Control) around June 2011. While waiting for BOLC to start, I attended the Center of Deployment Psychology (CDP) training February 1–10, 2011, in Bethesda, Maryland.

The CDP trains all military branches of social workers, psychologists, and chaplains. Many of the attendees were near the end of their schooling and some were already licensed. We focused on traumatic brain injury (TBI) and posttraumatic stress disorder (PTSD), as well as sleep hygiene (a variety of different practices that are necessary to have normal, quality nighttime sleep and full daytime alertness), Prolonged Exposure (PE), and Cognitive Processing Technique. Experts in the field provided the training. As I chose to focus on PE, I went through the research-based protocol as a "clinician" and as a "client." PE is a type of therapy that helps decrease distress about one's trauma. This therapy focuses on repeated exposure to traumatic thoughts, feelings, and situations to help reduce the power they have at causing distress. Overall, it was a good, organized overview of best practices of treating military personnel with PTSD.

What is PTSD? It's an anxiety disorder from exposure to an extremely traumatic event that evokes intense fear or horror that persists long after the event is over. After experiencing the training, I must admit that I wouldn't use PE, as it was too structured, required too many sessions, and was too painful for the client to relive the trauma. I believed in another therapy that would be more successful and better utilized by soldiers.

———————

In nearly two decades in the field of psychotherapy, I was trained in many therapy approaches. I wasn't committed to any particular approach, but constantly in search of techniques that would help my many complex clients. I studied marital counseling, psychodynamic therapy, cognitive behavioral therapy, Eye Movement Desensitization and Reprocessing (EMDR,) hypnosis, Neuro-Linguistic Programming, and, finally, Emotional Freedom Techniques (EFT). I particularly found the EFT material effective for many therapeutic issues since it reduces the stress response and helps restore balance to the mind and body.

––––––––––––––––

Where CDP moved smoothly, BOLC was definitely more challenging. First, I didn't receive orders to attend the class until the morning I had to leave for Fort Sam Houston. Apparently, it turned out I didn't have a reserved spot. But at the last minute, there was an opening in the class. After a few stressful phone calls from my unit to confirm flight times and that I was able to attend, I packed quickly, headed to the airport in the late afternoon, and arrived at the fort at 0200 hours (2 a.m.). During the lodging check-in, I noted a post that my report time to class was at 0415 hours sharp—two hours later. So no sleep that night. After I unpacked, I waited uneasily in the lobby and then followed other soldiers to the meeting site.

The processing included briefings, paperwork, and height and weigh-in. Dressed in my PT (physical training) uniform, I measured 64.5 inches tall and weighed 110 pounds. Then we were issued our TA-50s: sleeping bag, Kevlar (helmet), LBV (load bearing vest), two canteens, canteen cups, canteen pouches, ammo pouches, rainwear, rain boots, laundry bag, protective eyewear, and a duffle bag.

Fort Sam Houston is located in the heart of San Antonio, Texas. The post is the birthplace of military aviation and the concept of airborne operations. The post evolved into the "Home of Army Medicine" after WWII and into the "Home of Military Medicine" with the establishment of the Medical Education and Training Campus in 2010. Most of our "classroom" lectures were in a large, modern auditorium. My entering class had 125 students, approximately one-third women. We were part of a larger training group already in process, so in total the AMEDD BOLC Class 11-112 was 380 army strong, approximately one-quarter women.

What really surprised me, though, was the fact that the classes at Fort Sam Houston were only for a few days, and the bulk of the training was on the field at Camp Bullis, about an hour and a half away by bus. We would only return to Fort Sam on the weekends. In the middle of the day, the camp was blistering hot, and as soon as the sun set, the temperature dropped quickly to a bone-chilling cold. At Camp Bullis, everyone lived in large green tents that housed 30 soldiers, sleeping on narrow canvas cots, with our duffle bags being our only private spaces. Generally, we had one or two hot meals a day; the rest of the time, we ate MREs (meals, ready to eat). We were only allowed one shower a week—in a trailer. Depending on your unit and gender, the shower days and times rotated from week to week. My tent smelled of foot powder and baby wipes. I really missed a daily shower.

Now at 58 years old, the oldest female in the BOLC class, did I regret joining the army? Without hesitation, the answer is no. There was one moment, however, the first night in the tent, shivering from the cold, stuffed in my sleeping bag, lying on my cot in complete darkness, I confess I wanted to quit. Of course I realized that I couldn't quit, that I wouldn't quit. I peeled back my sleeping bag, fished in my duffle bag for my army fleece jacket, and wrapped myself in it. Once warm, I felt better and fell asleep.

If I experienced any doubts or fears, the sheer intensity and exhaustion of field training distracted me from them. I was assigned to the Alpha Company 187 Med Brigade, 3rd Platoon (66 soldiers). Each morning there was a formation of six platoons at 0500 hours for accountability, and then the reciting of the Soldier's Creed and singing of the Army Song. I often didn't return to the tent until 12 hours later. The evening continued with another formation to hear the announcement of the next day's tasks, a quick dinner, and night classes on medical operations. Then my day was over.

Field training rotated platoons through different phases: land navigation during the day and at night; convoy tactics, techniques, and procedures; shooting and taking apart and reconnecting the M16 rifle and

9mm handgun; low and high crawling; setting up perimeter security; setting up the radio and requesting a MEDEVAC 9-line radio; being strapped in and getting out of a controlled rolled-over Humvee; and Chemical Biological Radiological Nuclear training, which included donning a gas mask and then being gassed in a gas chamber.

My first field training was learning how to low crawl while cradling my rifle in my arms. Soon my brand-new uniform was filthy and my tan boots scuffed. My elbows and knees were scraped and bruised from jagged rocks on the ground. After 10 feet of crawling, I was exhausted, but I had another 15 feet to go. Determinedly, I completed it, albeit slowly.

In preparation for the APFT (Army Physical Fitness Test), we had PT training early mornings before breakfast. The outdoor field was dark, with an area lit by a portable generator light tower. The mornings were bitingly cold, so between our push-ups and sit-ups we would huddle briefly around the generator for warmth.

The chow hall at Camp Bullis was a large barren room with an entrance and an exit on opposite ends. Assigned soldiers were on two sides, dishing out hot and cold prepared food. There weren't tables but only outdoor benches or chest-high shelves where we could place our food trays and eat standing up. The food was far from the delicious variety and quality that I had enjoyed eating in San Francisco all my life. The city offers an array of delightful Burmese, French, Thai, Vietnamese, Italian, Mexican, Chinese, and African foods. Apparently the army embraces a set menu with identical preparations, with quality and taste akin to what I ate in my middle school's cafeteria—aka blah.

I had to eat quickly so that I had time to fill my water canteens, use the Porta Potty, attend class, prepare my uniform and equipment for the next day, wash up, and get to sleep on my cot as early as possible. With eyeshades and earplugs (and, of course, being exhausted), I fell asleep easily, despite the lights being on and other soldiers talking before the required lights-out at 2200 hours.

When we couldn't eat at the chow hall, we ate MREs. Eating my first MRE was fun. It was like a game, learning how to open the packets and heat it up. But after that, eating MREs was dreadful. The food was awful. It didn't matter what name was on the dish packet, such as barbecued pork rib or cheese tortellini in tomato sauce, it all tasted like cardboard. MREs have around 1,250 calories, and they made me constipated. The best food items were the occasional energy bars that I could save and eat later. I was always in awe watching soldiers devour the MREs, evidently enjoying every bite.

Though I wasn't fond of army chow, I did enjoy firearms training. With my prior law enforcement background, handling and shooting weapons was familiar and fun. Carrying the M16 rifle over my shoulder was tiring and painful, however, as it constantly kicked against one spot on the back of my leg. The resulting bruise turned colors that lasted the entire time I had to carry a rifle, and for weeks after. Imagine carrying an M16 wherever you go, even to the Porta Potty at three in the morning! During the first week at Camp Bullis, one soldier was missing his weapon, which was found by an instructor. Everyone was called to formation late in the evening and we stood there until the soldier who misplaced his weapon came forward. Surprisingly, that wasn't the only time a soldier misplaced his or her weapon during my stay at Camp Bullis. You'd think someone couldn't possibly misplace an M16!

Unlike weapons training, I wasn't fond of being gassed. I had previously experienced being gassed while training to become a police officer. When one leaves the chamber, it isn't pretty: gasping for air, uncontrollable coughing, snot dripping, and eyes shut tight with burning, watery pain. From past experiences, I knew to go with the first group, before the gas built up in the chamber.

I was grateful not only for having been a police officer but also for being a student of yoga. When you are upside down in a rolled-over Humvee, your head is pressed against the ceiling and it feels like your throat is being constricted, making it difficult to breathe. However, sitting there, upside down, I noticed it is similar to Halāsana, an inverted yoga pose, where the trunk and legs are taken over one's head. Since I had experienced this sensation many times in my yoga practice, I wasn't startled or fearful. I kept breathing evenly until I was released from all of my seat belts.

I anticipated the land navigation training would be the most challenging for me because my sense of direction is terrible. After the class instruction on how to determine location, distance, elevation, azimuth, and grid coordinates, I asked a young, impassive, no-nonsense army ranger if he'd be my partner during the practical exercise. Fortunately, he said yes. But unfortunately, he was determined to reach all four points, instead of the minimum three points needed before returning to the starting area within the time limit. Under the hot blazing sun, carrying my weapon and canteens of water, I walked up and down miles of mountainous terrain, trying to keep up with the vigorous ranger. We reached all four points, with plenty of time to spare, and as we walked back I asked him to teach me the words of the Army Song to help pass the time. "First to fight for the right, and to build the Nation's might…"

On the medical side of our training, we learned to set up tents, triage patients, carry litters, and load and unload patients from trucks and helicopters. This was extremely strenuous. When carrying soldiers on litters, I tried to grab the lightest end, the feet. Even then it's heavy and sometimes, depending on how far we had to walk or run, I needed help. Would I have to do this in a combat zone? I hoped not, but if necessary, I would.

Along the way of learning army terminology, meeting the physical demands of training, getting exhausted, sunburned, dirty, bruised, and adapting to the long days, I met some amazing people. I think this is one of the greatest benefits of being in the army. When I was in the police department in the early 1980s, most men weren't welcoming of women, and were generally not nice or supportive. I found men and women in the army, however, to be friendly, helpful, amusing, and considerate. Perhaps this was because it was 30 years later and I was working with health care professionals, or perhaps because we were a volunteer army, but I was grateful to find my colleagues comfortable to be with and engaging. I spoke with soldiers from different parts of the United States, some originally from Nigeria, Puerto Rico, and China—with first names of Olaigbe, Arcaya, and Xiao. They all had distinctive stories framed by their backgrounds, beliefs, and values.

Nearing the end of BOLC training was the dreaded four-mile road march. Some soldiers would say it's nothing, but wearing a Kevlar helmet and Mollie vest, and carrying two full canteens, an assault pack (25–30 pounds), and an M-16 rifle (7.5 pounds unloaded) under the hot sun was difficult for me. An earlier two-mile march to and from the gas chamber training revealed that I had a difficult time keeping up with the group. After being physically active my entire life, I was disappointed in myself. I hadn't anticipated this would be a drawback. Although I could complete the distance, I couldn't do it at the faster pace.

There were talks between my platoon leader and squad leader that I might be excused from doing the four-mile march, but on that morning, my platoon leader confirmed that I'd have to do it. I was placed in the front of my platoon to set the pace, but three-quarters of a mile into the march, a soldier tripped and hurt her arm badly. She needed a "battle buddy" until she could receive medical care. (We later learned she actually broke her arm.) I was "volunteered" by members of my platoon, so I rode in a truck the rest of the way, no longer holding back my group. It was funny how things turned out.

———————

Throughout my life, I treasured my athletic skill and considered it a blessing. It came to me easily. As a young girl, my athletic aptitude was developed during physical education classes and on weekends playing softball with my classmates at a playground. Or I'd just climb over the nearby schoolyard's seven-foot high fence and play tennis or basketball. Often I'd throw a softball or football with my brothers until it got dark. I was definitely a tomboy who preferred physical activities to cooking, sewing, or reading.

By the time I was in high school, I signed up for the afterschool activity of fencing. I was tired of participating in the usual sports like volleyball, tennis, and softball, and was curious. By the end of the semester, however, I decided to drop it, not caring for it and finding it rather difficult. But a few months later, a member of the high school fencing team asked if I would consider being on the team. Wow, I thought, to be on a school varsity team, wear the school's colors, and travel to other schools for competitions. I'd never done anything like that before, so of course I said yes.

Little did I know this decision would affect the rest of my life.

———————

After 26 days of intensive training, we had our graduation in an open field at 0800 hours. The ceremony was short, with one speaker, nothing inspirational, just a formality.

Only five days after returning home from BOLC, I flew back to San Antonio to attend the Combat and Operational Stress Control (COSC) class. This was a five-day course required by all behavioral health professionals ready to deploy. With no field training, the course was held in a comfortable, air-conditioned hotel conference room. It covered a wide range of situations one would encounter in Iraq and Afghanistan: traumatic event management, a unit needs assessment, drug/alcohol assessment and treatment, sleep hygiene, deaths, and deployment stresses. This was my first time meeting other psychologists in the army. As we had lunch together, I listened to their genuinely moving stories and their reasons for joining the military. Like me, they wanted to help soldiers.

I learned that the COSC program was the commander's program, which meant the commander of the unit—not the soldier—was the client. I would be able to make recommendations how best to help the soldier, but the unit commander would have the final say. My primary task would be to help soldiers return to the mission by learning coping skills. I was not to be seen as a travel agent who sent soldiers home. (Of course, there were circumstances when sending soldiers home was definitely justified and necessary.) All of the speakers emphasized the need for behavioral health professionals to be outside the wire (outside the base) to get to know the soldiers and their tasks. Bonding with the soldiers, becoming someone they trusted, would make it more probable that they would seek help.

The first day at COSC, I discovered that there were soldiers from the 113th CSC (Combat Stress Control) unit, the unit that I'd deploy with to Iraq. Halfway through the first day, however, someone from the 113th announced the unit's mission had changed from Iraq to Afghanistan.

Whoa! Wait a minute! I was mentally ready to go to Iraq, but not to Afghanistan, where the war was still in full tilt. To make matters worse, there was speculation that I would have to attend a 21-day pre-mobilization training at Fort Hunter-Liggett (in California) soon after the COSC class. Still recovering from field bruises and peeling sunburn, I was tired and didn't want any more training. I needed more time to adjust to the news, but time wasn't on my side.

Five days after I returned home from Texas, I was finishing lunch and cracked open a fortune cookie. The fortune read: "You will soon be crossing desert sands for a fun vacation." That evening, I received my orders: I was deploying with the 113th CSC to Afghanistan. I'd be there for nearly a year.

Since joining the Army, I'd been preparing myself for deployment by reading *The Girls Come Marching Home: Stories of Women Warriors Returning from the War in Iraq*, by Kirsten Holmstedt; *Rule Number Two: Lessons I Learned in a Combat Hospital*, by Dr. Heidi Squier Kraft; and *War*, by Sebastian Junger. Rob and I watched *Restrepo*, a documentary that chronicles the deployment of a platoon in Afghanistan. Watching the nightly news about the wars had only given me a detached feeling, but reading the books made it more real, albeit from each authorial point of view. In any case, I'd soon find out for myself what war is like.

Pre-Mobilization

On April 14, I hopped on a shuttle from my home to San Jose Airport's USO building, where I met my first sergeant from the 113th CSC unit. He was exactly what I imagined a career soldier to be: standing tall in a well-fitted uniform, with a ruddy chiseled face, gray hair in a crew cut, and a blunt personality. From there, 15 of us traveled by van for the three hours to Fort Hunter-Liggett, located 25 miles southwest of King City, California. Arriving at the fort, I carried my duffle bag to a 40-bunk barrack and ended up on a top bunk. I would have preferred a lower bunk, but there were none, as the 113th CSC women soldiers were sharing the barrack with another unit. I was at least happily satisfied that there were beds, lockers, showers, and flush toilets, unlike at Camp Bullis.

The 113th CSC Medical Detachment consisted of 44 soldiers. There was Col. Rabb, commander; his executive officer (XO), Capt. Gillespie; 1st Sgt. Schumacher; and several psychologists, social workers, occupational therapists, and behavioral health specialists, along with administrative staff. There was a wide range of ages, from 19 to me, the oldest member of the unit. The young soldiers were full of energy, both nervous and excited about the upcoming deployment. For some, there was endless chatter, laughter, and listening and dancing to music. Others were quiet, going off to the laundry room and talking softly on their cell phones. I had learned that a few had joined the army for the educational benefits while others were pursuing a career in the military. I learned of three soldiers in the unit who saw it as an opportunity to get away from poverty, dysfunctional families, and abuse, and as an opportunity to travel. One woman had enlisted and hoped to become an officer after completing her college degree.

Many of the older soldiers had careers as behavioral health professionals in their civilian lives and had joined the army to offer their expertise and support. My commander and another officer were previously deployed and worked for the Department of Veterans Affairs. As part-time soldiers and part-time civilians, they were already familiar with the challenges of deployment and soldiers returning home. Other officers in the unit had begun their career in the army as enlisted soldiers, who then moved up the ranks and received their commission (officer status) upon completing their college education. For many, this was their first deployment to the Middle East; it was necessary to go and they hoped they would be promoted later.

The older soldiers were mainly worried about surviving the next three weeks of training. I was, too. It wasn't clear how physically demanding it would be. At least a road march wasn't on the schedule!

What was on the schedule was an introduction to different weapons, qualification on the M16 rifle/M9 handgun, first aid, land navigation, combative training, urban operations, convoy operations, counter-IED (improvised explosive device) training, how to establish security, and how to evacuate a casualty. Most days began with waking up at five in the morning, breakfast at six, and first formation at seven. One benefit of sharing a barrack with 39 other soldiers was that I didn't have to set my alarm clock—at least 30 different alarms went off every morning.

The trainings themselves weren't difficult. All the instructors were excellent and wanted to ensure our success. What was difficult was wearing and carrying all the required equipment: boots, ACU (Army Combat Uniform), CamelBak hydration system, assault backpack, Kevlar (helmet), IBA (armor vest), and the M16 rifle with a scope. This collection of combat gear is called "full battle rattle," or "kit." It weighed 35–40 pounds. The weight was especially noticeable when walking up a hill, which we had to do most days in mid-80-degree temperatures. Once we got to the top of the hill, breathing heavily, sweating, and legs weak, we needed to rest a few minutes before continuing to the classroom.

One afternoon between trainings there was an informal competition to take apart and put together a M249 Squad Automatic Weapon (SAW) light machine gun. This was voluntary, and since I'd never touched one before, I wasn't interested. There were, however, seven male soldiers sitting on the floor each with a SAW, practicing for this event. I noticed one young junior enlisted soldier, "Mike," repeatedly complete the process with ease. In the meantime, Sgt. "Paul" was fast, but struggling from time to time, and therefore slower than Mike. During a break in the practice, I approached Paul.

"Sarge, I'm a sports psychologist. Would you mind trying something to help you perform better?"

I'm not sure if he was just humoring me or it was because of my rank, but Paul said, "Yes, Ma'am."

I quickly told him about EFT, or Emotional Freedom Techniques, also known as "tapping." It's a version of acupuncture, except it doesn't use needles. By tapping two fingers on certain (meridian) acupoints on the face and torso, it affects the flow of the body's energy and releases disturbing emotions, such as fear, depression, and anxiety. It also eases or eliminates physical pain, alleviates stress, clears limiting beliefs, and has been found to be helpful in cases of PTSD. I'd been using EFT for the previous six years in my private practice for sports performance enhancement, and I found it effective and easy to teach to others.

In Paul's case, feeling anxious and pressured to go as fast as possible, he made mistakes.

"Sarge, follow me and say what I say." While tapping on the side of the hand, we said, "Even though I'm nervous, I deeply and completely accept myself." We did this three times.

Next, Paul tapped a few times on his collarbone, then under his eye, his collarbone, and on his side under his arm as he said the word, "Nervous." (Generally, for sports, I learned to use this shortened version of the standard EFT tapping protocol.) Completing the tapping, I then had Paul slowly practice taking apart the SAW, placing each of the dozen pieces beside him on the floor in a specific place so that he could easily retrieve them. Just prior to the competition, I had Paul tap again for being nervous. Within minutes, the competition started. Mike and Paul were even, but soon Mike took the lead. Twenty seconds later Paul caught up, but Mike quickly went ahead again. Toward the end, a minute and a half into the competition, Paul took the lead and held on to win. Paul joyfully jumped up off the floor and pointed toward me and shouted, "My coach! My coach!"

I was thrilled for Paul's victory.

While at Fort Hunter-Liggett, I had to go through the Soldier Readiness Processing Center (SRP). The army wanted every soldier to have current immunization shots, blood draws for HIV and glucose (if over 40 years old), complete medical, dental, hearing, and vision exams, and to meet with legal, financial, human resources, as well as the chaplain. I had to go to each station, each of which required a sign-off. There wasn't a mandatory sequence, so I tried to find the shortest lines. Others had friends hold their place in one line while they went through another. Regardless, it was an all-day process, as nearly 150 other soldiers were preparing to go to Kuwait, Iraq, or Afghanistan. There was no formal lunch break. A book, a tablet, or a game on the smartphone helped pass the time.

During the 21 days of training, the 113th CSC unit transitioned from reservists to active-duty soldiers. About 40% of the unit was cross-level—that is, not originally assigned to the organic unit—so there were many new faces, different personalities, different ranks, and different expectations about deployment.

My commander, Col. Rabb, is African-American and a licensed social worker, which lent me some comfort, as he understood the profession from a minority point of view. The commander asked me to be the unit's counselor. This isn't an official army position, but the commander had found that having someone in this position had been helpful for him and his unit in Iraq seven years earlier. I was flattered but had mixed feelings about accepting the position. I was already overwhelmed with the day-to-day training and I was concerned that the added responsibilities might be too much. Other officers were more experienced than I was, and my lack of experience in the army might be seen as a limitation. Despite this awareness, I realized I could provide the unit with a fresh point of view.

So I said yes and asked the colonel for a written description of the position so that I fully understood my role.

This truly provided me a chance to do what I had originally desired to do: counsel soldiers. Within the first week of training, I was set to work, as several leaders were concerned about a young female soldier. Pfc. (Private 1st Class) Gestar was distracted, teary, and anxious.

"Your squad leader is worried about you," I said.

"I'm not sure I can do this…"

"What makes you think that?"

"I just don't want to make any mistakes. I don't want people to think I'm not a good soldier."

I discovered she had expectations of herself to perform her job perfectly, fighting her own high standards rather than any levied from the outside, and she was feeling uncertain of her skills.

I introduced tapping to her, tapping on her doubts, her limiting beliefs of being a good soldier. Tapping on the hand, I had her repeat after me:

"Even though I don't think I'm good enough, I am a good soldier."

"Even though I'm afraid of making mistakes, I am a good soldier."

"Even though I'm worried about what others might think of me, I am a good soldier."

Then we tapped the acupoints on the face and torso saying, "Not good enough. Mistakes. Worried."

Lastly, I asked, "Are you willing to learn and to ask questions?"

Looking down, she muttered a soft yes.

The next day I noticed a sense of calm and ease with Gestar.

"Do you want to deploy?" I asked.

With more assurance in her voice and looking directly into my eyes, she said, "Yes, Ma'am."

Her yes came with a caveat: as long as there was someone to teach her. I reassured her that she wouldn't be alone, that there would be noncommissioned officers and officers to advise her. Throughout the rest of training, she was the "perfect soldier"—punctual, first to qualify, first with a clean weapon, and participating wholeheartedly and confidently in all phases.

I became friends with three female captains: two social workers and one psychiatric nurse. The psych nurse was my bunkmate—she had the bottom bunk. All three captains had been in the army for more than 10 years. One captain had 17 years of experience. There were also three male psychologists in the unit. All were even-tempered and professional, in their 40s and 50s.

Unfortunately, within a week, the psych nurse had to return home, unable to deploy because of a recurring shoulder injury. The great perk was that now I slept in the lower bunk, making it much easier to go to the bathroom in the middle of the night!

On May 2, 2011, it was all over the news: US Navy SEALS and CIA paramilitary forces had killed Osama bin Laden at his compound in Pakistan. President Obama declared, "Justice has been done." Would this stop our deployment? I didn't know.

On May 4, the last day at Fort Hunter-Liggett, we turned in our bed linen and packed for the trip home. We also had to pack for Joint Base Lewis-McChord (JBLM) in Washington, our mobilization station, where we were to report on June 1, 2011. I had to decide what I'd need in JBLM, since the unit would transport the duffle bags for me.

In addition to spending quality time together before I had to report, my husband and I threw a party for his upcoming 60th birthday, our also upcoming 31st wedding anniversary, and my deployment. We hosted it at a neighborhood restaurant, whose owner and chef is the father of one of the students in the fencing program Rob and I run. Sixty people celebrated with us. Rob and I weren't able to sit or eat much, as we moved around the room talking to our friends, thanking them for coming. After dessert, we had a slide show. Rob had scanned dozens of old photos for it. It was a nice reflection of our lives together, the places we've traveled and the things we have accomplished.

Since the age of sixteen, I've been involved in the sport of fencing, first competing on the national and international levels, and now coaching. Six years ago, Rob—who is not only a French-trained fencing master but also a chiropractor—and I started a youth fencing program at Halberstadt Fencers' Club in San Francisco. We do this part-time, four days a week, developing youngsters into fencers. In our view, along with teaching the sport, we foster the children's attitudes, cultivating mental and physical flexibility that is fundamental to their happiness and well-being.

On my last day at the fencing club, Rob and I threw a pizza party for our young fencers. This was an opportunity for me to have some closure with my students, who I wouldn't be seeing for a year. I was touched by how the parents sincerely appreciated me for teaching their children. I always believed in helping children gain self-confidence, to deal with pressure and learn resiliency, as this is more important than the number of medals won.

During the remaining weeks before deploying, I packed for immediate travel and items I wanted Rob to send to me later. I filled small postal boxes with lotions, bed sheets, socks, vitamins, pistachio nuts—anything I thought I would need or want in Afghanistan. Fortunately, two days before leaving, I received an email from the 113th unit that each soldier would be issued a personal footlocker, which would be sent to Afghanistan. Feeling relieved, I packed all the boxes in my duffle bag for later repacking in my footlocker.

Mobilization

On May 28, 2011, Memorial Day weekend, I boarded a flight from San Francisco to Santa Ana, California. The 113th CSC home station is located in Garden Grove, where preparation and loading of equipment and a farewell luncheon were planned. It was the first time I traveled in my army uniform. There was a benefit to this: I was able to go through security in the first-class line and I didn't have to remove my boots.

While I was waiting for my flight, an elderly man thanked me for my service and reminisced about his time in the army 50 years earlier. A flight attendant told me I could enter the plane with the first-class customers. This was a kind gesture, but I believed I shouldn't be given preferential treatment, so I didn't take her up on the offer. Some people stared at me. I wasn't sure what they were thinking, and I wasn't used to the attention. Once seated, I retreated behind a book to avoid an uncomfortable conversation. Since San Francisco is an ultra-liberal city, I imagined that certain individuals might be unfriendly toward the military, since the limited federal funds are spent on national defense instead of health and welfare needs.

Along with other soldiers arriving at the Santa Ana Airport, I was picked up and taken to the 113th CSC unit, where we packed our footlockers. Now I had one less duffle bag to carry! After checking into the hotel, it was quiet—no rushing around, no worrying about what to pack—and I was finally able to settle in.

The next morning I was up at 0430 hours, knowing a van would take us to the unit for formation at 0600 hours. After formation, we had a gas-mask fitting and testing, and a pregnancy test—yes, I had to take one despite my age; no amount of common sense would change the nurse's mind. He was "just following procedures."

In the afternoon, the American Legion, Post 716, hosted the farewell party. Many families and friends of the deploying soldiers were there to enjoy a barbecue, live entertainment, slideshow, and guest speakers wishing us a productive and safe tour. It was a good opportunity to meet some of the soldiers' spouses, boyfriends, girlfriends, and family.

On June 1, the entire 113th unit traveled by plane to Joint Base Lewis-McChord (JBLM), Washington. Upon our arrival, it was raining and cooler than the nice warm weather of Garden Grove. Army housing was in trailers, with three to four soldiers per room and a shared bathroom—a great deal more privacy than the 40-person barracks at Fort Hunter-Liggett. JBLM is an enormous place. We needed to pack into rental vans to drive everywhere—chow hall, classes, and post exchange (PX; the military version of a general store).

If stress could be measured among members of the 113th CSC unit, being at JBLM sent the stress levels off the charts. With the realization that we were one step closer to deploying to Afghanistan, some members were having a variety of "meltdowns." Some of the younger female soldiers complained incessantly about the cramped accommodations, the endless training, and the poor food. One cried herself to sleep every night. Without mentioning names, I brought this matter to the commander's attention. But it only made the situation worse, because female soldiers stopped confiding in me. As the commander's counselor, I believed I had an obligation to tell him about the morale of his troops.

Everyone had to go through the Soldier Readiness Process Center (SRP) again. Financial, legal, vision, hearing, dental, immunization shots and medical all had to be cleared. It was rare to receive "a go" the first time through. It could take three to five times, and even more, to get that green light. Some soldiers never got it, receiving the red light because of high blood pressure, high cholesterol, sleep apnea, or high blood levels of copper, with the accompanying high levels of the enzyme creatine kinase, which is a marker for inflammation of the heart muscles. The screening was quite thorough, and the uncertainty of whether a soldier would be sent home or continue with the deployment was undeniably unsettling. Some admitted embarrassment at the thought of returning home, as they'd already had their farewell parties. Others didn't want to repeat the Regional Training Center and mobilization training in order to deploy later with another unit.

I had to go through SRP three times before I received the green light. This added two more days of returning to the hospital. I needed a current mammogram because of a history of two benign lumps in my left breast. If the result was negative, I would be good to go. In the meantime, attendance at mandatory training was nonstop, from classroom training to 10 days in the field at C.O.L. Eagle, about 20 minutes from the post.

Field housing at C.O.L. Eagle was half-shell aluminum buildings. The women's barracks had 20 beds, but not all of us made the trip. Within the first week, two women were considered non-deployable, but one returned to the unit after four days—a second chance to prove she could complete the training.

Field training required a pack for 10 days, living in a barrack, and eating at least one MRE a day. Shower trailers were available at certain hours. There was laundry service pick-up and delivery two days a week.

I had enjoyed the pre-mob training at Fort Hunter-Liggett, but the mob training at Fort Lewis was superb. Even the most seasoned soldiers thought it was the best training ever. We had classes on identifying IEDs, convoy training, urban operations, and lots of reflexive firing (shooting without using the sights), using our dominant and non-dominant hand during the day and night with the M16 rifle. By chance, next to me during the rifle trainings and earlier range trainings was the same young soldier, Sgt. Ramirez. As I hadn't shot an M16 before I joined the army, he taught me to take note of my breathing and to pull the trigger at the moment of not inhaling or exhaling, when the rifle was the most stable. Once the target was sighted, he suggested I fire in quick succession, instead of wasting time to re-sight for each round. I was grateful for his patience and sharing his shooting skill with me.

The trainings culminated in simulated convoy missions, where we encountered small-arms fire, mortar attacks, and IEDs. The purpose was to learn how to react to these situations. Most of the time I was in the first truck of the convoy, the worst position, as it was commonly attacked or imaginarily exploded. I was "injured or dead" and needed to be extracted from the truck, placed on a litter, and transferred into an evacuating vehicle.

During this time of stress, many soldiers often asked why. Why do we need this training? Did we as Combat Stress Control members really have to know this? Why do we have to bring this equipment? Why can't we go now? As many of us weren't trained as infantry soldiers and were in health care rather than combat, it was confusing why we had to learn certain skills. But we were going to a combat zone. We were all soldiers first. We needed to know the role of each soldier in the truck for when we traveled from one FOB (forward operating base) to another. The exercise also presented realistic knowledge of what infantry soldiers experience out in the field.

I learned not to ask why, mainly because we still had to do it, despite the answer (though mostly there wasn't an answer). I just accepted it and dealt with it in the moment. I didn't look ahead in the training schedule because it often changed. It was frustrating, but flexibility and adaptability were healthier ways to deal with never-ending changes. Often in the army I heard the assertion: "It is what it is." But I prefer: "Embrace the suck!"

During the last four days in the field, the 113th CSC unit split into five behavioral health centers. Role players came in with a variety of issues: soldiers wanting to go home to fix a broken marriage; suicidal and homicidal ideations because of posttraumatic reaction; paranoid ideations from soldiers experiencing their first psychotic break; depression because of multiple deployments; anger; and grief issues because of a lost battle buddy. Finally, I was in my area of comfort and professional competence. (Little did I know that I would later experience all this and more in my deployment.)

I adjusted to nearby notional mortar blasts by dropping to the floor and slipping into my body armor and helmet. (The word "notional" is commonly used in military exercises when pretend explosives are involved.) What an inconvenience, and it didn't help to establish rapport with my clients! We even simulated going into a bunker and making sure we had an accountability of staff and clients. In the evenings, we had classes on substance abuse, death and dying, and prisoners of war. These simulations and classes made it real and clear: We were going to war.

At this point, I had been in the army for 15 months. Similar to other organizations, the army collects its own set of expressions. Some of my favorites are: Jacked up! (not working properly or as intended). Stay in your lane (remain within your area of expertise, responsibility). Too easy! (a piece of cake). Are you tracking? (are you following the conversation, instruction?). Ate up! (messed up). Situational awareness (aware of one's immediate surrounding). High speed (a soldier who is all prepared and ready for whatever is next). Squared away (a soldier who presents a high level of order and discipline). And my beloved: Embrace the suck!

After 25 days of mobilization training, we earned a four-day pass. For many, this was the last chance to see family and friends before going to Afghanistan. I returned to San Francisco to see my husband and family, and to bring home a duffle bag of army-issued clothing and equipment I wouldn't need in country. For the next few days, I ate nothing but Chinese food. I hoped that I consumed enough monosodium glutamate to preserve me until I returned.

At home, I watched President Obama's speech on television about his plan to withdraw US troops from Afghanistan: 10,000 troops starting in July, and another 23,000 by the following summer. I didn't think this would affect me. At this point, I really wanted to go to Afghanistan. I had been through so much preparation. I wanted to earn my combat patch, which is presented to soldiers who have served in a combat zone. To receive it, I needed to be in country for at least three months. Part of me believed that being there for only a year might be too short a time to truly make a difference. I'd have to wait and see if I'd still think that after living in 110-degree heat.

Rob dropped me off at the airport for my return flight to JBLM in Washington. We didn't know if we'd ever see each other again.

Regrettably, there was an hour delay, and my heart sank as I realized we could have stayed home together longer. When I arrived in Seattle, I called Rob and he told me that after I walked into the San Francisco Airport terminal, he ran inside, wanting to see me and hold me one more time. But he couldn't find me. My eyes welled up. I'd hold on to the image of his smiling, yet concerned eyes for a long time to come.

More Training

The day after we got back from our four-day pass, some army dignitaries—a one-star general, a two-star general, a four-star general, and two
colonels—spoke to the unit, wishing us a safe journey and a successful
mission. Gen. Chiarelli, the four-star general, US Army vice chief of staff,
led the efforts on posttraumatic stress, traumatic brain injury, suicide
prevention, and implementing behavioral health programs. The general
said PTSD was fighting a culture that didn't believe that injuries you
couldn't see were as serious as injuries you could see. After the general's
presentation, we lined up single file and marched forward as he handed
everyone his or her "coin." (Military custom coins, dating back to WWI,
are a symbol of a bond, an indicator of the unique shared experiences.)

Then all behavioral health providers had the first of a four-day instruction on EMDR (Eye Movement Desensitization and Reprocessing), a
therapeutic technique that uses an eight-phase approach, which includes
having the client recall distressing images while receiving bilateral sensory
input, such as side-to-side eye movements. I had been certified in EMDR
in 1998.

During training, someone in the unit mentioned we'd leave for
Afghanistan in six days. I couldn't believe it was coming up so quickly. I
noticed a lump in my throat, a sense of excitement, and a trace of fear.

On our second day of EMDR, we did a practical exercise of a "client" bringing up a disturbing picture and a current negative belief about
himself/herself. The "therapist" would then use eye movements to
change the "client's" picture and eventually evolve it into a positive
cognition.

The commander called a meeting with all the officers. He was upset
at hearing that junior enlisted female soldiers were claiming he was
discriminating against them. Two females had been deemed unfit to
deploy, and the previous night a female was "smoked" for being late to
formation. I guessed some of the young female soldiers were feeling jit-

tery about the upcoming deployment. They were making mistakes. Yet when confronted, the young females alleged they were being disciplined unfairly. In my opinion, this wasn't so, but the discussion helped officers be aware of biased punishments.

During another full day of EMDR, I worked on my anticipatory anxiousness of the heat in Afghanistan. If the EMDR didn't work, I'd continue using EFT (Emotional Freedom Techniques).

What is EFT? This was the technique I had used with Sgt. Paul's machine gun competition and Pfc. Gestar's doubts of being a good soldier. The EFT process starts by the client choosing to bring to mind a distressing emotional trigger, which activates the amygdala—an almond-shaped mass of gray matter in the brain associated with feelings of fear and aggression—and arouses the threat response originally connected to the triggering event: fight, flight, or freeze. While picturing the scene, the tapping of certain acupoints with two fingers has a calming effect on the amygdala. The hippocampus—the part of our brain concerned with basic drives, emotions, and short-term memory—realizes that the trigger isn't as strong anymore. This changes our neural pathways, so that the trigger no longer creates distress.

I prefer EFT because a specific emotional pain can be released quickly. During the first session, the client can easily learn the mechanics of the technique. This means they aren't dependent thereafter on meeting with the therapist to feel better. The client can tap whenever necessary, while acknowledging his or her distress or negative beliefs. This takes about a minute to do. In deployment, I speculated that regular scheduled, multiple therapy sessions would be unlikely. This would make EFT the ideal technique.

After our last session of EMDR, we had a briefing on the Blackhawk helicopter. It was a dry run—learning how to enter, use the seat belts, and exit the helicopter safely. This briefing was for new soldiers as well as our canine member, Sgt. 1st Class Zeke. The rank of the dog was one higher than its handler! As a therapy dog, this black Labrador retriever had deployed two times already, in both Iraq and Afghanistan. This was the first time a reserved Combat Stress Control unit was going into country with a dog.

That evening, we received our team assignments. Some behavioral health specialists were pleased, while others wanted to know why they were on a certain team. Overall, many were concerned about the location of the camp and their safety. Bottom line, no camp was safe—after all, we were going into a war zone. This was exactly why we had been training so hard for so many months. Again, we are all soldiers first.

I was assigned to an outlying FOB to cover for about two months until the permanent provider and behavioral health specialist arrived. Then I was assigned to Team One, located at Kandahar Airfield, where my job would be to travel to other clinics and check on clinician's self-care. In addition, I'd assist the commander in negotiations for the benefit of the unit. This wasn't what I thought my role would be—I thought I'd be staying in one place. Nevertheless, it sounded like an exciting year!

The next day we had one more round at the Soldier Readiness Processing Center for medical clearance. For women, this meant another pregnancy test (not for me; I was finally exempt). Then off to a traumatic brain injury class, as the four-star general thought we needed a refresher course.

The afternoon helicopter ride was canceled for an administrative reason—whatever that meant—so I had free time. I packed my bags: a rucksack, 51 pounds; a rolling duffle bag, 70 pounds; and a three-day assault bag, 25 pounds. Much of the stuff was army equipment that we had to have when we landed in country: body armor, Kevlar, weapon, gas mask, and hazardous material suit.

We were told the temperature in Afghanistan was 75 degrees at six in the morning and should reach 105 degrees during the day. Hydration, hydration, hydration!

Deployment to Kandahar

On June 30, 2011, after cleaning the barracks, turning in bed linen, and picking up our weapons, we departed Joint Base Lewis-McChord. We arrived by bus at the airport terminal at 1730 hours and waited; our flight wasn't until 2200 hours. We received a box dinner and the USO had lots of snacks and drinks for us. I couldn't believe I was actually— finally—going to Kandahar Province in Afghanistan.

We flew from Fort McChord Air Force Base on a chartered North American airline, with the first stop in Leipzig, Germany, then to Manas International Airport in Bishkek, Kyrgyzstan. All in all, including layover times, the trip from Seattle to Kyrgyzstan took 24 hours. Sitting upright was difficult and uncomfortable. Nevertheless, I tried to sleep most of the time and didn't see any of the in-flight movies until the last one— *Gulliver's Travels* with Jack Black.

At Manas—a transit center operated by the US Air Force—we were processed and then sent to pick up our bags and grab enough clothing and personal hygiene items for 72 hours, as we didn't know when we'd fly to Kandahar. We stayed in a transient tent for 40 personnel and I was on a top bunk again. Manas was clean and relatively modern, and the DFAC (dining facility) was well stocked with snacks, drinks, sandwiches, and a variety of hot meals. It wasn't a bad place to be stationed. Of course, the weather was sizzling hot, with no shade to take a breather. Carrying and dragging my bags into the tent was slow and agonizing, and made me sweat nonstop. I went to the PX and loaded my Eagle Cash card (similar to an ATM card) so I could use it in military-run stores. After a long 24-plus hours, I took a much-needed cool shower and slept lying down—what a treat!

The next morning, July 3, we were up at 0700 hours and during formation were told we'd be leaving for Afghanistan around 1800 hours. Air Force personnel inspected our body armor ceramic plates, which weigh 28 pounds, replaced them if cracks were found, and then they loaded our gear onto huge pallets for the plane. For security purposes, before departing everyone on the manifest was locked down in a sweltering holding tent for a couple of hours. We spent the time playing cards and perspiring.

Then our unit and another were crammed in, along with the pallets, into a large C-5 military transport plane. Unlike commercial airplanes, all the seats are extremely close, with barely any elbow or legroom, but the cavernous ceiling is 13 and a half feet high. Moreover, when traveling on military planes to a war zone, everyone must be in "full battle rattle," wearing body armor, Kevlar, and carrying a weapon. This makes it difficult to be comfortable and to maneuver when using the one and only confined latrine on the plane. Lastly, the roaring of the engines was so loud that we were required to wear earplugs.

Last leg to Afghanistan on a military plane.

After a two-hour plane ride, we arrived at Kandahar International Airport, where we received a briefing. Although it was evening, the weather was hot and humid. The timeworn airport was faintly lit, with old plaster falling off the walls and ceiling, reminding me of the movie *Casablanca*. My unit was bused to Camp Roberts—a section in Kandahar Airfield (KAF)—and female soldiers were housed in a 12-person transient tent, where we'd stay until flights were set for each team to reach its final destination for the deployment.

My impressions of KAF: hot, really blistering hot, about 110 degrees Fahrenheit. There was annoying, fine white dust everywhere. KAF reminded me of the movie *Mad Max*—an endless span of desert under a brown, sunless, and cloudless sky, with the nonstop roaring noise of trucks, helicopters, planes, jets, and generators. The airfield was a small city, with at least 20,000 men and women. There was an array of uniformed soldiers from Australia, Canada, Italy, Bulgaria, Denmark, Germany, France, Spain, and other nations, as NATO had a strong presence there. Civilian contractors were from the Philippines, India, Bosnia, the UK, the United States, and other countries. When on duty, all military personnel had to wear their uniforms, or their assigned physical fitness uniforms, along with their weapons. The civilians had to have a photo ID card fastened to their outer garments. Night after night, there were flights taking off or coming in at all hours. Even with earplugs, it seemed like the planes were just over my head. I grimaced and inhaled the smells of the infamous poo-pond—a round lake in the middle of the base where raw sewage was treated.

In our free time, we could buy almost anything from the PX and stores along the Boardwalk (a strip mall) that sold knockoffs of brand-name items. Since the transient tents were so far from the center of the base, we had to take a bus to eat, shop, or go anywhere. For each bus ride, we had to wait nearly 30 minutes in the unbearable heat for the bus to arrive. I needed three hours just to do my laundry at KAF!

The day after our arrival, I thought, "I am one day closer to my mission, and one day closer to going home." Each day that passed was one day less in Afghanistan. I tried to sleep in the afternoon because the heat was so intolerable. But even with air conditioning in the tent, it was roasting. We had formation at 1900 hours for updates and to learn which teams would leave for their outlying camps. My team was scheduled to leave six days later, on July 10. I really wanted to leave as soon as possible so that I could learn my job and settle into a routine. After the formation, I decided to skip the delightful free army chow. Some of us went to the Boardwalk and ate at Mamma Mia restaurant. The pizza wasn't bad, considering the owners were Thai. There was karaoke in the square, with soldiers attempting to sing, their voices as dry, dusty, and crackly as the city. This was one Fourth of July I wouldn't forget.

Boardwalk at KAF.

113th CSC at KAF Camp Roberts.

The next day was my 31st wedding anniversary. I wasn't able to get to the MWR (Morale, Welfare, and Recreation) center to use the computer and wish Rob a happy anniversary. We had a KAF briefing in the morning, and another briefing in the afternoon about Role III—NATO hospital—where the center's commander detailed a sickening account of the number of legs and arms amputated because of IEDs (improvised explosive devices) this past year. Welcome to Kandahar!

In an outdoor ceremony, after just three days in the war zone, Col. Rabb presented each member of the unit with our combat patch. He thought this was an appropriate time, as it would be the last time the entire group would be together. I was happy to receive the patch and proud to wear it on my right shoulder. The patch represented the number of challenging obstacles I'd had to overcome to get to Afghanistan.

In the evening, we had night firing of our M-16 rifles to ensure they were working properly. We had to shoot ten rounds while wearing full battle rattle gear in the oppressive heat. When we were finished and about to walk back to the parking lot to board the bus, the camp's siren went off, indicating rocket attacks. Everyone dove to the ground. We waited for a couple of minutes and then ran into a nearby cement bunker. My heart pounded in my chest and a sour taste arose in my mouth (adrenaline). My brain on full alert, my mind said, "This is real. It's no longer practice or role-playing. It's real!" I listened, but there were no nearby explosions. Nevertheless, we stayed in the harsh heat of the bunker for half an hour, dreading and sweating, before the all-clear sign. Mercifully, we had bottles of water to drink. As we filed onto the bus afterward, there was some disquieting nervous energy among us.

My behavioral health team consisted of Pfc. Li and me. This was her first deployment, though she had been in the Army Reserves for about three years. Li was in her 20s and had recently married. She was observant and quiet, but with an air of self-confidence.

We now learned we were scheduled to leave Kandahar at 0300 hours for our FOB, Camp Nathan Smith. I was surprised, as the original schedule had been set for a few days later. I didn't get back from the firing range until 2300 hours, so there wouldn't be much sleep this night, as I had to repack my rucksack, rolling duffle bag, and three-day assault bag.

Our driver pulled into Ramp Lima around 0130 hours, but we didn't even get out of the vehicle because our flight was canceled due to a sandstorm. Back we went to Camp Roberts to try to sleep on our cots. Another team was going out, so it was noisy. I might have slept a couple of hours, but in the morning the generator went out, so no air conditioning and no more sleep. I headed to the DFAC for lunch, hoping the air conditioner would be working when I returned, but no such luck. I hung around the USO tent because it was slightly cooler there. Li and I were there for nearly three hours when my executive officer ran into the tent and shouted that we had to go to the air ramp immediately. I wasn't totally packed, so I ran back to my tent and threw everything together as quickly as I could. Sweat ran from every pore of my body.

Back at Ramp Lima, we loaded our bags into the Blackhawk helicopter and had buckled ourselves into our seats when the flight crew signaled to us to exit. We begrudgingly unloaded our bags and returned to the flight line to discover that a one-star general and his entourage were taking the bird. I was pissed. We were back at the ramp and waited for the next flight out, which was three hours later. *Arrggh!*

As I sat on the hard bench at the ramp waiting for transport, drenched with sweat, and with no electronics or a book to occupy my time, I was deep in my thoughts, reviewing the path that had led me to Afghanistan.

As a young girl, the middle child of five, I'd learned that I didn't garner the same attention from my parents that the oldest or youngest siblings received. This was fine. I was able to carve out my own identity and direction. I developed certain skills and, perhaps unconsciously, ventured into activities to seek attention.

Even though I grew up sharing a small home with two brothers and two sisters close in age, I was more comfortable being alone. I liked having my own space. I didn't have close friends or feel the need to have them. I didn't like being surrounded by people. I had friendly relationships with acquaintances, coworkers, classmates, and roommates, but once I didn't see them anymore, I hardly kept in contact. I liked to do what and when I wanted without waiting for a consensus or having a discussion. To me, this was simply more efficient.

In the military, surrounded by many people, I still preferred solitude. This was a good thing, since military personnel are constantly in transit. It is fruitless to make lasting friendships, as one was here and then transferred to another unit the following week. Another issue was the fact that, as an officer, I was not allowed to fraternize with non-officers. I could be friendly with other officers, but again, they would leave the military, or transfer, or had no time to socialize because of the demands of the job. Lastly, as a therapist, it was unethical for me to be friends with my clients. So it was a good thing I like being by myself.

I also thought my personality was well suited for the military. I was generally quiet, even-tempered and steady, without complaint, loss of temper, or irritation. If I was upset, my face rarely showed it. The circumstance had to be quite unacceptable for me to react. I think I'd learned this as a child. Attracting attention to myself wasn't what a good Chinese girl would do. I'd learned that many things weren't in my control, and being angry didn't change that fact.

———————

Maybe the third time would be a charm? Nope! After waiting three hours and carrying our bags to the flight line, we were again denied boarding because there was no space. We carried everything back to the vehicle and returned to our tent to spend another suffocating night at KAF. I was now exasperated.

We were up at 0300 hours for a 0430 hours pick-up to the ramp, but for the fifth time, we were denied access to a helicopter. By this point, I was seething, losing my patience. My first sergeant reminded me that I had volunteered for this, which helped me regain composure. Soon after, my first sergeant grabbed our bags and drove us to the Canadian air ramp, where we got on a Chinook helicopter to Camp Nathan Smith (CNS). Preparing to strap in, I was surprised the five-point seat harness we had used in training wasn't available; instead, there was only a simple lap seat belt.

We were finally on our way.

Aboard a Canadian Chinook from KAF to CNS.

Not five minutes into the trip, the rear and side gunners engaged their machine guns—*brat-ta-tat-tat*—loud enough to be heard above all helicopter noises. The gunners were firing at someone or groups of insurgents on the ground. In disbelief, I glanced over at Li, my stomach rolling, thinking that we could be killed before reaching our FOB. With cold fingers, I cinched the seat belt tighter across my lap. The gunners fired a few more times. As far as I could tell, no one was shooting back at us. All nine passengers had tense faces, lost in their own thoughts, but they didn't look scared, which was good because it kept me calm. To avoid possible ground fire, the pilot flew the helicopter circuitously up, down, and sideways, making the flight a longer, more intense, but safer trip.

We finally arrived at CNS where we were met by the outgoing behavioral health team, Capt. Rivas and Staff Sgt. Little. They helped carry our bags and showed us the camp. We settled in transient housing, a narrow room with eight bunk beds. This time, I snagged a bottom bunk! Resting for a minute, I reflected slightly on my trip here—frightening, surreal—but there was no time to dwell on it, as I had to adjust to my new surroundings.

Camp Nathan Smith

Camp Nathan Smith was a former Canadian and later American military base in the heart of Kandahar City, Afghanistan. In November 2003, US Army from Fort Bragg, North Carolina, reconstructed the site from an abandoned fruit factory. The camp was turned over to the Canadian Army in 2005 and named for Private Nathan Smith, after he was killed in a "friendly fire" incident. Currently, it is a headquarters of the provincial reconstruction team, which houses State Department officials and US soldiers to improve governance and development in the area. It's a small FOB, with about 1,500 soldiers, 10% of them female. The 1-10th Cavalry, 4th Infantry Division, 1st Brigade Combat Team, is in command. There is a small PX, a local bazaar, an aid station, a gym, a swimming pool, and two dining facilities.

The camp didn't have sidewalks, and walking on uneven rocks shimmering with heat was a challenge. There was chalk-like powdery dust everywhere and a foul stench when the wind shifted. It got extremely dark in the evening, so carrying a flashlight was necessary. Flush toilets were few, but there were plenty of Porta Potties—some clean, some better not to eye too closely, and all better not to smell. There were abundant, baked, plastic drinking water bottles piled high on wooden pallets along the roadways. The weather was searing—around 115 degrees Fahrenheit—and wearing the uniform and boots made it even hotter. Soldiers already in Afghanistan said it took a month to get used to the heat.

The food served in the DFAC at the camp was quite good, with a variety of dishes: chicken wings, pull-pork, beef stew, and fresh salads. I learned they served lobster tails every Friday night! It was definitely better than the Army DFAC back in the States. There was plenty of food and drinks, so maybe I'd be able to regain some of the weight I'd lost.

Each FOB hosts a Mayor Cell, operated by military personnel responsible for the daily living and working conditions. The Mayor Cell handles the trash and supplies, processes work orders, provides housing for temporary residents, tracks the population, and employs and supervises local nationals.

The Mayor Cell assigned me my permanent sleeping quarter—one room of six in a narrow one-story building. The room was two and a half meters by four and a half meters, built of plywood, with one metal-framed twin bed, one wobbly folding chair, one thin metal locker, and no windows, but the air conditioning worked great! This was the first time since joining the army that I'd have my own room. It was strange not to have other people's energy around me. I'd miss some of the entertaining conversations, but I was sure glad to have a little place of my own. I wanted to buy some bed sheets so that I didn't have to keep sleeping in my hot, confining sleeping bag.

Author's room at CNS.

To make life a bit more comfortable in Afghanistan, I quickly learned to keep certain items in my pockets: antacid, Chap Stick, reading glasses, hand cream, flashlight, eye drops, pens, writing pad, protein bars, handkerchief, small camera, and tissues. Conveniently, the army uniform includes a gazillion pockets.

Li and I worked with the exiting team, Rivas and Little, to learn the job, set up computer access and accounts, conduct inventory, and take over responsibility for the office equipment. After transferring in from another forward operating base, they had been at the camp for about four months.

The next day, Friday, July 8, I met my first two clients: a female private, a sexual assault case; and a male sergeant, for anger management. I sensed an urgency to establish rapport and help them quickly, as I didn't know whether these soldiers would return or not. Although they came to our session wearing a uniform, their presenting problems were not largely different from the many clients I've worked with. I was knowledgeable, patient, and conveyed an openness and curiosity about each soldier's experiences.

It was horrifically hot, but, fortunately, my small, narrow office also had a working air conditioner. Much of the equipment had a noticeable layer of dirt. There was only one cracked black vinyl office chair, one small canvas folding stool, a relatively new inflatable swimming pool chair, and two rectangular folding tables. Of all the counseling rooms I'd worked in, this was by far the least "touchy feely" one. But the soldiers seemed unfazed by the poorly furnished, tight space. I think they were just glad to talk to someone with a sympathetic ear.

July 9 was the last full day with the outgoing behavioral health team—more forms to learn and how to complete a clinical note with the computer program (AHLTA-T). We had a photo taken of the two teams in front of the Camp Nathan Smith sign and had dinner together one last time. On our way back to the office, Li and I spied an empty wood locker outside in a common area and we quickly carried it off. As the locker had a key, we could place our weapons in there. We were laughing hard at our quickness and boldness. From then on, we were on constant lookout for other things we could "procure."

———————————

Now as an army officer, being in a position to lead others wasn't unusual to me. I was grateful for all of the early positions of leadership that helped shape me. They taught me to function under stress, apply critical thinking skills, and make immediate, accurate decisions as a police officer and as a soldier.

My first leadership role was in junior high school. I ran for president of the Girl's Athletic Association, an after-school club. A physical education teacher approached me and asked that I consider running for the position. I had never been a class officer or team leader before and I was running against a very popular and extremely athletic girl. The worst thing that could happen was that I would lose. To my surprise, and, I think, to that of many of my classmates, I won.

In high school, I honed my skills as a leader. I was elected class president three times. I exhibited good organizational skills and a rather serious, no-nonsense persona that people felt was needed to do the job. My style of leadership was to delegate responsibilities and to encourage each activity leader to speak to the group instead of me. I was actually uncomfortable being the center of attention.

After high school, I attended City College of San Francisco. I didn't score well on my SAT, so attending the University of California at Berkeley as a freshman was out of the question. Unlike the stereotype of Chinese boys and girls performing well in math and science, I was awful in those subjects. I remember my mother telling me not to attend college since I didn't like school, but once she said that, I did the opposite. In fact, I excelled at City College.

There, for the first time, I had classes with older students, Vietnam veterans, and students of other ethnic backgrounds. Living in San Francisco, near Chinatown, from elementary school through high school, Chinese students were close to 80% of the school population. I wasn't a minority, but a member of the majority. Now at City College, I realized and experienced racial discrimination more fully. For example, although next in line to be helped in the bookstore, I was overlooked and a white male was served instead. I felt invisible at times and, conversely, targeted when the offensive ethnic slur "Chink" was used. In my second year, I was elected a member of the school's city council, served as captain of the school's fencing team, and earned excellent marks. I did so well that in my junior year I transferred to UC Berkeley, to my parents' surprise and disbelief. My mother asked me why I wanted to go to Cal, and I said, "To meet my future husband," which turned out to be true.

Counseling

July 10, the first day Li and I were on our own, began with a phone call requesting behavioral health services for a male soldier, Spc. Ingram, who admitted suicidal tendencies. Ingram was rather shortish in height but well built, with frizzy brown hair. After Ingram was escorted in (meaning the soldier is non-voluntarily taken to the center by a higher ranked soldier), I introduced myself.

"Hello, I'm Captain Louie—"

"I don't care about the army," Ingram blurted. "Why should I since the army don't care about me?"

"I heard you were thinking of hurting yourself. Is that right?"

"Why not? No one likes me. No one would miss me."

"And how would you hurt yourself?"

"I don't know yet...I'm just sayin'..."

"No specific plan?"

"No. I hate this place, I hate the frickin' army!"

His weapon had been taken from him. As we continued to talk, I learned that the soldier had spoken to two chaplains in the last 24 hours. The accumulation of home-front issues, medical issues, and frustrations with the army had resulted in him walking away angrily from his platoon sergeant, with a comment that he'd kill himself if he could. I did not use EMDR or EFT. With supportive counseling and compassionate listening, I just allowed Spc. Ingram to vent, to take the wind out of his sail. My quiet presence was enough to calm him. After our session, I released him to his escort. I didn't know then that I wouldn't see him again or even hear what happened.

Next, Maj. Stefani (brigade surgeon) wanted a second opinion regarding a sergeant with a history of dissociative and psychotic symptoms. The sergeant had managed his symptoms in an earlier deployment, but the current deployment had irregular hours and his symptoms worsened, blurring the lines of reality and fantasy. The brigade surgeon observed the sergeant could jeopardize his own safety and that of his unit. With the surgeon's agreement, I recommended that he go to KAF for a medication evaluation. The sergeant agreed to this, saying, "Anything to get better."

While I was working in the office that evening, another soldier walked in to let me know that he was going to KAF, then to Germany, then to the States because of severe panic attacks after two months in theater (in a theater of combat operations). I was happy for him to receive the immediate attention and care he needed.

At last, all the training and traveling were over. I could finally do the job I had signed up to do: help soldiers heal. The number of soldiers Li and I saw on the first day surprised us and the cases were more serious than we had anticipated. This was the main Taliban fighting season—March to December—and soldiers were stressed to the max. Long hours, less sleep, inadequate nutrition, and lack of free time added to the problem.

On Monday, July 11, we saw only one client as a follow-up. This provided us a chance to clean and organize the file cabinets. I typed up some notes and reviewed computer files from the previous team. I had been trying to meet the 1-10 Cavalry commander, Lt. Col. Cook, to introduce ourselves as the new behavioral health (BH) team. By coincidence, I bumped into the Command Sgt. Maj. Veneklasen, as I stepped out of the office. Our predecessors had forewarned me that there was a problem in sharing the narrow office space with Finance because Veneklasen insisted that BH vacate the space when Finance came to CNS. Sure enough, Veneklasen echoed that. He told me that my team could stay in our quarters and read. But I couldn't predict when soldiers would be in crisis and would require behavioral health support. I hoped the space issue could be resolved before I transferred out, to make it easier for my replacement, whom I had been informed might arrive in early August, sooner than previously thought.

Though the days passed slowly, I was intrigued by what each day might bring. Of course, a part of me wanted to return to the comfort of my home, but most of me wasn't ready to end this adventure. As I adjusted to the many inconveniences of life in Afghanistan—generators not working, dust-filled air, unbearably hot dry weather, and poor living conditions—I continued to feel the strong desire to help soldiers when given the opportunity and their trust. Li and I planned some walkabouts in the camp to introduce ourselves, let soldiers know the location of our office, and encourage them to come in for counseling if needed.

On Tuesday morning, my Afghan cell phone rang with a request to counsel a soldier. Spc. Fisher was escorted in because of her abusive outburst to her platoon sergeant. She looked at me angrily from dark, almond-shaped eyes.

"I'm pissed. This shit-bag is spreading lies about me."

"Who?" I asked.

"My platoon sergeant, and when I point-blank confronted him, he lied right to my face! So I went ballistic! I was really upset, cussing him out. I wanted to belt him."

After I encouraged Fisher to take some deep breaths and reassured her that we had plenty of time, she admitted to a history of anger issues prior to joining the army four years earlier. We used Emotional Freedom Techniques (EFT) to release old negative emotions, with her tapping on acupoints as she narrated her uncontrollable anger.

"When I'm angry, all I see is red...and then I yell, scream, punch."

"When did you first learn to do this?"

"Probably around 4 or 5 years old...Boys used to pick on me cause I was skinny with long braids my mom made we wear."

My tapping protocol usually went like this: Establish a rapport with the soldier, listen to their complaints, and then ask what they think of Einstein's theory that everything with mass contains energy, even things we cannot hear or see. I further explain that five thousand years ago the Chinese realized that there are highways of energy in our bodies called meridians. Acupuncture and acupressure use these meridians. And the conventional medical world uses EKG and EEG to measure energy in the body. The soldier was generally in agreement with the concept of energy when I explained it this way.

I'd then say, "Let me tell you a story in which a soldier was driving on the highway when another car swerved into his lane. He quickly swerved out of the way and applied the brakes. His heart was beating faster, he was breathing faster, his muscles tightened up, and he was frightened. Luckily, nothing happened, and as he passed the car that almost crashed into him, he might have uttered some choice words, and even flipped a bird. When he arrived home, he immediately told his wife. Then he went to the gym and told his buddies. And upon returning home, he told his neighbor. So how many times did the near accident actually happen?"

Whether the answer was one or five times, the soldier would be right.

"Every time you tell the story, you relive it. Your body relives it, and your mind relives the fear, the anxiety, and the heart rate and blood pressure increase as if it were real. Your body doesn't recognize the difference with what was imagined and what was real, so by reliving the story you are practicing to be angry, to be scared, to be stressed. The trick is to let it go, instead of repeating and keeping the negative emotions."

I'd then ask the soldier, "Would you be interested in learning a tool that you can use anytime to lessen the emotional charge? You would still remember the event, but it wouldn't be so upsetting." If the soldier agreed, I then said, "Before I teach it to you, I want you to experience the technique first, and then I'll explain more about it. I want you to think of an event, past or recent, that was emotionally disturbing."

As this would be the first time, it was best if the event was a 7 or 8 on a Subjective Units of Distress (SUD) scale, where 0 was neutral and 10 highly emotionally charged.

"I want you to see the event in color, hear it, smell it, taste it, and touch it as much as possible." By "touch it," I meant to experience any tactile sensations associated with the event.

Once the soldier had an event in mind, I would ask him or her to tell me just a bit of it. Notably, it often wasn't the initial complaint the soldier expressed, but another event. When the soldier was connected with the event in his thoughts, in his feelings, in his body, I'd say, "For the next minute, just trust me and do what I do and say what I say. If you feel uncomfortable, you can change the words, or even stop."

For Spc. Fisher's anger issues, a high distress level, I had her say, while tapping on her hand (the Setup): "Even though I have all this uncontrollable anger, I'm still a good soldier."

This was repeated two more times. Then Fisher mirrored me as I tapped on the acupoints on the top of my head, face, and torso where the energy highways end, saying the word, "Anger." A minute later, when the tapping was done, I had Fisher take a deep breath.

There was a stunned but pleasant look on her face. She said with a wide grin, "What happened?"

Fisher was surprised she wasn't as angry. Instead, she was smiling and, in a light voice, said, "My mind feels calmer."

At this point, I presented my EFT book, which I'd brought from home, and offered certain websites where she could get additional information about the technique. I encouraged her to use tapping for her anger, and to use it to anticipate triggers, as it is easy and quick to do.

As this session was ending, another soldier was escorted in for counseling. Pfc. Matthews had received an Article 15 (of the Uniform Code of Military Justice, the foundation of military law) for falling asleep on guard duty. Under Article 15, for minor disciplinary offenses, a commanding officer can award certain limited punishments. In this case, Matthews received a fine, a loss of rank, and days of extra duty. He could fight the punishment, but he chose not to and used his mistake as a learning experience. Matthews planned to make a career in the army. The counseling enabled the soldier to vent if he wanted to, and for me to assess for possible harm to self or others.

Thinking I was finished with the morning and having missed breakfast, I walked around the FOB before heading off to lunch, when Sgt.
1st Class Dixon stopped me. Her sandy-colored hair was pulled back in
a tight bun. She looked older than her age.

"Ma'am, can I talk with you?"

"Of course. Why don't you come into my office," I said.

"No...how about my office?" She pointed nearby.

Her office was the largest room I'd seen at the camp, with a welcoming black leather couch. After I sat down, she told me about her melancholy and difficulties at work.

"Thanks for coming here. I don't want to be seen going to Behavioral
Health," she said.

"Why not?"

"I know some of my soldiers are going to dog me. They'll think I'm
nuts."

I was distraught at hearing this. Unfortunately, no matter how often
Big Army (Regular Army as opposed to Army Reserve) attempts to des-
tigmatize mental health, it has sadly not trickled down to the enlisted
soldiers. Dixon suffered a mild traumatic brain injury (mTBI) after a
fall and now had vertigo from time to time, as well as blackout spells.
Treated at Landstuhl Regional Medical Center in Germany, she should
have gone home but somehow returned to duty. I suggested she retake
the ANAM (Automated Neuropsychological Assessment Metrics) test so
that there was a comparison of her cognitive ability. Prior to deployment,
every soldier took a computer test to establish a cognitive functioning
baseline. The comparison would be helpful with her treatment and any
entitled health benefits.

The next day, Chaplain Arguello (one of the two CNS chaplains)
dropped by the office to introduce himself. In his thirties, with an athletic build and a warm smile, he was easy to engage with. I was sure we'd
see him again.

The FOB had been bustling since the assassination of President Karzai's half-brother the day before. Everybody was preparing for possible fall-out from this event, because Ahmed Wali Karzai was a negotiator for the insurgents and the United States in the Kandahar region. During the evening, the dark sky lit up. I saw a few orange glows in the distance and had to remind myself they weren't remnants of fireworks, which was my immediate thought before I remembered where I was. The glow was from rocket or mortar explosions.

I saw a couple of clients that day and administered the ANAM test to Dixon. Then I had to figure out how to retrieve the old test to make the comparison.

For most of the day we were unsuccessfully trying to get on Outlook accounts for both unclassified and classified levels of emails. We had to go to the civilian contractors who run the help desk for phones and computers in the camp. I'd overheard that they make a generous salary because the position requires high-security clearance and they work in a war zone for one to two years. After a couple of hours, with the contractor's assistance, I was finally able to log into my Afghan Outlook account, where I discovered I had 21 emails, the bulk generated from headquarters in KAF. Luckily, none of the emails were critical or time-sensitive.

The following morning, I received another call on my Afghan cell phone about a soldier being escorted to me for counseling. Pfc. Monroe had been forgetful and unable to focus on his job working in the prison. He was jittery. There was a sense of anxiety and uncertainty about him.

After a brief awkward pause, he said, "I had a brain cramp...I left my weapon in the truck last night. That's my bad...good thing it was locked."

There had been other incidents in the last three months, probably stemming from a yearlong home-front issue with his now ex-wife. He was scheduled to leave the theater in two weeks and he anticipated more legal battles over child custody and alimony payments. What he needed was just to talk, which we did.

The formerly angry Spc. Fisher dropped in as a follow-up. She laughed cheerfully and said, "I'm better. I've been tapping. I'm not afraid of exploding anymore."

After Fisher, a master sergeant walked in, asking for resources to handle his anticipated divorce when he finished his deployment. This was his fourth deployment. In response to an earlier suggestion from me, he had begun writing in a journal and said he found it helpful. I taught him how to tap for stress, as well as what to say while tapping:

"Even though I can't get myself straight, I'm stressed, I accept myself. I choose to breathe. I choose peace, joy, calmness, and laughter."

These were my words. Usually, after repeating the client's words as the first two EFT Setup Statements, the third time I would include "I choose to…" The words I added to that phrase often brought about some nodding, a deep breath, a smile—signs of resonance.

Settling In

Seeking as much shade as possible, I was finding shortcuts to and from my room, to the office, to the latrine. My sleeping quarter and office were in separate buildings, and I had to walk outside to different buildings to shower and to eat. It was still in the 115-degree range. The evenings were comfortable, however, and I could wear just an army T-shirt and PT (physical training) shorts. The FOB was a salute zone, though, so I couldn't daydream when I walked around. A soldier might salute me whether I was in uniform or in my PTs, and I'd have to return the salute. Sometimes I didn't see a salute but heard, "Ma'am," and I hurriedly saluted back, embarrassed.

Though it was hot, we were lucky that the mosquitoes in the area were tiny and sparse. Li had been bitten a couple of times, but I hadn't been bitten, probably because I wore my uniform as much as possible. The long sleeves helped, plus the uniform had built-in insect repellant. In regards to animals, there were some skinny stray cats and dogs, usually hanging around the DFAC trashcans. We were warned not to feed or pet them because of rabies. Earlier, I observed two German shepherds, with handlers, sniffing for possible explosives at a checkpoint—a dangerous duty.

From time to time, I visited the FOB's small PX to see what items might be on the shelves. There had been no shipment since I arrived, so the shelves remained bare. The manager told me I'd know when trucks arrived with supplies because there'd be a long line of soldiers outside waiting to get in.

On a quiet day, with just a couple of clients, my clinical director, Maj. Diaz, requested some paperwork and informed us that our footlockers were in country. Li and I requested that our lockers stay in KAF and not be sent to us, as we weren't staying at Camp Nathan Smith for long. When would we leave? We didn't know. In the meantime, stress was at a minimal yet constant level, considering we were in a war zone. No rocket or mortar attacks...yet.

We were settling in. Li and I were running the office without anyone peering over our shoulders. The meals were plentiful and good. My belly was starting to show again. It was time to cut back on the ice cream and do more walking.

This deployment wasn't my first time being away from home for a prolonged period of time. After I graduated from Cal, I went to work as a social worker in Chinatown for a youth organization. After eight months of working, I became disillusioned about how well the agency could help troubled teens from broken homes and poverty when gangs and drugs offered an attractive escape. I was young and ready for an adventure. Rob wrote me a letter of introduction to his fencing school in Paris that would allow me to train with the French national team for one year.

I'd saved up enough money for the airfare and expenses, but then I had to convince my parents that I would travel and live alone in a foreign country. At 22 years old, armed with fencing gear and high-school French, I was determined to go. My mother was not thrilled, but in the end, when she realized that I wasn't going to change my mind, she helped upgrade my plane ticket so that I could fly directly to France. That's love expressed in Chinese.

Living in Paris was difficult. My high-school French was useless. I couldn't get an apartment, because only French citizens could sign the rental agreement. Eventually, I met an English-speaking French school-teacher who needed a roommate and we moved into an apartment in St. Maur, a suburb of Paris. I would train with the French fencing team and have lunch at the school, return back to the apartment, and then go off to a fencing club in the evening. I didn't fence every day, though. Occasionally, I would walk around Paris, in the Latin Quarter, window-shop on the Champs-Élysée, and see a French movie, even though I didn't understand much. I carried a French-English dictionary with me all the time, and my roommate would help me with my French. By the time I left France, I was proficient in day-to-day conversation.

There were a couple of times during the first few months when I wanted to return home. Everything was so different. A mailbox there is much smaller than ours, and in order to use the pay phone you had to first buy a *jeton*. And Parisians are not the friendliest people. The most bizarre thing was seeing Asians and Africans speaking fluent French on the metro and buses. I told myself that I didn't have to stay, but maybe I saw it as a weakness, so I willed myself to stick it out. I'm glad I did. I met some wonderful people through my roommate. We were all in our 20s and many of them had traveled in the States. French people like to get together over food, with wine and cheese, of course, and talk. It would take at least half an hour to say good-bye to everyone, with the double to quadruple kisses on the cheeks. I never knew how many to do, so I just kept kissing until the other person stopped.

On a Saturday, July 16, a soldier walked in after being referred by her sergeant because of poor sleep. Li handled this case. I wanted her to do as much as possible to build up her skills and confidence.

The 113th Clinical Director emailed everyone to stipulate that all cases must be documented on the MC4 laptop electronic health record, which was not the way the outgoing BH team had trained us. I couldn't get on the program all day. I called the service desk, a technician came over, and I was finally able to log in. The technician even helped me uninstall and reinstall the video media player program on my personal laptop computer. The previous night I had realized I couldn't open any movies my brother Randy had downloaded to my computer. I was so happy when the reinstalled media player worked. I was going to watch a movie that night!

Then I received a call on my cell phone. Dixon, with the traumatic brain injury, had gone to the aid station and wanted me to share the intake form I'd done on her with the treating physician, who would send her home due to her many medical issues. I hoped her ANAM comparison report would come back before she headed out of CNS.

As I stepped inside the aid station with Dixon's intake form, I unexpectedly discovered a flush toilet—only for urine, not even toilet paper. Smiling and feeling a jolt of excitement, I realized I could use it during the night, as it was in the building next door to my sleeping quarter. It was so much closer and safer than walking in the dark to a smelly, filthy Porta Potty.

Sundays were time to get my laundry done. Laundry service was free. There were two ways to do it. I could drop my bag at a laundry service—nice, but it was a bit far and took one to two days to get the laundry back. Or I could take my clothes to the laundromat near the office and an elderly Afghan man would stuff it in the washer and dryer. He'd sometimes even fold the clothes. This was a better option, as my clothes would be clean and returned within two hours.

But that Sunday morning two soldiers came with escorts, back-to-back. One was Pvt. Nolan. In his early 20s, he admitted to suicidal/homicidal ideations and auditory hallucinations.

"I cut my wrists with a razor blade once in a while. It feels good…"

"When did you start this?" I asked.

"After high school."

"Do you cut to feel something?"

"I don't know…maybe."

"And when do you cut?"

"When I think about my dad…he's dead…"

'You miss him?"

"I'm angry…really angry at him!"

Nolan had previously worked with a civilian psychologist about his anger toward his absent father. I didn't identify whether he was exaggerating his symptoms, but since he entertained thoughts of hurting himself and others, he certainly didn't belong in theater. I referred him to the brigade surgeon in the aid station, who would probably refer him to KAF for a medication evaluation.

The second soldier was Spc. Pruett, who was brought in by his unit.

"Ma'am, can you say I'm not fit to stay in the army, that I'm crazy?"

After an assessment, I said, "You're not crazy, but it seems you're going through some difficulties."

"I have a bunch of problems here and at home. But I don't like people to know my business."

Pruett was facing multiple disciplinary charges. I recommended he stay in CNS for a couple of days for R&R (rest and recuperation): eat, sleep, and contact his family. This might give him renewed energy to face his upcoming court-martial.

Later Li and I had lunch with a civilian contractor. He called himself Dido and worked as a mechanic. We mentioned that we had a box of carpentry tools in the office, left behind by Sgt. Little. Dido was glad to come pick up the tools, which opened more space for us in our tiny office.

Many civilian contractors work in the camp. Their jobs range from cooks, custodians, interpreters, analysts, and mechanics to jobs in security, information technology, and logistics. They generally work 12 hours a day, seven days a week, for months, with opportunities to renew their job. All require a security clearance.

To my surprise, the next day, Pruett showed up, elated. The little amount of R&R he'd had was already leaving him smiling. "I had four hours of sleep," he said. "I even Skyped with my wife. I'm cool."

On our way to lunch, Fisher, whom I saw a week earlier, stopped me and giggled, "Things are goin' good. I'm still doing the tapping, it's working." She was especially joyful because she was leaving country a few days later.

Li and I tried to meet Lt. Col. Cook again, but he wasn't in his office.

Dixon gave me some wonderful news. She offered us her office space, saying that her unit didn't need it. The space was about three times the size of our current clinic. It had an outer office and a larger inner office perfect for running groups. I called Col. Rabb about this possible space, and he called the CNS Mayor Cell. They and the commander agreed to give it to us. We'd get a place all to ourselves—no need to share with Finance!

Col. Rabb told us that our replacement might not get into country until mid-August, meaning we'd have at least another month at Camp Nathan Smith.

I bought a couple of knockoff DVDs from the local bazaar, at two bucks each: *Captain America: The First Avenger* and *Mission Impossible 4: Ghost Protocol*. In our office we had a projector, and watched them on the wall. Movies helped pass the time, and temporarily made us forget that we were in Afghanistan with its endless dust, intense heat, and bleakness.

During the first few weeks, Li and I began to recognize some soldiers and locals on base. Generally, however, I found most soldiers problematic to individualize. Everyone wore the same uniform and mandatory eye protection (dark sunglasses) and headgear. On the other hand, Li and I—two Asian females—were easy to distinguish, so people recognized us. Many soldiers also recognized that Li and I were Behavioral Health. I asked one sergeant in the PX how he knew I was BH, and he said, "Just look for a captain with an M-16 rifle." Most officers didn't carry a rifle—rather an M9 handgun—but my unit had issued me a rifle. Li thought that was because our unit was poor, with only a few handguns in its armory.

One evening while typing on my laptop in my room, I was startled when a tiny brown mouse scurried along the wall. He stopped by my luggage and stared curiously up at me with his dark eyes. My initial thought was that he was cute and maybe I should feed him. But my better judgment kicked in and I got up and opened the door. As I moved the luggage, the mouse retraced his footsteps and scarpered out of the room. I quickly closed the door and then slept deeply and soundly.

The next day, Tuesday, July 19, I worked 12 hours. Even though I was scheduled to start work at 1200 hours, I had to go in early to see Pruett, with the disciplinary problems. He was happy and rejuvenated; he was ready for whatever the army was going to throw at him. He had contacted his chaplain, who'd agreed to assist him. He was supposed to be picked up at 1200 hours but came in the office at 1600 hours, saying no one from his company had come to get him. He would stay another night at CNS.

Dixon's ANAM pre-test came in. I met with her and compared her past and current tests. It was clear that her current cognitive ability was well below average. She knew of her difficulties and this provided some relief, as it was tangible proof. The brigade doctor had arranged for her to leave theater soon. Although Dixon expressed reluctance to leave, she realized she could harm herself and others if she were unable to do her job.

My daily schedule was to wake up at 0730 hours, walk a block to wash up, do a bit of exercise in the room (yoga handstands, arm curls with my rifle, push-ups, and sit-ups), get dressed, and go off to breakfast, which was another block away. After that, I'd head to the office around 0830 hours, see clients that dropped in or came by appointment, catch up on emails on my Afghan, Yahoo, and AKO (Army Knowledge Online) accounts and, of course, paperwork.

If it wasn't too hot, Li and I conducted some walkabouts to introduce ourselves and generate some business. We would stop by the smoke pits (outdoor areas designated for smoking), the gym, the PX, and anywhere else where off-duty soldiers would chill so that we could exchange pleasantries or share a joke or two. These face-to-face meetings helped break the ice and to encourage them to visit us if they wanted to, either to talk or just out of curiosity.

Lunch was at 1130 hours. I was usually hungry and ate a large meal. Back to the office for more phone and computer work, maybe see some clients, and check emails. The afternoons were slow, partly because of the heat (110+ degrees) and leaving the office wasn't a good option. By the time 1730 hours rolled around, Li and I were starving. We didn't understand why we were so hungry. We weren't exercising much, yet we were constantly thinking about food between meals. Maybe eating provided steady blood sugar and, being so far from home, we were constantly hoping for some familiar comfort foods.

At 2230 hours, I was in my room watching the movie *The Hangover* when my cell phone rang. Reorienting myself quickly, I answered the phone. The manager of the PX, a sergeant, was calling me for help with his distressed soldier, Spc. Pacheco. I quickly dressed and went to the PX. Even in the dim light, I could see that Pacheco's eyes were red and swollen.

"How can I help?" I asked.

"My wife hasn't been eating. I think she's lost 15 to 20 pounds in three weeks."

"Has she seen a doctor?"

"Yeah. She went to the doctors, even two trips to the ER. The doctors don't know what's going on..." Pacheco quickly added, "I want to go home to be with her, but my commander won't give me leave."

We brainstormed. Pacheco made a call and was able to convince his wife's sister to help. This provided some momentary relief for him.

The following morning began with Sgt. Smith and another soldier with an Article 15 (violation of the Uniform Code of Military Justice) for disrespecting a female officer. The two soldiers had shared a couple of sexist jokes with the female officer. Even after she told them it was inappropriate and to stop, both soldiers continued their bantering. She notified her superior officer. They'd had their disciplinary hearing the night before and now would be discharged from the army. It may sound unforgiving, but as a female I was glad the army wasn't tolerating sexual harassment. I must admit, however, that I felt sorry for Smith. He would lose his career in the army, and after six years, it wasn't the way to leave.

Even though Thursday's hours didn't officially start until noon, I went into the office in the morning at the usual time. This allowed me time to do the perpetual dusting, email Rob, and catch up on other paperwork. As each day went by, the 113th unit demanded more reports or for us to follow more SOPs (standard operating procedures). The clinic director, Maj. Diaz, called me and we went over the documentation procedure and clinic protocols. Moreover, he no longer wanted the clinic referred to as Behavioral Health, but rather "Combat Stress Control Center." The former implied a diagnosis, a "crazy" label, whereas the latter referred to normal reactions to combat and operational stress-related issues, such as dealing with leadership, being away from family, financial concerns, traumatic incidents, injuries, and death. I agreed with this.

Pruett dropped by and said, "My unit is going to pick me up today." Two days later than planned. But with his newly acquired happy-go-lucky attitude, the lateness didn't bother the soldier. In fact, he would have been glad just hanging around the camp for the rest of the deployment.

I saw a new client, Staff Sgt. Vasquez. Tall and striking, she had hazel eyes that seemed dull and blood-shot, with dark shadows underneath.

"I can't think, can't sleep, I can't turn things off," she said. "This is my second deployment...I should be used to this, but..."

"What else is going on?"

"I miss my husband and baby girl. She's two."

"What else?"

"I hate my job, it's meaningless..."

I taught her tapping. Vasquez chose to tap on "information overload" at work. She copied me and tapped, starting on the side of her hand and then the top of her head, eyebrow, side of the eye, under the eye, under the nose, the chin, collarbone, and, lastly, on her side under the arm. Her initial Subjective Units of Distress (SUD) scale rating was a 10 (10 indicating the highest level). After one round, it went down to an 8.

"What makes it an 8?" I asked.

"Well, there's work, lots of it, but it doesn't go anywhere. Just shuffling paper from one pile to another pile," she replied.

We tapped for, "Shuffling paper, lots of it." Then the SUD went to a 5.

"What's left, what does the 5 represent?" I said.

"It's a waste of my time, my talents. I could do more."

We tapped for, "Could do more. Waste of talent." Then the SUD went to a 0. In a matter of minutes, with three rounds of tapping, her distress was neutralized. The stunned glow on her face was priceless. She asked more about tapping, and I demonstrated to her how to use it for falling asleep.

"Tap 30 minutes before you sleep, since you are putting energy into your body," I explained.

"Tap on the side of the hand and say, 'Even though my mind is racing 1,000 miles an hour, I choose to turn it off. I choose to be pleasantly drowsy, to have peaceful dreams, to sleep throughout the night, to be rested, and to be ready for the day's challenge.'"

Vasquez shook my hand and said, "Thank you for joining the army to help soldiers."

Her sincere response helped me keep going.

We didn't have any clients the following day. It was a good thing, as the opportunity came for moving into our new space. We "procured" furniture from the old office—anything that wasn't nailed to the floor. Combined with what remained in the new office, when we were finished, we had two desks, two office chairs, file cabinets, pillows, a folding table, two folding chairs for clients, and a large, rectangular, red wool carpet. All of this created an open, inviting area. Without the advocacy of Dixon, this wouldn't have happened. On behalf of all soldiers needing combat stress control support, I couldn't thank her enough. Now it was just get-ting the computers and phones working. I hoped that everything would be ready to go by the next day.

That night I wrote Rob an email. Actually, I told him, some things in Afghanistan were better than at home: 1) free laundry service; 2) no need to shop, prepare, cook, or wash dishes for any meal (plus there was plenty of food and drinks—all you wanted); 3) not much cleaning to do (no mop or vacuum cleaner—yet); 4) free gym membership, even though I wasn't using it; and 5) time to catch up on my movies. I must think of the positive stuff.

Rob's response to this list was that Camp Nathan Smith was ideal for retirement. Yeah, right!

On Saturday, we were getting the phone lines and computer lines connected in the new office. At least the right people were coming in to do the work. I told Col. Rabb about our space and that we had to share it with Preventive Medicine (PM). I thought it would be good if PM could use the Finance office space instead and had suggested this to Capt. Maxim. She hesitantly agreed, but later told me she needed our new space and the partnership of helping one another. I acknowledged the help medical had given us and that we definitely wanted to continue that relationship. So we returned to the original agreement of sharing space in the new office. Everyone was happy. The captain guided me to two conference rooms, one next to our office and one behind our office, which we could use for therapy if need be. One conference room had a large wall-mounted monitor; with a laptop, we could show weekly mov-ies in the room. I mentioned this idea to the Mayor Cell, and it was a go. All we had to do was pick a day for Movie Night.

By Sunday our office was fully functioning, with phones and com-puters. I sat at my desk, looking around and enjoying the comfortable space. It was another quiet day, with only one client. Pvt. Joseph ambled in, standing six-foot-two and weighing two hundred pounds. With a red face and in a prickly tone, Joseph said, "I'm mad as hell. I just found out my wife wants a divorce."

"And what do you want?" I asked.

"I want to go home and fix this."

After taking a thorough history, I advised him to seek legal consultation from a local attorney in his city. Joseph revealed he was sleeping only three hours a night. Since Joseph understood he couldn't go home until his tour was over, he was willing to learn tapping to lower his anxiety.

Tapping on the side of his hand, Joseph repeated after me, "Even though I'm mad...I'm angry. How dare she want a divorce...I deeply and completely accept myself."

Then tapping on the acupoints on his head, face, and torso, Joseph said, "I'm mad. Divorce. Angry. Mad as hell."

Joseph initially reported a SUD level of 8. After one round, it went to a 4. Joseph said he was pissed, and now being more specific, Joseph echoed my words, "Even though I still have some anger, even though I'm still pissed, I deeply and completely accept myself." Then tapping on his head, face, and torso, Joseph said, "This remaining anger." After the second round, his SUD went to a 1. The edge in his voice was gone. He was visibly calmer and gave me a grateful smile. I also taught him how to tap for sleep, encouraging him to use it before lights out.

Missing the Comforts of Home

I always thought myself to be an appreciative person, but the many things that I took for granted at home were made apparent at Camp Nathan Smith. For example, at CNS hardly anything was new; we had decaying furniture, desks, shelves, walls, and ceilings. In my "new" office, there was an old chair permanently in the recline position because of missing screws and bolts. Normally, I would discard such a chair and buy a new one from Office Max. But at CNS I had to repair it, because where would I get another one? Fortunately, Dido, the mechanic, had agreed to fix the chair. If not for our friendship, I'd always be reclining!

Even a single wall nail was precious. After I found one and pounded it into the wall, I was finally able to hang up my wet towel in my room. I used a plastic bag for garbage, emptying it out from time to time so that I could reuse it. Li and I had arrived here with no resources at our disposal. We used our wit and charm to network and improvise. We bartered bags of Seattle's Best Coffee (entrusted to us by our predecessors) for items or services. There was still nothing on the PX shelves.

There wasn't even a post office. Ordering merchandise online was fine, but the mailing system to and from Afghanistan was unreliable. I was told one story about it taking three and a half months for a soldier's laptop to arrive. The soldier had figured it was lost and bought another one during his R&R. Now he had two.

I was able to Skype with Rob on Monday morning. I'd had been worried about not making enough contact with him. We saw each other for only a brief moment because the connectivity was poor. We exchanged some nervous small talk, both of us smiling at nothing, but after the Internet dropped so many times, we finally gave up. Nevertheless, it was well worth the few seconds of seeing Rob's face again.

Before announcing Movie Night at CNS, I bought an HDMI cable from the local bazaar and made sure my laptop worked with the monitor in the conference room. The image and sound were clear. Li got busy making flyers and we ran around the FOB posting them. While at the gym, Terence of MWR (Morale, Welfare, and Recreation) handed us boxes of used DVDs. We borrowed five of them so that soldiers could choose the next movie. Li would make popcorn. Terence's office had an array of colorful magazine pages taped up over the walls. We thought this was a great idea to cover one side of our office wall, where the plaster was falling off. We spent the afternoon making a large collage, holding it down with strips of gray duct tape. Not an art piece one would find in a museum, but good enough for this base in Afghanistan.

I received an email from 1st Sgt. Schumacher that he, Sgt. McCollough, Cpl. Vo, and Zeke, the therapy dog, would come to CNS August 5–8. This visit would fulfill a dual purpose: walkabout with Zeke and a surprise promotion for Li, from private first class to specialist (E-4). Schumacher asked me to find an embroidered E-4 rank and pin for her.

The PX received a small shipment on Monday night and opened early the next morning, with nonstop customers thereafter. I bought two bottles of shampoo, one for Li and one for myself, and my favorite snacks: Cheez-Its and white cheddar popcorn—something crunchy and salty. At last, civilization had arrived! Well, at least until everything ran out, which would probably be that afternoon.

While I was in the Mayor Cell to arrange housing for my first sergeant and group, I asked a sergeant if he was recently promoted and whether he had his old specialist rank. Spc. Delgado overheard me and confidently said he could get them to me. I went back to my office and gladly gave Delgado my box of Cheez-Its in appreciation. Later in the day, Delgado came into my office and shook my hand. As he did, I felt something in my palm. When I glanced down, I saw an embroidered E-4 rank and pin. I thanked him.

The next morning was extremely quiet, until after lunch when two soldiers walked-in. Staff Sgt. Wallace was crying and I thought Capt. Riley was escorting her. Both had come in, however, worried about retaliation by their company's commander for their lodging an IG (Inspector General) complaint against him. Rumor had it that the commander had found out who had made the complaint and was going to make life hell for them. It was the uncertainty of when and what would happen that was most distressing for them. After reviewing that they had documentation to support their position, I suggested they follow up with the Equal Opportunity officer for harassment in the workplace and to go over the commander's head with their concerns. Wallace would return to the clinic the next day.

At the same time, Spc. Morales came for his weekly appointment, requiring Li to see him in the outer office. As soon as I was finished with Riley and Wallace, a civilian named David walked in requesting to talk to someone. He didn't look good: unshaven, sorrowful eyes, and slumped posture. Employed by the State Department, David was a public diplomacy officer at CNS.

"I just found out my friend, a close friend, just died…in an accident in New York. What am I doing here?" He lamented, "I haven't done shit in my 33 years of life. No wife, no kids, no house, no graduate degree…"

I focused on his strengths and achievements, but it wasn't convincing. A review of his depression revealed a history of taking anti-anxiety and antidepressant medications. I asked if he wanted to go back on antidepressants and he agreed. I walked him over to the aid station.

After one last appointment, I finally called it a day—another 12-hour workday.

On Wednesday, July 27, the temperature reached 120 degrees. In my new office, the air conditioner blew hot air—it was broken. We had Seabees (US Navy personnel) check the system and they declared it fried, kaput, and dead. The worst part was that the Mayor Cell had given away the last new air conditioner a week earlier and didn't anticipate getting any more in the near future. This wasn't good.

We had just two clients that day: a follow-up with insomnia, and Wallace from the day before. Wallace was less emotional, although still teary at times. During the session, she received a text that a suicide bomber had assassinated the mayor of Kandahar City, the second leader from the Kandahar region to be killed that month. With a sense of dread, I understood the war was getting closer to me.

I came in earlier on Thursday morning. It was quiet and I could check my emails, and, at times, soldiers would drop in, as they did that day. Pfc. Aviles was escorted in for anger management.

Cracking her knuckles, she said in a deep tone, "He wouldn't shut up…he kept saying my name…so I grabbed and pushed him."

"Do you regret what you did?" I asked.

"Yeah, I know it's wrong, but I couldn't stop myself…"

Prior to the military, she had a history of impulsive behavior and making negative and critical remarks of others. Her anger was a problem and she wanted to learn how to control it to avoid getting into trouble. She was up for a promotion and didn't want her unfiltered outbursts to get in the way. I taught her tapping to lower her anxiety and to increase calmness.

In the afternoon, a first sergeant wanted one of his soldiers to be seen. Cpl. Abraham was the driver of a vehicle that had rolled over weeks earlier. In his early 20s, with neatly combed auburn hair, he spoke softly.

"The…the…truck hit…hit…something…I don't know what… before I knew it, I…I was upside down. I haven't driven since."

"What else is going on?" I asked.

"I…I fell asleep while on guard duty the…the night before the accident."

"Oh?"

"Yeah…Sarge snuck in and took my rifle when I was asleep."

Abraham completed the PCL-M (Posttraumatic Checklist–Military Version) inventory that indicated PTSD. He reported a disturbing image that he couldn't let go of, in which the gunner was cut in half after a rollover. This hadn't actually happened, but for this soldier it was a reminder that it could happen if he wasn't careful. Abraham also realized that if he were preoccupied with this image, he wouldn't be able to focus on the current situation.

"Corporal, I would like you to copy my tapping and repeat after me. Okay?" He narrowed his eyes but nodded in agreement.

"Even though I can't let go of this image, this large image, this bright colorful image, I choose to shift it to black and white…shrinking it, and it gets smaller and blurrier into a tiny spot, becoming so tiny that I can't see it anymore."

When we finished tapping, Abraham squeezed his eyes shut and then opened them again. "Oh wow," he said. His worried face transformed into a bemused expression. I scheduled him to return to the clinic the next day.

Layla, a civilian contractor with DoD (Department of Defense) Civil Affairs, came into our office to reclaim a small black table. She had been away on a mission when we moved in. In Afghanistan for 10 months, she was ready for a month of R&R. After that, she would work another six months. She described Camp Nathan Smith as home, saying that it wasn't too large, had people she could trust, and everything was accessible by foot. I was reassured to hear this.

I watched *Thor* that night in my room and the little mouse visited me again. There was a slight gap under the door through which the mouse could easily squeeze. Again after opening the door, I was able to scare it out of my room. I thought I should give the mouse a name.

The next day, more weekly reports (JMEW and SITREP) were due. Li was on top of it. I saw three clients. One was a walk-in referred by the aid station because of stress. Every little thing was bothering her. When I told her about tapping and how it could be helpful, she thought it was silly and wasn't interested in trying it. I discussed meditation, deep breathing exercises, increasing physical exercise, and a better sleep cycle. With eyes rolling and arms and legs crossed, she showed what she thought of these suggestions. She had numerous problems and wanted medication to solve them. I asked her to return for a follow-up, but I didn't think she would.

Wallace was doing better. She was no longer overly emotional, so we would decrease our sessions. Abraham, who had been involved in the rollover, returned. He was no longer bothered by the image, but he readily mentioned incidents of losing his temper and fighting when in high school. He realized that his behavior would get him into trouble, perhaps serious trouble if he didn't find a way to control his anger. Abraham would return the next day with a technique of his choice (after researching it on the Internet) that he wanted to use for anger management.

It was Friday night, which meant lobster tail for dinner! But it was a bit overcooked and not as delicious as I remembered. Everything was beginning to get old… and I still had how many months to go? Eight to 10 more months!

A sergeant came in for a behavioral health evaluation as part of her application to Recruitment and Retention School. This evaluation was necessary for any soldiers interested in being a recruiter. A possible benefit as a recruiter was an assignment closer to home for three years. This was my first recruiter application; luckily, there were old reports that I used as templates.

Abraham came in. When he sat down, his head lowered to his chest. With a long sigh, he said, "This is my last appointment. The guys in my platoon are dogging me because I come here."

"Does coming here help?" I asked.

"Yeah, sure."

This made me furious. I spoke with the first sergeant about this "dogging" and he said he would talk to the platoon. Many soldiers believe that seeking help would harm their career or they would be considered weak for seeking help, and many are afraid that their peers would lose confidence in their abilities. I introduced Abraham to a martial arts instructor, Dido (the civilian mechanic). If I couldn't counsel him, I hoped martial arts would help relieve this young soldier's stress.

I was about to go for dinner when a soldier from the aid station came in and told us we had mail. Li went to pick it up and returned to the clinic. The first box was shampoo and conditioner Li had purchased from Amazon. The second box was from HQ with our extra issued PT uniform. I decided not to keep the jacket, pants, and shorts. I just didn't need them, or the extra weight in my luggage. I planned to give them to the Civil Affairs supply sergeant when I picked up the Shop-Vac. I'd discovered they had a vacuum cleaner, which I badly needed to borrow.

My "Home" Away from Home

On the last day of July, I realized I had been out of the United States for one month. It felt like a lot longer. In the morning, I strapped on my body armor (IOTV), carried my weapon, and walked around the camp. I needed to get back in shape, able to tolerate wearing the IOTV, for when I checked out of CNS. I couldn't believe it had been three weeks since I had last worn it. Though that quickly became evident—within five minutes my left shoulder throbbed from the weight.

I saw only one client that day, a civilian who complained about sometimes not being able to fall asleep. Once he was asleep, he could sleep 10 to 12 hours straight. I reviewed his current sleep hygiene and discovered he had a good regular sleep schedule and no computer use, exercising, or eating protein close to bedtime. I offered a muscle relaxation exercise, counting backward by threes or sevens, and visualizing a calm, peaceful place. He soaked up the advice and quick-stepped out of the clinic, pleased with some new options.

I wanted to be productive, so I searched information on the Internet for dealing with anxiety, anger management, and sleep hygiene and printed them as handouts. I pinned them up on the bulletin board in the foyer of our office for soldiers and civilians to pick up. These were the most common complaints of those who came to see us.

August 1 was the first day of Ramadan, the Muslim holy month. From dawn to dusk Muslims need to refrain from eating, drinking, smoking, and having sex. By evening, insurgents are peeved, I presumed, because August is usually the deadliest month of the war.

I started my day eagerly waiting for the PX to open. I rushed to the store to find boxes stacked up everywhere, making it difficult to maneuver. Many of the shelves were still bare, however, except for the snacks section. Most of the merchandise delivered was junk food: chips, pretzels, popcorn, cookies, and a variety of candies—all tempting and tasty, but not good for me.

I wore my body armor again and was relieved to find I was able to wear it longer without the aching pain in my left shoulder. I hoped to build my stamina to half an hour; it was a good workout.

Just one soldier came in for an R&R briefing in the morning. Occasionally, when the chaplain is busy, Combat Stress provides this required briefing to soldiers wanting to return home. It occurs about halfway through their deployment and covers what to say, what not to say, and to take things slowly with their children.

In the afternoon, Li and I attempted for the fifth time to meet Lt. Col. Cook of the 1-10 Cavalry. Even though I might be at Camp Nathan Smith for a short time, I felt it was essential to introduce Combat Stress to the FOB's commander and his staff, emphasizing how we could assist in keeping his soldiers combat ready. Instead, we talked with Maj. Krattiger, who suggested I send Cook an email as a reminder. He would also check the colonel's schedule, so we'd know when to come.

As much as I condemned the infernal heat, I enjoyed the mornings and evenings wearing my running shoes, PT shorts, and short-sleeve T-shirt. I marched around lighter and freer, just carrying my rifle. It was very comfortable and so unusual for me to do this, especially coming from cool and foggy San Francisco.

Dido, the contractor, came by and fixed my desk drawers. Time after time, I had to gingerly open the draw or I'd find a panel of fake pressed wood in my hand. I was glad we had become friends. Besides being a mechanic, Dido, who was about to turn 61, was an eighth-degree black belt in Kajukenbo (a martial arts style), a great fix-it man, and an all-around good guy.

Maj. Krattiger returned my email and suggested we meet the staff during their weekly meeting, which was the next morning. I replied that Li and I would be happy to attend. I wanted Li to develop a one-page handout and prepare a short, concise introduction of what services we provided. I was responsible for reporting things we had accomplished in the past month: move into a new office space; combat stress flyers; creation of Movie Nights; handouts on handling stress, sleep hygiene, and anger management in the foyer; and a check-and-balance system when soldiers needed to leave Afghanistan. By "check-and-balance-system," I meant I wouldn't solely decide who had to leave but would seek out a second opinion. I also wanted to speak about the stigma of seeking help. Unfortunately, this stigma remained strong, in society as a whole but especially in the military. Yet when soldiers didn't get help, unnecessary suffering occurred, even to the point of suicide. I was hoping to encourage the command staff to recommend counseling to their troubled soldiers.

I finally received my dates for R&R: November 7–21, 2011. This would be halfway through my deployment, if I returned home March or April 2012. Rob hoped my break was in January, when it wouldn't affect his competitive fencing season, but as an officer I didn't have a choice. Junior enlisted soldiers had first priority.

In the morning, Col. Rabb called to inform us that there was a possibility the Taliban might attack CNS. My heart skipped a beat. There was no known timeline. I told him I'd inform my Mayor Cell office. While I had the colonel on the phone, I asked him about our replacements. As a reply, he spoke about the big picture: There was a request for more Combat Stress Control personnel at more FOBs; current 113th CSC teams with more than four members would split up to cover more FOBs; and as there were only the two of us, Li and I would be staying at Camp Nathan Smith. The colonel's original plan had been for me to travel to other FOBs to relieve providers on R&R. I was glad this wasn't going to happen. I detested having to pack and haul my gear to the flight line. Doing it multiple times in the frustrating attempts to get from KAF to CNS had been enough.

When I grasped I'd be staying at CNS, I sighed in relief, overjoyed and greatly thankful. I now knew where I'd be hanging up my hat—or helmet—for the duration of my deployment. The first thing I did was email my supply sergeant, asking for our footlockers to be sent from KAF. Li was also thrilled because now she could order things online and her husband could send her favorite things. For the past month, we had been unsure of our situation and hadn't wanted to settle in, but now we were going to shop for items to make our home-away-from-home as comfortable as possible.

In our office the following day, Li practiced her presentation to the 1-10 Cavalry command staff. After finding the right words from four rehearsals, Li was prepared. We were both nervous about speaking before a group we had never met. I had written a summary note and rehearsed it at night and again in the morning.

We arrived early at Maj. Krattiger's office and he escorted us to the meeting room. As we sat there, more and more soldiers and officers crowded into the room. When it was time for our presentation, there were at least 20 people. Everything went as planned; Li did a great job. The best part was when I mentioned we had moved out of the Finance office. Command Sgt. Maj. Veneklasen lifted up his head in disbelief—it was priceless! Veneklasen wasn't supportive of Combat Stress Control and when Finance came to the camp, he said we were to stay in our quarters. Now we weren't required to!

The group also nodded their heads when I described a check-and-balance system for sending soldiers home if needed. I could make the initial determination and then refer the case to the brigade surgeon. If necessary, he would refer the case to the psychiatrist at KAF.

Many commanders believe that Combat Stress Control is a travel agency that sends soldiers home. This is just not true. Every soldier deployed is a valuable part of the mission. Every soldier that leaves theater requires one to two additional soldiers to escort the departing soldier home. No commander can afford to be understaffed. The counseling in theater is preventive: to identify and treat issues before they become full-blown depression and posttraumatic stress. Our goal was to teach soldiers to cope so that they could stay in the fight. Combat Stress Control is a force multiplier.

One member of the command staff asked if we would travel to COBs (Combat Operating Bases) and to COPs (Combat Outposts), essentially going where the soldiers were. Without hesitation, I said yes. I learned that other 113th CSC teams were doing this. Moreover, it would be good to leave the camp and see what was out there.

After the meeting, I went on Amazon and ordered a handheld vacuum cleaner. I couldn't believe this was the first thing I wanted after learning that I was staying at CNS. The dirt on the thin carpet in my room and in the office was driving me mad!

I went to see Terence at MWR about getting some space in the gym for a fencing program. I thought this would be an unusual, exciting, mentally and physically challenging activity for soldiers to do when not working. Terence was very supportive, saying, "Anything for the soldiers." I had lost the contact email to Blue Gauntlet Fencing store, so I wrote to the company. I hoped they would offer a generous donation of fencing equipment for the soldiers.

It was so hot that day I couldn't sit on the Porta Potty toilet seat. Even worse, our office's broken air conditioner blew scorching hot air during the warmest period of the day. Li and I removed our uniform blouses, and we were slightly cooler. But when a soldier came in for counseling, we had to dress quickly.

Veneklasen was the first person I saw on Thursday morning. As I was walking into my office, he joked about needing counseling and wanted to see what building I had confiscated for Combat Stress Control. Fortunately, Capt. Ferrell, the Officer in Charge of the Mayor Cell, was there, too, and he asserted it wasn't a building but an office. Veneklasen walked away. Ferrell stayed and inspected the new space. He knew that we were sharing space with Preventive Medicine.

After Ferrell left, two soldiers walked in for services: Pfc. Aviles, who I had seen the previous week for anger issues, and her sergeant. I met with Sgt. Moore first. I noticed his slow shuffle and downcast eyes as he expressed worries about his seriously ill 2-year-old son. He had known about his son's illness for the past eight months, and being in theater for six weeks hadn't helped. He spent his off-duty time constantly worried and feeling helpless. I taught him tapping to release some of the stress, and recommended a book written by Susan Jeffrey Busen, *Tap into Joy: A Guide to Emotional Freedom Techniques for Kids and Their Parents*. I encouraged him to do more research on how tapping could help with health issues.

Then I listened to Aviles, who had angrily grabbed a soldier the week before. As she informed me that there had been no incidents since then, her eyes twinkled.

"Things don't bother me anymore," she said. "My platoon leader and sarge even noticed it. I'm just more chill."

The next morning, Sgt. Smith walked into the office. He had dark circles under his eyes, his hair was unkempt, and his uniform loosely worn. I had met with him nearly two weeks earlier, for disrespecting a female officer. After his Article 15 hearing, he was to return to the States.

"Ma'am, do you remember me?"

"Yes, of course, Sergeant."

"I'm still waiting for my orders to leave theater, but I can't. The battalion commander won't sign it. I think they forgot about me…"

Smith became more agitated as he talked. He wanted to move on but felt unimportant. He reported only two to three hours of sleep a night and no appetite. When he did eat, he was unable to keep his food down. He firmly denied suicidal ideations and homicidal ideations. He had a girlfriend and a son.

I went to Capt. Ferrell, who learned about the situation, and said he planned to see the colonel that evening, hoping to get the required signature. I scheduled to meet with Smith the next morning.

At noon, Smith lumbered into the office.

"Sorry, I'm late, Ma'am. I just woke up. I finally fell asleep this morning."

I again went to Ferrell's office and he said the main office was closed until 1400 hours, since it was Sunday, and for me to return then. At 1410 hours, Ferrell said orders were set for Smith to fly out of CNS at 1800 hours. At least one emergency MEDEVAC was diverted.

On Monday I spoke to Capt. Gillespie (my XO) and told him that the 1-10 Cavalry wanted Li and me to go to the COBs (Combat Operating Bases). The captain asked for the names of the COBs so that he could figure the routes to these places. I told him I'd contact the 1-10 Cavalry and get the information. Things might shape up to where Li and I could go outside the wire (out of the camp) to help soldiers or at least let them know who we were and what we were doing.

I wrote to the executive officer of 1-10 Calvary about Li and my willingness (and approval from our command) to visit outer COBs. Unfortunately, ground convoys were the only way to reach the COBs and Col. Rabb emphasized we could only go where there were critical, pressing issues, such as Unit Needs Assessment and Traumatic Event Management. Therefore, I didn't know how much we could actually serve the outer COBs.

There were no clients that day, but Terence gave us some paint and Kleenex (clients were using toilet paper to wipe away tears). With the paint, I hoped Li would make a bigger, better sign for the clinic. Desiring physical activity, I suggested we play Ping-Pong in the cooler part of the afternoon. Weight machines, treadmills, and stationary exercise bikes in the gym were the only other physical activities we could do indoors. And these aren't as fun as Ping-Pong.

Tuesday was another scorching day. August was definitely hotter than July. The mornings and evenings when I ventured out felt like being in an oven. Even though I had a convenient excuse not to wear my body armor and walk around with it, I did anyway. I also did my usual handstand, push-ups, and sit-ups in my room. Maybe one day I'd get up early and work out in the gym, shower, and then go to work. Yeah, right!

That morning, a sergeant brought in Pvt. Rae, frazzled by his unit and a home issue. Although the sergeant had tried to stop the harassing,

Rae continued to be the brunt of jokes, mocked for his clumsiness and targeted for extra duties.

Rae bit his lower lip. "I'm jacked up. I cry every night...I shouldn't, but I tell my fiancée when I call her. She has her own problems...her health isn't good."

"Maybe talking about it would help," I said. "You also have the option of filing an EO complaint about a hostile work environment."

Then I taught him how to tap to release some anger and stress. I scheduled him to return in three days to check on his progress.

In the afternoon, angry young Cpl. Abraham came in for his weekly visit, even angrier now that his R&R had been pushed back a week. He raged about the many ways he could get out of the army, or rather how the army could throw him out. I discussed the possible ramifications and consequences. I was thinking he'd find a way, the least damaging one, I hoped, and not one where he'd end up facing a court-martial.

The last weekly client for the evening was Capt. Benton.

"I know I'm better," he told me. "I was able to control my temper for about a month now. There was one recent incident where I could have chewed my colleague's head off, but I didn't."

More important, his relationship with his girlfriend continued to thrive. And he had just found out that in two months he'd start a new job in his unit, though he admitted, "There are times I don't want to be in Afghanistan. I miss being with my friends, the fishing and hunting trips."

"What would you say is a positive aspect of deployment?" I asked.

Without hesitation Benton said, "The money." He hoped to buy a home when he returned.

In the office on Wednesday, I tried taking the Commanders Safety Course online, a required training. But the Internet was so slow I decided to take just the test without studying the material. Of course, I failed.

It had been rumored that a new Internet company would be coming to CNS by the end of the month—a faster, more reliable service at a lower monthly cost.

I had a welcome surprise in the morning: My footlocker had arrived from KAF. The first thing I did was to refill my vitamin chest. I'd been out of everything for a couple of weeks. At the same time, I'd gone one month without missing other things that were in the footlocker and I wondered why I had packed an extra pair of combat boots, extra T-shirts, combination locks, towels, and washcloths. Moreover, a large USO box came filled with shampoos, toothpastes, snacks, batteries, and free AT&T calling cards. Just like Christmas! Now I needed to rearrange my tiny sleeping quarter to fit a footlocker.

I finally went for a haircut. I normally wear my hair short, but the most recent time I'd had it cut was in San Francisco, when I was there on my four-day pass in June. The barbers in the camp were two local Afghan brothers. Haircuts cost $3 for men and $7 for women. While waiting for my haircut, I eavesdropped on two soldiers' account of a Taliban insurgent firing a mortar into Camp Nathan Smith. When the warlord found out who had done it, he captured the man, skinned him, and hung him up for others to see. Since then, there had been no more attacks. Was this true? I didn't put much stock in the bizarre story, but after that, I heard the same story from three other people, one of whom was an army chaplain. This gave me some assurance that the camp was safe.

After being at CNS for two months, my surroundings seemed normal. I remember how unfamiliar everything had been when I arrived. I had only known three people out of the 1,500 there. It was dark, dirty, and dusty. Now it wasn't as alarming, even with the incessant helicopter, generator, and truck engine noises, the constant Muslim call to prayer, and the Afghans speaking brashly in the early mornings and late into the evenings.

Overall, the work Li and I did was relatively easy at Camp Nathan Smith. By this, I mean there were just the two of us from the 113th CSC unit. No bosses scrutinizing our work and telling us what to do or not do, at least not onsite. I enjoyed working with soldiers. I could teach soldiers coping skills, offer guidance, be realistic and confrontational if necessary. It was easy to be lazy, to just surf the Internet, especially on the many quiet, monotonous days, but doing this would make it a terribly long tour. I wanted to change the routine, introduce new activities with physical and mental challenges so that we wouldn't be bored. Or maybe really so I wouldn't be bored.

Outside the Wire

Friday, August 12 started as usual, but I ate or drank something that sent me to the Porta Potty five times in between two clients. Sgt. Somers, who worked with Military Intelligence, came in wearing an army uniform but also sporting a thick beard.

"I'm keyed up. I just need to let off some steam. My first sergeant is always on my case." He complained about the emotional abuse from his superior. "Why is he doing it? I think he's egging me on so that I'll lose it. It's not right." This had been ongoing, but recently the sergeant believed his life threatened. "The other day, we got into it, and he made a move for his side arm. I was really scared."

Somers later transferred to another unit, in another location. An investigation was pending.

Pfc. O'Keefe was a follow-up regarding a hostile work environment. He talked quickly, as if out of breath, getting things off his chest. He was waiting for a transfer out of his unit.

Before we had a chance to write up our clinical notes, Maj. Krattiger came into the office. He told us that near COB Little Blue, north of CNS, there was a KIA (killed in action) and two WIA (wounded in action). A master sergeant stepped on an IED. He and the wounded soldiers were part of a team clearing roads of explosives. Maj. Krattiger wanted to know if we would go. I quickly informed my command and we received the green light.

We hastily crammed our three-day assault packs and grabbed our sleeping bags, anticipating a one-night stay. Within an hour and a half, Li and I were on a Blackhawk flying out of CNS. This was our first time outside the wire. We were anxious, concerned about our safety, and uncertain of what we'd encounter.

In 30 minutes, we arrived at Little Blue, where the team's commander, Lt. Col. Raule, met us. He told us about the team's mission, the number of trucks and soldiers involved, and the event resulting in their first casualty of this deployment.

Li and I planned to conduct two debriefings: Traumatic Event Management for those involved with the IED blast, and use of the Kuhlmann Model to debrief the members not at the scene but affected by the loss. The purpose of both debriefing models is to help stabilize soldiers by addressing conflict in their cognitive, emotional, physical, and spiritual reactions to a sudden loss, thus to help soldiers work through the sequelae of the traumatic event. First, however, we had to wait for the soldiers to return from the field.

Finally, an hour and a half later, they arrived, in a heavy, somber mood, hugging and consoling each other. The unit's chaplain and his assistant also arrived; both had been in the field helping to recover the remains. The chaplain had arranged to meet with the soldiers after dinner chow. I knew that the soldiers had a connection with the chaplain, and Li and I were strangers. So I offered our support and assistance to the chaplain during the heartfelt meeting with the soldiers. Many soldiers were in disbelief, angry, and crying.

After the evening debriefing, Li and I slept on sagging canvas cots in a tent shared with four other women soldiers from the COB. We couldn't shower that night, as the only shower facility was scheduled for men. Having missed the shower time, a couple of women soldiers used bottled water, shielding themselves behind the tent and pouring water over each other in turn. Just six steps from the tent was a Porta Potty, which, though convenient, meant there was a strong odor of human waste throughout the night.

The following morning, the chaplain wanted us to go to FOB Frontenac, approximately 20 minutes away by ground convoy, since the affected soldiers would travel there for truck maintenance. This would give us a chance to talk with the soldiers, but I knew the ground convoy was dangerous and my commander wouldn't approve it. Unfortunately, I only had 15 minutes to pack and get into a truck. I had no way to contact my commander. But I hadn't done my job yet, so I decided that we would go, without approval, and hoped that nothing would happen to us.

As we approached the FOB, I was relieved: no contact with insurgents, IEDs, mortars, or rockets. I called my commander and told him where we were. Li and I set up in the chaplain's office, but the soldiers hadn't arrived in Frontenac yet. To be helpful, we offered to shelve donated care packages. The soldiers finally arrived, but late in the evening, so it was another day of not working with them. However, Sgt. 1st Class Martin, a medic from the Frontenac aid station, got wind that Combat Stress was in the FOB. He asked if we would meet with some of his medics and with the S-1 staff (personnel). I told him yes, of course, and we scheduled a meeting for the next day.

In the morning, we went to the motor pool where we spoke with Sgt. Humphrey of the affected team. Humphrey mentioned that one soldier was having a difficult time, but that working on the trucks helped the soldier deal with the emotional pain. He was refusing Combat Stress Control service at this time but would seek help when his team arrived later at Kandahar Airfield to visit with their injured battle buddies.

In the afternoon, I sat with the FOB's chaplain, who had requested some counseling time for himself, to process some personal and deployment strains. His job was to listen to soldiers' problems, offer compassion, untangle spiritual challenges, and sorrowfully put friends in body bags. He needed a colleague to process his emotional memories.

Then Li and I gathered with the S-1 team and the medics to discuss critical incident debriefing and self-care. We also debriefed the medics about trauma: the effects of the fight, flight, and freeze (stress) response. This is the body's automatic and natural response to stress and threat—it is not the result of choice or a person's character. As medics, they were familiar with the sympathetic nervous system. In fight or flight, the body uses an adrenaline rush to increase heart rate and respiration, causing muscles to tense and a surge of energy that prepares for action. And when it isn't safe to flee or fight, the parasympathetic nervous system slows heart rate and respiration, leading to physical collapse, exhaustion, trembling, and the survival responses of freeze and submit. I emphasized the need to be grounded; maintain a healthy regimen of exercise, eating, and sleeping; and stay in contact with family and friends. I was finally working on this mission as a psychologist.

Now we had to figure out how to get back to CNS. Ground convoy was available on Monday morning, but I knew my commander wouldn't agree to it, because there would be a chance of IEDs or insurgent attacks. We eventually found a flight leaving Monday, 1240 hours, directly from Frontenac to CNS, but we didn't know whether this would happen or not.

On Monday we packed up, conveyed our good-byes to the chaplain and his assistant, and walked to the landing zone. This was a long, hot, slow walk with a helmet, body armor, rifle, and assault pack. Sweat was spewing. We had been hoping for a ride, but the FOB's two Gators (6x4 military utility vehicles) weren't available. Then after waiting for nearly an hour at the landing zone, a copter flew in and we were able to board and take off. Forty minutes later, as the helicopter slowly lowered to Camp Nathan Smith, I sized up Kandahar City for the first time. It was a larger area than I thought—flat, sandy, with scant, crumbling, grimy white, one-story buildings.

Aerial shot of Camp Nathan Smith.

Helicopter flight over southern Afghanistan.

Back on the FOB, I called and provided a briefing to my commander, executive officer, and first sergeant. I'd had to make the difficult choice of taking the ground convoy to Frontenac and the commander reassured me that I'd made the right decision. But if anything had happened to us, he said, he and his XO would have been hanging by their toenails.

My overall impression of the mission was that we arrived too early and departed too soon. The soldiers didn't have enough time to process and integrate the trauma and loss. Many were numb, caught off guard. We traveled out before the memorial service. If we had stayed, we could have collected some soldiers in crisis and worked with them. I was second-guessing my decision to leave Frontenac. But realizing that we had no coverage at CNS for crisis drop-ins or clients already scheduled, I had decided to leave. I definitely learned a lot from this mission and, in the end, Combat Stress presence and support in the field was acknowledged and appreciated.

I especially learned that what I had at CNS wasn't that bad, after all. In fact, I really appreciated my situation: the familiarity of the place, the people, my office, and my small but private sleeping quarter. It was much better than sleeping on a cot in a tent with other women and a foul-smelling Porta Potty nearby.

My commander said Li and I should take a couple of days off after a mission, but I felt fine. I went to the office at my regular time, but I also did my laundry and repacked my three-day assault pack, in case of another emergency mission. Li got the CNS landing zone phone number so that next time we could call them and arrange our round-trip flights. Now that we had gone outside the wire, we were no longer "Fobbits"— Army slang for forward operating base + hobbit = fobbit, a soldier stationed at a "secure" forward operating base who doesn't leave the base during deployment.

The best thing about being in the office after we returned was that the Navy Seabees had come and installed a new air conditioner. A Connex (shipping container) had arrived with 80 air conditioners. The air conditioner was a welcome sight, but, unfortunately, the electric socket was so old the new plug wasn't compatible. I needed to wait another day for the electrician to correct the problem before I could feel cool air at work.

A recent client came by to say hello and told me that there had been a rocket attack at Camp Nathan Smith while we were away. Apparently, two 40-mm grenades had been launched: One hit the landing zone, an open area, resulting in no damage; and one landed on top of a building, but that one didn't explode. Explosive Ordnance Disposal later detonated it. This was the first attack on the base in a couple of years…and, I hoped, the last.

During my next phone call with Rob, I didn't mention my outside-the-wire mission. I didn't want him to worry about me being off the FOB. I figured I'd tell him about it in person.

I'd been using USO prepaid phone cards. The phone connection wasn't bad, but there was a slight delay, which caused the conversation to be intermittent. Sometimes we had to check to see if the other person was still on the line.

These phone calls were gratifying, though, keeping me current with the news at home. We were trying to coordinate a November trip to Genoa, Italy, when I had my R&R. Rob had been busy researching his flights and finalizing his itinerary. I would leave CNS on November 2, fly to KAF, then to Kuwait, then to Germany, then to Italy, and return on November 21. Because of flight delays in reaching the initial destination, my HQ allowed me to leave five days earlier than the scheduled date. I could hardly wait. But November was a long way away.

Behavioral Health Deployment Stress

I did my first Mental Status Evaluation for Spc. Danczak who was facing a UCMJ Article 112a following a positive urine analysis for "spice" (synthetic marijuana). The smoking and test for spice happened in garrison prior to deployment. The results had just come in. The soldier's immediate supervisor wanted him to stay in theater and the soldier also wanted to stay. He was cooperative during the interview and knew the consequences of his action. The decision about whether he stayed was beyond my control, but I did check the box that he was fit for duty.

Just before dinner, a soldier walked in and asked about smoking cessation. I pointed to Li, as she was trained in this, indicating that he needed to speak with her. She conducted the interview, got some history, and offered some suggestions.

On the morning of August 18, I donned my body armor and walked over to the Seabees HQ to help Preventive Medicine submit a work order for two non-working 110 electrical outlets. Then I walked over to the motor pool. I spoke with Dido, whom I hadn't seen in a while, and we caught up on some news. While I was there, one worker asked what happened to Movie Night. I told him Li and I had been away on a mission, but I promised next Wednesday we'd show *Rise of the Planet of the Apes*.

I saw a new client, 1st Lt. Autry, referred by one of her soldiers, Jane, whom I had treated for being overly emotional and stressed at work. Autry had similar problems. Her anger was "through the roof." This was a common theme, and I needed to create a handout about how to use tapping to relieve tension. This was the third soldier Jane had referred to Combat Stress.

In the afternoon, Li and I had a scare when our phones suddenly weren't working. The last time this happened was the day a master sergeant was killed and we went to COP Little Blue. When there's a death, the army blocks all communication until the deceased soldier's family is notified. Li and I were afraid that soon the 1-10 Cavalry executive officer or chaplain would walk into our office and tell us to go to a COB. We walked around outside to see if anyone knew anything. The Mayor Cell said the phone system was down. I hoped this was true. Two hours later, the phones were working again, and no one had told us to go outside the wire. Whew!

Li and I spent the next morning surfing the Internet to find organizations that donate clothing, toiletries, and books to deployed soldiers. There are many military-friendly organizations, but there didn't seem to be an easy method to request donations. We even wrote to the USO. If we had some things soldiers needed, they might be more likely to come into Combat Stress Control, giving us a chance to talk with them.

In the afternoon, Maj. Michaels came in asking for help to compose an email to his wife. His wife had many problems: her father's health, a special needs child, and her own poor health. She essentially wanted her husband to leave Afghanistan and return home. We discussed possible support systems for her, but no option was viable. Eventually, Michaels remembered his wife had been independent and self-determined when he first met her. This was reflected in his email to her, but she threw it aside and told him that he cared more about his job than her. She no longer wanted to talk to him and ended her email with "have fun over there doing what u do and who you do."

After Michaels left, Cpl. Mayer was escorted in. Mayer had a characteristic well-built military physique, but he couldn't hide his contemptuous tone. Ten days earlier, Mayer was on patrol when an insurgent shot him, injuring his right side. Fortunately, the body armor plate stopped the bullet.

"I can't sleep. I keep thinking of being shot over and over again. I was knocked down but was able to crawl behind the truck for cover."

"What happened next?" I asked.

"I fired back, but no else did...just me."

"Why not?"

"I don't know...I looked around...they all looked scared."

Mayer had had continuous flashbacks, insomnia, and anger about the lack of support from his team. There were approximately 15 soldiers dismounted from their trucks when he was shot, but he was the only one that returned fire. I taught him how to tap for his anger and for his insomnia. Mayer should return to the clinic the next day.

Li and I returned to the office after our lobster-tail dinner. I almost asked for three tails since I had missed the previous Friday. Li needed to write her clinical notes for Cpl. Mayer but couldn't log in to the AHLTA-T program. This had been a problem for the last week and we finally phoned the administrator for help. Luckily, the administrator was in his office at 2030 hours. After half an hour, Li was able to get in and complete her notes.

As I was still in the office, I called Rob. Nine-thirty in the evening in Kandahar is nine in the morning in San Francisco. (Afghanistan is 11.5 hours ahead of California.) As always, it was comforting and grounding to hear Rob's voice. It made me feel less far away from him. After we finished the call, Rob wrote me an email: "Thanks for calling. As always, I love to hear your voice. Funny, I keep a voicemail of you on our home phone and sometimes I play it just to hear you. Your grunt, Rob."

On Saturday, at 1130 hours, I was enjoying the now-functioning air conditioning in our office when there was a loud boom and the building shook. I stared at Li with wide eyes and she stared back. I didn't register what it was, but I knew it was serious. I ran outside and looked toward the Mayor Cell's office. People were scattering and yelling. I ran back to tell Li and we quickly heaved on our body armor and helmets—these are kept in the office, since that's where we spend most of our time. I snatched an eight-pack of water and was ready to run to the bunker when Li told me I had forgotten my rifle. Well, that was embarrassing! I gripped my rifle, but now I saw people calmly walking away from the bunker. They were saying, "Con det." What was con det? A passing soldier told us it meant, "Controlled detonation."

Oh, thanks for the advance warning. Adrenaline rush for nothing!

Cpl. Mayer returned for a follow-up visit. "I still can't sleep. I keep playing this movie over and over in my head...being shot...knocked down...hurting..."

Li gave him an audiotape to help him relax for the night. Li also administered the PTSD checklist (PCL-M) and his score indicated that he was experiencing many reactions of posttraumatic stress: flashbacks, insomnia, irritability, and rage.

"Let's schedule your next appointment," I said.

"Ah, no. The guys already think I'm crazy. I can't keep coming here."

I explained to him the importance of fully processing the trauma so he didn't get stuck, which could result in long-term problems. He made a commitment to come back.

War trauma (now called posttraumatic stress disorder) was first chronicled in the eighth century, with Homer's recounting of Odysseus's rage, violence, and inability to adjust to civilian life after returning from war. During the American Civil War, soldiers were diagnosed with "soldier's heart," and WWI soldiers were diagnosed with "shell shock." WWII called it "combat exhaustion" or "battle fatigue." By 1952, the American Psychiatric Association's *Diagnostic and Statistical Manual of Mental Disorders,* Second Edition (DSM-II) included a diagnosis for "gross stress reaction." It wasn't until 1980 that the DSM-III used the term "post-traumatic stress disorder." (In the DSM-V, the term is no longer hyphenated: posttraumatic stress disorder.) Soldiers with PTSD commonly report symptoms of hypervigilance, anger, insomnia, numbness, flashbacks, and sensitivity to loud noise.

On Sunday, Mayer came in and paraded a copy of the official storyboard of his shooting incident. "Look, here's some bullshit creative writing...that way we followed the proper protocol. For example, 'Question: Why did all the soldiers dismount from the vehicles before higher-ranking personnel gave the order? Answer: To meet up with the Afghan National Police.' But they weren't there!"

The corporal also presented pictures of the round that he caught on his body armor and the ensuing damage. Fortunately, most of the damage was on his vest and ammo magazine. Mayer suffered a neck injury, back injury, and bruises in his rib area.

"Oh, by the way, I heard the camp might be attacked soon," Mayer said.

This was distressing news.

"Yeah," he continued, "the latest rumor was that the US government stopped paying the warlord the monthly rent of $93,000."

Was it true, $93,000 a month? It was a great sum of money. I received the information with skepticism, however. Although, since CNS was attacked on August 13, why continue paying warlords for protection if CNS wasn't protected?

Security had increased around the camp. Locals, civilian contractors, and soldiers wearing PT uniform had to show their identification cards in certain areas: dining facilities, gym, and certain buildings. At dinner, I asked the brigade surgeon about the increased security. He understood the entire RC-S (Regional Command South) had gone to this measure. I felt slightly relieved that CNS wasn't the only base targeted. And perhaps this was happening because August was usually the deadliest month of the war.

Sure enough, at 2230 hours, there was a loud explosion. I recognized the now familiar sound and went outside to get some information. A soldier from the aid station said there was an IDF (indirect fire) near CNS. Later this information changed to an IED (improvised explosive device) one kilometer away. Li called me on my cell phone and I joined her in our office, where we stayed until we got the all-clear. I couldn't believe that CNS didn't have a working siren. We were in a war zone and the camp couldn't tell people to run to the bunkers or to signal the all-clear. Super distressing! As if it were the 19th century, we depended on word of mouth, and we hoped the information was accurate. I could hardly wait for the end of August—a holy month yet the most deadly. It just didn't make sense to me…but war doesn't make sense.

When I went to breakfast the next morning, I was asked to present my identification card before I got to the entrance. This was new. I was in my uniform, yet 100% ID was required. There was also a guard stationed at the dining facility's exit.

I got my government computer back from being reimaged after it stopped working and all the programs were functional again. So I started my Commander Safety Course, which would take eight hours. Some of the information was boring, but it was necessary to read if I wanted to pass the test this time. When I was barely a quarter of the way through the course, Mayer came in complaining.

"I'm not doing well…can't sleep. The blast bothered me a lot. And my neck is still killing me."

He wasn't interested in tapping for his anxiety, pain, or sleep. Instead he wanted medication for sleep, so I encouraged him to see the doctor in the aid station.

Then Sgt. Gallego came in. He was directed to us because of stress, home-front issues, poor sleep, and flashbacks of his friend dying. Scarred from the inside out, his work performance had deteriorated, with poor concentration and repeated tardiness. We discussed his wife's support system, which was adequate, and how she could ask for additional help to relieve his worries. Then we discussed ways he could improve his sleep by eliminating noise and light, as he was sharing a tent with 15 other soldiers, all with different work schedules. Lastly, I taught him how to tap to diminish the triggers that set off the flashback of his friend's death.

"Even though I miss my friend, even though I'm reminded of him from time to time, I deeply and completely accept myself. I choose to celebrate his life," we tapped.

I asked him to return to check on his progress.

In the late afternoon, there was a drill in the camp. I couldn't really hear what was going on because we had clients and the speaker system didn't work. I moved outside and saw a soldier riding around in a utility vehicle with a handheld loudspeaker saying something that I couldn't understand. At first I was worried. But once I heard him say, "...this is a drill," I was thankful.

At ten at night, I was in bed reading another thriller book when there was a loud knock on my door. When I opened it, I was alarmed to see a massive German shepherd tethered to a burly civilian contractor, accompanied by a soldier.

Staring up at the soldier, I said, "Yes?"

"We're conducting a room-to-room search, Ma'am," he said.

"For what..."

"Um...alcohol."

Since I didn't drink, I wasn't concerned and opened the door for the dog to sniff around, and they quickly left. But really...alcohol?

The next morning, Li went around and learned from some soldiers at the PX and the aid station that the dog was actually searching for a bomb. There was speculation that there might be a bomb in CNS, and it might be in the dining facilities, gym, or sewer system. Everyone was on edge, sharing a mixture of facts and rumors. Later in the afternoon, Li and I understood that a bomb had been discovered in the local bazaar. During our walks around the camp, we noticed more razor-sharp wire around central buildings and markedly heightened security.

Going out for lunch, we gazed up and saw a huge banner introducing Instatelecom, a new Internet service at CNS. The cost was $50 a month for unlimited service. Apparently, another Internet company called Sniperhill would arrive here the following week. The current service was expensive with poor and frustrating connectivity. I hoped that one or both of these companies would be better.

I finished the Commander Safety course. I barely passed, as I only read three of the 10 chapters. But at least I was done with it!

Buddy Watch

Li and I were shocked when Command Sgt. Maj. Veneklasen marched into our office one morning. I wasn't sure if he had come in for therapeutic help or just to harass us. But he was relaxed. In fact, he was extraordinarily nice and shared with us that this was his 10th deployment. When he returned home, he'd submit his retirement packet, which by then would be 24 years in the army. Apparently, he just came by to chat.

Veneklasen didn't stay long, as Capt. Edwards came into the office. Edwards was there for a command-directed evaluation because, during a urine collection for drug testing, he dropped his trousers down to his ankles in view of many soldiers—inappropriate behavior, especially for an officer. Higher command wanted an evaluation to see if other things were going on with the captain.

"You know all urine samples have to be witnessed, but the Porta Potty is too small. So my witness stood outside. I left the door wide open. What's wrong with that?" he said.

The captain was cooperative during the interview and completed a 45-question survey, assessing symptoms of distress, social roles, and interpersonal relationships. He'd return for a computer personality inventory assessment.

Soon after Edwards walked off, a platoon sergeant escorted in Pfc. Turner. His face was thin, freckled, with a frown. Turner had been in the camp one month and found it difficult adjusting to deployment.

"How can I help?" I asked.

Turner said, "I'm not happy with life. My sergeant says I'm a slacker. I'm not...just miserable all the time."

"Miserable about...?"

"My aunt and two cousins died before I left for Afghanistan. I want to go home to my wife and kid."

He admitted having anxiety attacks and thoughts of hurting himself and others. I referred Turner to the brigade surgeon for a medication evaluation. The doctor placed him on an intense 24-hour buddy watch and prescribed Ambien and Paxil. Turner and his escort would return to the aid station the next morning.

It was Movie Night. We showed *Rise of the Planet of the Apes* and we had the largest crowd yet—10, if you count Li and me. Just as we were starting the movie, the mail came, and I finally received my vacuum cleaner. We also received a large box of Seattle's Best coffee from Soldiers' Angels. Now we had more bartering power!

On Thursday, I went to the aid station at 0800 hours to meet with Turner, from the day before. While Turner was having his vitals checked, his escort told me that the soldier admitted lying about the death of his relatives and his threat about harming himself and others. During the session with the brigade surgeon and me, Turner confessed.

"I know I shouldn't have lied. I just want to go home."

I advised Turner of the drawbacks if he couldn't complete his tour and to reflect on the reasons he'd joined the army a year earlier.

"I joined to support my wife and son, and to make my sister and brother proud of me."

Turner would remain on buddy watch, return to work, and use the MWR (computer/phone) to contact his wife.

Edwards came back and completed 344 computer questions to scan for primary clinical issues. The results indicated nothing significant in the area of depression, anxiety, or psychotic disorders. So now I just needed to complete a Mental Status Evaluation report for his commander.

After Edwards left, I went to the aid station again so I could meet with the brigade surgeon and Turner. This time Turner flashed a grin.

"I talked to my wife. She's doing good. She even sent me a picture of my son holding a stuffed black-and-white pony. I'm ready to go back to work."

Apparently, when a soldier is on buddy watch, they generally sleep in the TOC (Tactical Operations Center) where there is always someone watching the soldier, so that they can't harm anyone, including themselves. In this case, Turner slept without a blanket, because there wasn't one there, and he swept and mopped the place. He missed his usual freedom and comfort, which, compared to the previous two days, was quite good. Everything is relative. The brigade surgeon called this "Plan B," and in this case it worked quite well. Turner was motivated to return to work and to finish his deployment, realizing that he could ask for help from the chaplain, Combat Stress, and the aid station if needed.

Edwards came in to hear the results of his mental status evaluation.

"Captain, your report showed no clinical evidence of mental or personality disorder at this time. You're fit for continued duty," I said.

Pleased, the captain said, "I joke around sometimes, maybe too much. I guess I better tone it down." The captain had good insight; he didn't want his chain of command to take any more notice of him—unless he was receiving an award for outstanding service. "You won't see me again," he said as he turned for the door.

After Edwards left, Mayer (who had been shot) came in after his appointment with the brigade surgeon, which, for the third time, had been rescheduled.

"For some reason, the doctor is too busy to see me..." With a tired sigh, Mayer added, "I still can't sleep, I have night sweats sometimes...I even took three of the four sleeping pills, but it only worked one night." Grabbing his neck with one hand, he winced in pain.

Wishing I could do more (as noted earlier, he wasn't interested in continuing with the tapping), I said in a quiet voice, "I suggest you keep trying to meet with the doctor."

Outside the Wire Again

On Saturday, August 27, Li worked with an escorted soldier regarding a home-front issue: the questionable death of his father. His weapon was taken away when he disclosed that he would harm himself. But after an hour of venting, detailing his story, the soldier felt much better.

At about 1430 hours, a distant-sounding boom shook the office wall. I didn't feel it, but Li did, and she went outside to find out what had happened. A half hour later, we found out it was a VBIED (vehicle bomb improvised explosive device) that exploded at nearby PSS-1 (Police Substation One). The initial word was one KIA (killed in action), Spc. Roberts, and six WIA (wounded in action). Soon I received a call from Maj. Krattiger to report to the TOC. We rushed over.

Krattiger said succinctly, "I need your team to report to PSS-1. You may know, one was killed, two were wounded, and they will be transported to CNS. Four others will go to KAF, to the NATO hospital. Here are the grid coordinates of PSS-1."

After returning to my office, I called Col. Rabb and provided him with the information.

Hero's flight for Spc. Roberts.

At 1830 hours, everyone at CNS lined up at the landing zone to pay our last respects to a fallen hero, Spc. Roberts. Within a minute, the body was loaded onto the helicopter and flown off. As everyone was solemnly walking away, a civilian in the background played "Amazing Grace" on the bagpipes. It was touchingly sad. Soldiers were crying. I was crying. The reality of war really struck home for me this time.

I knew we could be leaving for PSS-1 with little notice. I told Li to be ready. Sure enough, on Sunday at around 0900 hours, I received an email from Maj. Krattiger requesting that we leave that day. After my unit's executive officer and Krattiger conferred via phone regarding the safety of the route, Li and I received the green light to travel by ground convoy. Krattiger warned us to expect to stay overnight, so I packed my sleeping bag. Dressed in our full battle rattle, we met our drivers and they guaranteed that we'd return that night. I was pleased to hear this.

At 1200 hours, Li and I boarded different MRAPs (Mine Resistant Ambush Protected vehicles) in a four-truck convoy. Li was in the first vehicle; I was in the third. The MRAP vehicle's underbody has thick, armored plating supposedly effective against IEDs. Inside, the vehicle was dark, hot, stuffy, and claustrophobic. Everyone in the truck holds a position and a job: driver, truck commander, and gunner. As "cargo," it was difficult for me to find a place to sit, but I found a small metal ammo box. In about 20 minutes, we arrived at PSS-1.

While I was in the truck, I tried to peek through the scratched front and narrow side two-inch-thick Plexiglas windows as much as possible. This was my first time traveling the roads of Kandahar City. The dusty streets filled with rubbish and hazy sights reminded me of when I visited India in 2004. There were faded billboards, donkey-drawn carts, and timeworn automobiles prowling the rundown streets, abandoned old mangled bicycles, wandering farm animals, and dilapidated hole-in-the-wall shops. Unlike in India, here men dressed in drab *shalwar kameez* (mid-thigh length tunic and wide-legged trouser), earthy colored turbans or *pakol* hats, well-worn sandals, and scruffy beards—the length of a clenched fist, as required by the Taliban. Traveling next to my truck was a noisy struggling motorcycle. A man was driving and a woman wearing a pale blue burka rode sidesaddle on the back. Most striking were the Afghan men carrying rusting AK-47 rifles.

PSS-1 is a small police substation where US soldiers and Afghan National Police live in the same compound. This was where Spc. Roberts had been killed and six soldiers injured. The conditions were poor. The VBIED damaged the TOC, sleeping quarters, and the shower Connex, which were now all structurally unsafe.

Capt. Douglass, the commanding officer, and Chaplin Williams briefed Li and me. The driver of the VBIED had attempted two to three times to ram through the south gate of PSS-1. After failing to break through, the driver had detonated the explosives. Roberts was killed instantly as he was running out of the TOC to warn others. He was 23 years old, a well-liked, hard-working soldier who made his fellow soldiers laugh with his "party boy" dance.

After the briefing by Douglass and Williams, we discovered their main concerns were Sgt. Nickel and Spc. Stahl, close friends of the deceased. Li and I found a deserted corner in the open-air courtyard and talked with Nickel. He was pale, had a vacant stare, and was visibly shaken. As we were ending the session with him, everyone was told to slap on our kits because of possible attacks. The surrounding streets were abruptly quiet, with few vehicles. Everyone sat silently and nervously on alert, baking in the sun.

About half an hour later, CNS's command staff arrived—Lt. Col. Cook, Command Sgt. Maj. Veneklasen, 1st Sgt. Freeman, and Maj. Stefani (brigade surgeon)—to talk to the soldiers and to treat them. After they took off, Li and I were able to run the Traumatic Event Management (TEM) to approximately 30 soldiers.

Sitting or standing anywhere they could in the courtyard, I introduced Li and myself. I glanced at my prepared and studied script, and said, "This meeting is designed to talk about the death of Spc. Roberts. Other soldiers have found this kind of discussion helpful, to grieve, to remember the qualities of Roberts. Unfortunately, the time for this discussion will not be sufficient to grieve the loss, but it's a beginning. It's something you can continue as a group or on your own."

I had butterflies in my stomach. This was my first TEM outside of training. My mouth was dry, but I attempted to speak naturally and made as much eye contact as possible.

"It's a discussion about what happened, and a chance to hear different perspectives and reactions to that event. Everyone has a piece to the puzzle and this discussion will hopefully complete the picture. This stops the second-guessing—if I had done this or if I had known that. The reality is you still have a mission to do, and this discussion can help you maintain focus and support each other as a team.

"Let me tell you what this discussion is not...this is not therapy, this is not an investigation, and it's not a critique of your job." I peeked down at my script, and continued, "Here are the ground rules for this discussion:

1. This will take about one hour—it depends how you want to use the time. There will be no breaks.

2. This meeting is confidential. That means what is said here stays here. What we discuss here is not shared with anyone outside of this group. However, there is a limit of what is confidential. For example, if something is said that has a bearing on a UCMJ (Uniform Code of Military Justice) action, then we have a duty to report it to your leadership.

3. We want everyone to participate. We want you to talk only about what you feel comfortable talking about. Part of this discussion is learning how to express yourself so your buddies can help you and each other.

4. Speak only for yourself. Don't judge what others say.

5. All opinions are important but be respectful of rank.

6. No leadership bashing. That's not the point of this meeting.

7. You may ask questions at any time.

8.   Lastly, we will be around at the end for individual talks."

I started at one end of the group and went around. Soldiers could pass if they wanted to. I asked what they saw, where they were, and what they did when the event happened. This was followed by their reactions, their first thoughts after they went off autopilot, and what was the worst part. It was important for me to take a breath, to be patient and encouraging by nodding, repeating their last few words, and allowing them to talk. Once soldiers started to open up, I was relieved. My job was then to listen, facilitate more discussions if necessary, and to sum up the variety of perspectives. In this discussion, one soldier said, "I'm not going to lie, I was scared shitless." Others were angry, but their training kicked in with situational awareness and helped the injured. Another soldier said, "I prayed. I thought I was going to die."

The next part of the TEM was self and buddy aid. I looked down at my script more often now, as this was especially important.

"After an event like this, soldiers can become angry and aggressive; they have a very short fuse and they may want payback for what happened. It's okay to be angry, but you can't act on anger. You must ensure that you and your buddies follow the rules of engagement. You are a professional warrior. You treat noncombatants with dignity and respect whether you think they deserve it not. Again, you are a professional warrior and that's what distinguishes you from the insurgents. It's tempting to cross the line, but much more difficult to cross back. Once you cross that line, you'll know that you are no longer a professional warrior.

"Another common reaction is shutting down, like you can't continue. You know this is happening when you or your buddy get out of routine."

I asked the group what routine could change. One soldier said, "No longer a gamer." Another said, "Not eating, showering, or working out."

"Yes," I said. "And perhaps not calling or emailing home as often. Shutting down can be a normal reaction, but it can be harmful because it keeps you from using your support system—your battle buddies, your family. Staying shut down can also make it difficult to be mission focused.

"So, if you see your buddy has shut down, you have to get into his business. If your buddy won't talk to you, you have to take him to the chaplain or Combat Stress Control. You need to personally take your buddy to get help.

"In the next few days, you may find yourself having difficulties sleeping; some of you may already have problems—a hard time falling asleep, staying asleep, or nightmares. It's important to get good sleep, otherwise your performance will be affected. As professional warriors, alert, quick decision making is critical—your buddies' lives depend on it."

I asked the group, "What are some things you guys can do for better sleep?"

"Just kickin' it," said one soldier.

"Rocking out," said another.

"Read, watch funny movies," said another.

"Correct," I said. "You can also work out with your buddy. If these things don't help, and you're still having problems, go see Combat Stress or to the aid station."

To bring the discussion back to Spc. Roberts, I asked, "Although Roberts is gone, you will always have fond memories of him. What did you like about him? And since no one is perfect, what was annoying about him?" There were some funny comments about his dancing, his silliness, and his annoying habit of waking people up. There were smiles in the group, and even some mild laughter. Tension lifted.

The last question I asked was, "How can we pay respect and honor Roberts?"

"I think Roberts would want us to complete the mission," said one soldier.

Another said, "Let's create a Facebook page so that his friends, family, and army buddies can share photos and stories of him."

Many were nodding in agreement.

The next and final part of the TEM was resilience focus.

"You know firsthand that combat is hard. You've experienced a loss, but you can still move forward and complete your mission. You might find yourself second-guessing decisions you've made, but trust your training. Trust your ability to bounce back, to be resilient. It takes confidence and mental focus. Your leaders care about you, but sometimes they don't show that very well. Go to them if you or your buddies are having a problem. If you are a leader, be receptive when a soldier comes to you with an issue."

In closing, I said, "Each of you will handle things in your own way, in your own time, and most of you are going to be fine, but one of your buddies might not. Recognize this and get you or your buddy help. This is a sign of leadership and strength. Thank you for what you're doing and the sacrifices you are making." I choked up when I spoke the last few words.

The unit's medic spoke next and reinforced the need to talk to a buddy, chaplain, or him, or to Combat Stress. He also shared an update on the wounded. All were doing well and in good spirits. After the group was dismissed from the TEM, I counseled four soldiers individually.

On our trip back to CNS, there was a tense moment when the ground convoy came to a complete halt. During our pre-deployment training, we were taught that when a convoy made an unexpected stop, it could mean a possible attack. Everyone in the truck was keenly alert. No one said anything. I looked out the window but couldn't see anything. I was mentally preparing for an explosion, but after a couple of minutes we continued without incident. Li later told me that an Afghan boy had stood in front of the lead truck—the one she was in—but eventually moved out of the roadway.

We returned to CNS by 1930 hours. It was a good thing we weren't staying the night at PSS-1. The only available sleeping space was outdoors and the mosquitoes were ravenous. Overall impression: We were glad we were able to go, glad we were of some help. Our arrival may have been too early for some soldiers, as they were still on "autopilot," but for those close to Roberts, our arrival had been just right. We were able to soften the impact of the blow. More important, the PSS-1 soldiers now knew who we were, and when they traveled to CNS they could come to Combat Stress to process their loss. At the moment, there was no news of when and where there would be a memorial service.

After throwing off our gear, Li and I devoured a quick dinner. I took a long, cool shower, attempting not only to wash away the sweat and grime, but the sorrow, pain, and anger I was feeling. This unit had only been in Afghanistan for two months. So quickly they had lost one of their own. War is truly horrible! All the books and news reports didn't prepare me for the harsh firsthand realities of senseless killing of young people in war.

I told Li not to come in until noon the next day. A period is needed to process and to recharge after a mission. That night I went to sleep without difficulty, but I woke up several times with thoughts and images of the day, resulting in a fitful sleep.

I had to be in the office early the next morning to give my command a briefing of our mission to PSS-1. I was glad the clinic was quiet. It gave me a chance to unwind mentally and physically. While at PSS-1, I had been working, watching, and connecting with as many soldiers as possible. I took in the horrific accounts of the incident, the descriptions of the aftermath, and the gruesome cleanup. When I worked with individual soldiers and had them tapping, I tapped along with them on their feelings of fear, anger, helplessness, and sometimes guilt for not doing enough. The tapping helped me process the material so that I could release the trauma as well.

At 1300 hours, our unit had its first phone conference. It was good to hear news from HQ and colleagues from the other FOBs. It could be acutely isolating with just the two of us. After the call, I felt more connected with the 113th. I reported our recent missions outside the wire and that we were still waiting for a printer and, we hoped, even a small fridge. The conference calls would continue every two weeks.

I usually wore earplugs in the evening because of the constant noise, but after this attack I wore them only in one ear. I wanted to recognize quickly whether to go under my bed for cover or to run to the nearest bunker.

Tuesday, August 30 was the beginning of the festival of Eid-al-Fitr, a three-day Muslim celebration that marks the end of Ramadan. Everyone was hoping the killing spree would end with the festival. CNN had reported 71 US soldiers killed in August, the most in one month since the initial invasion in 2001. Sadly, this statistic included 30 troops killed on August 6, when their CH-47 Chinook helicopter was shot down by a Taliban rocket-propelled grenade in the remote Tangi Valley.

That morning, Chaplain Williams's assistant, Staff Sgt. Howes, checked in with us at the urging of the chaplain. Howes appeared more rested than he had on Sunday at PSS-1. He blushed when describing that his sleep was fine, except for the mosquitoes, as he slept outdoors there. Shifting his weight, he admitted feeling guilty that he was able to return to CNS, to his air-conditioned room, while the soldiers at PSS-1 had so few amenities. I shared that Li and I had the same guilty feelings.

During lunch, in line at the dining facility, I was surprised to see Nickel from PSS-1.

"Sergeant, how are you doing?" I asked.

"Ma'am, I'm doing better. I'm here for some medical appointments."

Composed, looking directly at me, he added, "Thank you for helping me. I was really hurting and you helped me."

Speechless, I felt some weightlessness when I heard this. With a slight nod, I smiled to acknowledge he was welcome.

Nickel also informed me the memorial service for Spc. Roberts would be the next day at 1000 hours in the CNS dining facility.

Later Sgt. Cunningham was escorted in for severe sleeping problems. He had nightmares every night. He wore his dirty-blond hair short, so short that he appeared bald. He spoke nervously, pulling at a loose thread on his sleeve.

"For three months, I collected DNA samples from dead detainees... that meant I had to cut into the bodies. I believe desecration of the body is wrong, but I had no choice."

"What else is bothering you?" I asked.

"Every night I have strange dreams...detainees sitting up, pointing at me, asking why I was cutting them."

Recently, the sergeant changed duties, but he was still haunted nightly. I taught him how to tap to erase the image and to help him sleep.

"Even though I see the large image of the dead in color, I choose to switch it to black and white, and shrink the image smaller and smaller, so small and blurry that I can't see it anymore."

His initial Subjective Units of Distress (SUD) score was an 8, and at the end of the session it was a 4. He would return the next day.

At six in the evening, Li and I were ready to leave the office to go play Ping-Pong when two soldiers came in, both wanting to work on anger management. Li worked with the specialist and I worked with Sgt. Decarli. It turned out they were both mad at their chain of command for not doing their jobs, ordering the lower enlisted to do the bulk of the work instead. The sergeant wanted to protect his soldiers who were working long hours and weren't allowed access to the MWR to connect with their families. He was so angry, "blowing spit," he was ready to punch out his superior. But he knew the serious consequences if he did, and he had too much to lose, with a newborn on the way. I discussed the options of an Inspector General and Equal Opportunity complaint and/or going to the first sergeant for assistance. Moreover, I taught him tapping to release his anger and to relax.

In truth, there were many days when I didn't want to be in Afghanistan. There was a persistent feeling of menace. My life was perpetually threatened and this was always gnawing at my mind. I was fearful that in my unit I'd be the first one to mentally break and be required to be sent home. There were days—actually most days—when I was afraid of mortar attacks coming into the camp. Yet every day I looked forward to meeting with those I could help. And every day I looked forward to marking off the date on the calendar—one day closer to going home.

I became friends with some Afghans at CNS. Local Afghans work in the camp, which gives them a steady salary, far more than they could ever earn in the old regime. My friends were interpreters and were in favor of Americans being in Afghanistan. They said that with the arrival of Americans they got better roads, schools, hospitals, improved farming techniques, animal care, and women's rights, to name a few of the benefits. One interpreter proudly announced that more people owned radios and listened to the BBC World Service, and some even owned televisions. They no longer depended on the village leader for "news."

Of course, there were insurgents fighting the American soldiers—the infidels who have trampled on holy Muslim soil—a fight that America will never win. The Afghans are one of the oldest civilizations in the world, yet the poorest. The British in the 19th century and then the Russians in the 20th invaded Afghanistan, and now the Americans in the 21st. They were tired of being invaded, but they were also tired of the Mujahedeen, the Taliban, and civil war. Religion and war have been the main way of life for centuries and war would most likely continue despite the US effort to bring peace to the region.

On the last day of August, I noticed that the weather was changing: cooler in the mornings and evenings, with more clouds and more wind. We were approaching monsoon season, and the camp staff was filling sandbags. For my first two months, it had been rare to see clouds in the sky, and every day had been hot and dry. But now with fall approaching, I'd need to rummage through my duffle bag and find my wet-weather gear.

The memorial service was assembled for Spc. Michael C. Roberts, born November 24, 1987, and died August 27, 2011, just 23 years old. Mourners filled the DFAC. At the front of the room were a picture of Roberts, his boots, his rifle, and his ID tags. The chaplain opened the ceremony with the invocation, which was followed by leadership's remarks, heartwarming tributes by his fellow soldiers, silent prayer, final roll call, taps, the firing of volleys, and final salute. The final salute was a formal marching up by attendees—two at a time—to Robert's picture, where they slowly saluted him and touched his dog tags or helmet. All this was quite moving and sad to see. Many people, including me, quietly shed tears.

Back in the office, Cunningham came in for a follow-up, reporting a slight improvement. But he was still experiencing nightmares. "I feel guilty for what I did to those bodies."

Cunningham also spoke more openly of the death of his parents and the closeness it brought him with his older sister. We discussed the five stages of grieving: shock/denial, anger, bargaining, depression, and acceptance. Lastly, I emphasized the importance of processing his feelings of loss.

It was near dinnertime when we discovered we had mail. We received seven boxes: four from donors of Any Soldier, two from HQ with our monthly allotment of replacement uniform and PT clothing, and one from my ACMHS Sistas (my former female coworkers at Asian Community Mental Health Services). It was great—like all the holidays and my birthday rolled into one day! It definitely lifted my spirits to receive treats from home and to feel remembered.

More Missions

It had been two months since I'd left the States. It seemed much, much longer. It would be another two months before I could go on my mid-tour R&R break in November—still a long time away.

Decarli returned for a follow-up regarding his anger toward his immediate superior. He reported feeling slightly less animosity toward this individual. "The best way I've found is to avoid him," he said. "He goes one way, I'll go another."

We discussed Decarli's history of anger problems, where he learned this behavior, and how he could unlearn it: by replacing the behavior with a healthier way, such as taking deep breaths to remain calm, "Focus on your breath because it's in the present—you can't breathe in the past or in future," and not allowing others to dictate his emotions. The sergeant found talking helpful and was willing to practice new skills.

After Decarli left, I wrote to a couple of more companies asking for donations: Kimberly-Clark for Kleenex, Pampers for baby wipes. Who knows? They can only say yes or no. I also helped the PX manager request Xbox games and television sets.

Cunningham returned in the afternoon. He was still experiencing nightmares, but with the tapping he was able to get back to sleep. We worked on being more specific about the nightmare so that we could collapse it further with the tapping.

"Even though I can't forget that I dishonored the dead, it wasn't right, I was doing my job, I deeply and completely accept myself."

Afterward, he shuddered as he said, "I tried to get the dead detainee's fingerprint. I tried so hard that I broke the knuckle. The body was in rigor mortis."

Cunningham felt guilty and shameful. "It's wrong for me to violate the body. Even though they were insurgents, it's wrong."

We tapped on, "Even though I could hear the sound, the feeling of breaking the knuckle, I accept myself. Perhaps I can forgive myself."

Staring off at nothing, with a heavy sigh, he said, "I think all humans should be laid to rest without any more harm…" He was a deeply feeling man.

Later the aid station referred Staff Sgt. Young because of daily panic attacks he had been experiencing in the previous week and a half. Although he was on medication, it hadn't helped. He spoke in a monotone and his face was void of expression. Young had been having panic attacks since 2004, when he first returned from Iraq.

"I feel closed in. I sweat…my heart pounds. It feels like I'm dying."

"How long does this last?" I asked.

"Maybe half an hour."

After I gave Young an overview of EFT, we tapped for the attacks, the physical symptoms of an attack, and on future attacks.

"Even though I don't understand why I get them, I don't need them anymore, and I choose for my body to release them, for my body to heal, to feel peace and joy again."

I didn't know if the tapping was going to work this time, as I'd forgotten to ask for his starting SUD rating so couldn't compare it to an ending SUD level. Young was cooperative, but lackluster.

The day after meeting with Young, I received a phone call requesting that we conduct a TEM (traumatic event management) at Check Point 8.1, a compound near our FOB. At nearly the same time as the August 27 VBIED attack on PSS-1, another suicide car bomb had attacked this checkpoint. There was an American casualty, one seriously wounded, resulting in that soldier being brain dead. After a week, the soldier's family made the grim decision to take him off life support. The unit was requesting Combat Stress to come process with the soldiers affected by this tragic event. I notified my command. They had to review and approve route and transportation before we could leave CNS.

As I was waiting to hear from command about our upcoming mission to CP 8.1, the Internet went down. I figured it wasn't a big issue.

Maybe the new Internet company was working on it. But later, Maj. Stefani came into my office.

"Did you hear there was a KIA at PSS-9?"

"No, sir. What happened…where's PSS-9?"

"Not far, about two kilometers from here. Spc. Scott dismounted from his vehicle to conduct some meet and greet with local merchants when an assassin came from behind and shot him in the back of the head."

The Internet wasn't working because of communication blackout.

Soon Maj. Krattiger came into our office with the grid coordinates of PSS-9 and wanted us to respond there. We forwarded the information to our unit operations officer for approval.

Much to my surprise, in the middle of all this, Young came back in. I thought he wouldn't return.

"I had no panic attacks the day and night after our last meeting."

"That's great news," I said.

"But I had one this morning. But it was less intense."

We had made some progress. He was amazed.

"I don't understand how it works…"

"I can provide you a scientific, medical, or holistic explanation. But do you really want to know how it works?"

He shook his head no. "I know it works…I don't understand it, but it works."

"Do you want to continue the sessions and figure out what might cause these panic attacks?"

He said, "Yes."

My hypothesis was his deployment stresses in Iraq.

While we were still waiting to hear about our departure for PSS-9, Gallego returned for a follow-up. He reported better sleep since his last visit late August, but for the previous two nights, he had been waking up every 45 minutes, thinking about his family and his last tour. Recent events at work had triggered these troubling memories.

"I can't stay motivated at work," he said. "No one appreciates my initiative or my work mentoring soldiers. I might as well leave."

"There are consequences to leaving," I said. "You could lose rank and receive a dishonorable discharge. How will you support your family? It can also affect your future employment with federal jobs, too."

He nodded that he understood.

"I know it seems like this will never end, but deployment isn't permanent. For every day that passes, we are one day closer to going home. How about hanging in a little longer?"

"Yeah, I guess I can do it."

"Stay in contact with your wife and children. Look for any positives."

With a sudden lightness, he said, "Yeah, I can think of the motorboat I want...to take my kids fishing."

After Gallego left, I found out that Maj. Michaels, who had asked for my help in writing to his wife, had flown out of Afghanistan. I learned this accidentally, by talking to his replacement. Michaels's wife had managed to convince a physician to say she needed her husband to return home because of her poor health. It had worked!

Li and I waited the whole day for the green light to go to CP 8.1. Apparently, the hold-up was the transportation. Who would take us there and bring us back? We wouldn't know until later. Maybe not even until the next day.

We submitted a tentative mission schedule of the dates and places so that HQ could track us, but the road safety conditions had to be verified first. Hurry up and wait—it was the army way. If everything worked out, Li and I would be gone on Monday and Tuesday on our two missions.

In the late afternoon, our command finally gave us the go signal for PSS-9. Now I had to confirm my transportation to and from CNS.

I couldn't believe how difficult and time-consuming this was. Before I went to dinner, I received confirmation for the CP 8.1 mission as well.

That night I borrowed the *Green Lantern,* a bad Chinese DVD copy, bad because the dialogue wasn't in sync with the actors' lips. It was so distracting I had to stop watching it and just listen. Kind of boring, but at least it was a diversion from the daily grind.

On Monday, September 5, I received the departure time to PSS-9 to provide psychological support on the death of Spc. Scott. But I was upset with a second lieutenant who was supposed to report the transportation schedule to me. I had waited for two hours in my office the night before, because I was told he would come by, but he didn't. When he finally came the next day, the lieutenant knew from my stern look that I wasn't pleased with his lateness. He mumbled it was a "miscommunication" and apologized. Finally, Li and I rode off around 1400 hours, and we were at the site in just 10 minutes.

After a briefing with the PSS-9 commanding officer, Li and I gathered with 15 soldiers in a small dining facility. There were no tables or chairs set up, just a bare room. The soldiers sat on the dusty, dirty floor, or leaned against the walls, looking down, a few quietly crying.

The group was initially reluctant to talk, but with patience and words of encouragement, everyone participated. There were two sergeants and one soldier extremely close to Scott. He had died en route to the NATO hospital at KAF. He was 21 years old, just eight days from his R&R, during which he was to marry his fiancée. Well-respected, Scott was funny, the go-to soldier of the unit.

Another young soldier was taken from us much too soon. The memorial service for Spc. Scott was scheduled for Wednesday, September 7 at CNS.

On the ride back in an MRAP vehicle, I squinted through the thick, dull windows and spotted some Afghan boys with matted hair, dirty faces and hands, some with dusty sandals, others with bare feet standing in the streets. Some waved at us; others threw rocks. I could understand why soldiers could become so angry after losing a fellow soldier. Many soldiers believed they were helping local Afghan National Police (ANP) learn how to provide better security for their city, so that people could enjoy a more peaceful life. Yet at the same time, many soldiers didn't trust the ANP—they didn't trust people with whom they were living. Some soldiers whispered the timing of attacks was well orchestrated, perhaps with information from ANP. Many were resigned to the fact that at the end of all this, after the US military left, the Afghan people, with their deep pride and fierce tribal loyalties, would continue their warfare.

The mission to CP 8.1 went like clockwork. A captain called in the morning and confirmed the pickup time. Li and I rode in a Stryker, a tank that was large and roomy, but hot and airless. Our predecessors never went outside the wire during the months they were at CNS because their command wouldn't allow it. Whenever we were outside the wire, we were at risk of insurgent attacks. Fortuitously, nothing happened. We arrived in 20 minutes.

After our briefing from command about the brain-dead soldier, Li and I decided to run two groups, back-to-back: one group of 15, and one group of 16.

One soldier said, "I wished I had said good-bye to him."

"It's funny, he wouldn't eat the MREs, just peanut butter and bread," said another.

"I'll miss his smart-ass remarks."

"I made a promise to him to stay connected after we got back..."

Others expressed feeling empty, hollow, wishing he were still with them.

Based on their participation, tears, and anger, the debriefing helped the soldiers process their loss, begin healing, and refocus on their mission.

On September 7, Li and I attended the somber memorial service for Spc. Christopher John Scott, born November 17, 1989, and died

September 3, 2011. It was depressing to acknowledge another young soldier's death, especially as he was the second soldier killed from the company that had lost Spc. Roberts the week before.

After the service, I met with Sgt. Quinlan because his command was concerned about his ability to lead a group of soldiers outside the wire. The sergeant spoke with the slowness of a Southern accent and there was stiffness in the way he moved. For the past week, he'd had only a couple hours of sleep per night. And because of the sleep deprivation, it was difficult for him to make decisions. He was constantly worried, stressed, and depressed. He was also having nightmares, a common side effect of a malaria medication. He didn't want to make a mistake in which soldiers might be hurt. I requested his command to allow him to stay at CNS, to rest and meet with the brigade surgeon regarding the problems with his medication. I wanted to see if having more sleep and a change in medication would help him function better. Quinlan wanted to stay in theater and complete his tour.

While I was meeting with Quinlan in the outside office, Staff Sgt. Osei came in. Standing nearly six feet tall and muscular, he reeked of cigarettes.

"I was told I had to come here before my team could leave."

Wondering what he meant by that, I said, "Okay, can you fill out this intake form?"

Li talked with Osei in the inner office. About 10 minutes later, Li quickly rushed out of the room to the outer office and shrieked that Osei had removed his handgun from his holster. Li continued saying he was acting strange and saying strange things. She was afraid to go back in.

I went into the room. I saw that Osei had his M9 handgun in his hand.

Calmly, I said, "Hey, what's going on?"

"I just wanted to show her how a round was placed in the chamber," Osei stated matter-of-factly.

"Did you know you're freaking out my behavioral health tech?"

"Oh, I'm sorry. I didn't mean to. Hey, don't worry. I'm not going to hurt her, or anyone."

"Would it be okay if you give me your gun? It's making me a little nervous."

"Sure, I know you're a good person, cuz you're a captain wearing an army uniform."

He handed me his gun without hesitation.

From my police training I knew to ask, "Do you have another weapon?"

Osei reached into his pocket and handed me his matte-black Gerber knife.

With a friendly tone, I asked, "So why are you here?"

"Well, after the memorial service I wanted to hurt an ANP because he gave me the look."

Apparently, Osei lunged after an ANP, but his fellow soldiers pulled him back before he did any harm.

"So what did you learn from this incident?"

"I shouldn't have walked toward him but should have *run* and killed him!"

Feeling a quick adrenaline spike, thinking he was psychotic, I said, "How about staying at CNS and taking a couple of days off to rest?"

"No, no…" he pleaded. "You can't take me away from my soldiers. My soldiers are nothing without me, cuz I'm the Ghost Rider."

Meanwhile, Li had contacted Maj. Stefani, the brigade surgeon. When the major came in, I told him that Osei wanted to return to his unit, but he wasn't mentally fit. After the major met with Osei, he told me that he wanted Osei to go to KAF for observation and evaluation. I agreed, but knew Osei probably wouldn't be willing to go.

When it was time for Maj. Stefani to tell him, Osei gritted his teeth, gripped his chair seat, and uttered, "I am trying really hard to keep my cool!" Everyone in the room was afraid he was going to be violent. Fortunately, Osei had enough respect and training to obey his superiors. He stomped out angrily but peacefully. Eventually, he was medically evacuated to KAF, to Germany, and subsequently to the US.

———————

After this incident, I flashed back to my police training. Why did I become a police officer?

I thought about what happened when I returned home after nearly a year in France. I competed in the US Fencing Nationals in Florida and was eliminated earlier than I hoped. I was devastated, after all my training and experience in Europe. I couldn't adjust to the slower tempo of American fencers and I was making actions that my opponents couldn't or wouldn't respond to. I was so upset that I quit fencing for nearly two years.

It was time to find another adventure. I needed a job, but social work positions were limited because Proposition 13 had eliminated many city and county jobs in California. The San Francisco Police Department was hiring, however, after a long court battle that forced the city into hiring more minorities and females. I took the written exam and scored well enough to be in the first group of the civil service list. The physical exam wasn't too difficult, since I was still in good physical shape and had practiced the dummy drag on Rob many times. What I was most worried about was my weight. For my height, 5 foot 3.5 inches, I was supposed to be 110 pounds. But I was only 99.5 pounds, no matter how many banana shakes I drank before the medical exam. Fortunately, the city's physician asked if I was always on the light side, as he could tell I was fit. I passed the vision and background checks, and I went into the Police Academy on November 13, 1979, as a member of the 133rd recruit class.

A month after entering the police academy, Rob proposed to me. By this time, even though Rob loved fencing, it was time for a career change for him. Prior to the wedding, Rob was completing prerequisite courses in bio and organic chemistry before starting chiropractic college. Rob was a believer in holistic medicine and, as a patient of chiropractic care for several years, Rob knew firsthand the benefits of this alternative approach. We wed in July. With me being 27 years old and the last daughter to get married, I think my parents were just happy *someone* wanted me, even if he wasn't a Chinese man.

After the field training, I patrolled in uniform on the midnight watch in the city's Richmond District. The department was so thin in personnel that I was a solo unit from time to time. Having a partner was safer and helped pass the time. Patrolling was excruciatingly boring. Even the dispatcher had nothing to say after four in the morning. Occasionally, I would respond to a bar fight, domestic violence call, or burglary or arrest drunk drivers. But most nights I would drive around the district citing vehicles with expired registration tabs just to pass the time. I was going brain dead. I considered resigning after 10 months in the department. But one day my sergeant said I was transferred to the Street Crimes Unit in the Tactical Division. My name had come up for this specialized unit, which I had signed up for after I completed my probation. I didn't know what the new job entailed, but this was a chance to get off midnights and to work the day shift.

The morning I walked into the Tactical Division, the lieutenant laughed and said, "You look like a victim to me." What did he mean by that? What had I gotten myself into?

The lieutenant told us that the Street Crimes Unit was starting up again to arrest and to deter pickpockets and purse-snatchers in high crime areas of the city. There were four black male police officers, a white female officer, and me. My role was to look and act like a victim, essentially inviting would-be bad guys to separate me from my valuables. I learned to put on make-up of facial bruises, put my arm in a sling, walk with my eyes cast downward—fundamentally everything opposite to a self-assured police officer. At times, I dressed in my mother's old coat and scarf, shuffled along the streets with my purse over my shoulder, and waited for someone to take it. Other times, I wore a gray Mickey Mouse sweatshirt and carried a camera. This wasn't entrapment. Entrapment required a police officer to put the idea of committing a crime into the suspect's head. There was never any verbal exchange between the decoy and suspect.

This woman has been robbed 115 times in the past 18 months while walking the streets of San Francisco. But she's no easy target. Story is on Page 4.

I admit at times it was scary being the decoy. I wore an earpiece so I could hear when possible suspects were approaching me. My heart would pound. I couldn't transmit if something went wrong, nor could I carry my service revolver, because it was too large and bulky under my clothes. Sometimes I was on the back-up team to arrest suspects when others were the decoys. My lieutenant, a six-foot-two white male, was a great decoy. This part was dangerous, as suspects don't want to give up their prize or go to jail. Often they tried to run, fight, or even use weapons. I had my share of rumbles in the streets because suspects often didn't believe I was a police officer. I was in plain clothes, Asian, and slightly built, and showing my police star didn't matter; they were going to fight. Overall, the work was exciting and satisfying. We were able to put many career criminals behind bars through this process.

Author as police decoy. Source: *San Francisco Chronicle*, February 1983; photo by Frederic Larson.

Movie Night

Sgt. 1st Class Park and Sgt. Ramirez, from 113th HQ, arrived from KAF with supplies for us: a computer, coffee machine, printer, office supplies, and a small used refrigerator. They were both young and energetic. Even though they woke up at 0300 hours to travel to CNS, they explored the FOB, checked out the swimming pool, and played Ping-Pong most of the day.

Quinlan returned as requested, so that I could continue my evaluation of his cognitive ability and emotional state. He had a brighter disposition, and said he was sleeping better. He also met with the brigade surgeon, who prescribed another malaria medication, which we hoped would have fewer side effects. He would stay another night at CNS.

Young came back in for his panic attacks. Although initially he'd had a minor success—when he didn't suffer an attack the evening of our first session—he continued to experience them.

"Let's see if there's a pattern to your panic attacks. Are you on a particular diet?" I asked.

"Yes, I take protein supplements daily. I could stop them for a few days and see if that's it."

I also suggested, "Every night before sleep write down five things for which you are grateful."

"Okay."

We also examined his stress levels and discussed different ways to release or lessen them.

Cunningham returned and with a brilliant smile reported good things over the previous few days. "Ma'am, I don't have any more nightmares... and I decided to sign up for classes to earn my associate of arts degree. Also, I want to switch from military police to chief warrant officer."

I was delighted with his report.

"But I seemed to have put my problems on the back burner..."

"What do you mean, what problems?" I asked.

"You know, my nightmares, my guilt for desecrating bodies."

"Your problems have been processed and released through the tapping, and so you don't need to remember them any longer."

He shook his head in disbelief. "I thought it would take months to get rid of these problems. I feel a heavy weight lifted from my shoulders..."

I was so happy for him.

Late at night, unable to sleep, tossing and turning in my bed, I reminisced about my decision to change careers, to go back to school and study counseling.

After two years, I transferred out of the Street Crimes Unit and returned to district uniform patrol. A few months later, I injured my ankle pursuing a robbery suspect. My ankle required surgery, so I was on disability for several months. When I returned to work in light-duty capacity, I was assigned to the department's video unit. I was initially assisting a sergeant, but when he got transferred to patrol, the department sent me to Hollywood, California, to learn how to shoot and edit video. My primary job was to make training tapes for the department. I learned how to use a teleprompter, worked on scripts, shot at different locations, and edited late into the night. This was definitely better than handling death cases and taking burglary reports. The officer-in-charge (that's me in charge of myself) of the Video Unit reported to the lieutenant of the Police Academy, so the video gig subsequently lead me to be a recruit training officer for police recruit classes.

My first police training class was the 163rd Recruit Class. This was 30 classes after the one I had been in and they had it so much easier—a lot less yelling, more support for their academic studies, less running, less marching, and a "you-will-succeed" attitude from the friendlier training staff.

During this time, the police department was starting up a peer support group. I remembered seeing the flyer for an upcoming training as a peer counselor, but I had no interest at the time. Somehow the flyer kept appearing in my mailbox and on my desk, so I signed up. This training turned out to be the spark that ignited my interest in counseling. Soon I was counseling police recruits, but I wasn't confident about my skills. So I went to the University of San Francisco in the evenings and earned my master's degree in family and child counseling. Still, my thirst for knowledge wasn't satisfied, so I resigned from the department, took my retirement money, and pursued a full-time doctorate degree in clinical psychology. Some friends said I was foolish to leave such a cushy nine-to-five civil service job. But after 11 years with the police department, I was ready to do something new. I had no idea what my degree would mean in terms of either employment or financial security, but I was interested in how I could help people.

One morning Sgt. Quinlan came in again. (His command was concerned about his ability to lead a group of soldiers outside the wire.)

"I have some concern about your slow speech, whether it is due to neurological problems, fatigue, or both," I said.

"Well, I speak slowly…that's what we do in the South, where I was raised." He added, "I also speak slowly because I want to select the right words so my soldiers can understand me."

I decided to give the sergeant the ANAM test to see how well he was processing information. His scores ranged from average to above average, indicating no significant difficulties.

"Sergeant, you're fit for duty, and if possible, I want you to maintain a regular sleep cycle so that you can function at your best."

He sighed with relief and nodded gratefully. Later, he came in to tell me he was returning to his unit in the evening.

Spc. Safdari arrived and protested about the lack of sleep her unit (PSS-1) was experiencing. "The lieutenant got us on guard duty and running missions all the time. We're all tired, maybe sleeping two or three hours a night. It's gotten so bad that some of us are thinking of hurting ourselves so that we can go to medical just for a break."

Their morale was already low from losing their fallen brother, and now even lower. I emailed their commanding officer and reported the problem. The commander was tracking the problem and he disapproved of the working schedule. He mentioned immediate changes. I appreciated his cooperation.

It was a quiet day with just a couple of clients. Li and I were satisfied. It gave us time to catch our breath, do laundry, and clean the office. We also received a few care packages, so now I had plenty of toothbrushes, dental floss, baby wipes, and packaged soup noodles—yum!

On Saturday, three soldiers came in to debrief after receiving Article 15s (where command is authorized to deal with minor violations of the Uniform Code of Military Justice). One was for falling asleep on guard duty, one for not wearing his body armor on duty, and one for failing to attend class and lying about it. The punishment was extra days of duty and decrease in pay. All three accepted their punishment without much argument.

For most of the rest of the day, Park, Ramirez, Li, and I played doubles in Ping-Pong. I enjoyed the game for the quickness, agility, sweating, and lots of laughter.

Li told me that Capt. Ferrell, commander of the Mayor Cell, wanted to move our Movie Night to a better venue. Apparently, there was an unused TOC and it had been converted into a theater with surround sound. The captain ushered us to the new site. It was large and the sound was excellent. We could use it the following Wednesday. This came about because Veneklasen didn't want any social activities in the conference rooms. However, the Mayor Cell wanted to continue to support Combat Stress and found us another venue. Soldiers would be able to watch Armed Forces Network programming, which airs football games and television shows, in addition to movies. Who would imagine that our little weekly Movie Night would turn into something much larger?

On Sunday, the tenth anniversary of 9/11, everyone was a bit on edge because of possible attacks. It turned out to be a slow day, so I got a haircut—not a good one. I wanted my hair neater before I headed off to KAF the following week, as requested by Col. Rabb for a meeting with the Gray Team, a civilian group surveying military behavioral health problems in certain areas of Afghanistan.

Just before dinner, we found out that 77 US soldiers had been wounded and five Afghans killed by a suicide bomb at US Combat Outpost Sayed Abad, in the eastern Wardak province. The Taliban claimed responsibility for the attack. The first thing I thought was: how sad. And the second thought was that I was glad it hadn't been at CNS. Throughout the rest of the evening, there was talk of soldiers being on standby, of needing to wear our kit (body armor and helmet). But it didn't happen.

It was the last night for Park and Ramirez, and around midnight we ate packaged soup noodles in the office. I guess they didn't want to end their time with us. They were a great diversion for us, too, given that the first half of the week had been extremely exhausting and stressful, with our two missions and the increased attacks.

The next morning, Ramirez and Park lifted off on time to return to KAF. Half an hour later, Maj. Reagan, a clinical social worker, came from KAF to cover for me while I'd be at KAF. HQ wanted her to come in a few days earlier to learn what I do. There wasn't much to learn. We had one client, a civilian contractor who needed a mental status examination. Li played the tour guide again, showing Reagan the few sites of interest in our small FOB.

The mail came that day, bringing Li and me four more boxes from donors: coffee, shower shoes, white socks, and cans of Chef Boyardee. Rob sent me my fencing teaching gear, so now I had everything I needed to start the sabre program. I was planning to begin when I returned from KAF. My sister Jenny sent me an enormous box of treats. There were so many bags of dried fruit and beef jerky that I gave some to a soldier to share with his unit while they went out on daily missions.

On Tuesday, a platoon sergeant escorted in a soldier who had discovered the day before that his wife was Skyping with his male friend. She was posing provocatively. The soldier was devastated.

"I want to go home...I love her...maybe she did this because she misses me..."

"While you wait to go on your R&R, to go back home, consider separate checking/savings accounts to protect your deployment money," I said. "Also think about couple's counseling with a clergy or a counselor to help you and your wife work this out."

We also practiced assertive communication skills, beginning with the word "I" instead of "why" or "you," which automatically puts people on the defensive.

While I was with this soldier, Li had been busy with the opening of CNS Theater. She made the movie flyer and helped with the setting up of the room. There was a sense of excitement. Tomorrow would be Movie Night in the new theater, and we would serve free popcorn and drinks.

There was a great turnout for the opening night of the new CNS Theater with the showing of *Battle: Los Angeles*. I was feeling great to be a part of this. I knew that on the weekends the theater would be packed, because of NFL football games. This was good—anything to help soldiers and civilian contractors release stress.

The next day, four clients came in, all without appointments. A captain was depressed due to work and he wanted some medication to help him complete the last few months of deployment. After an evaluation, Reagan, who handled this case, referred him to the brigade surgeon for medication assessment. Another soldier was worried about his depressed wife at home, probably postpartum depression. She was under a doctor's care and we explored who could provide support for her.

Another client that day was Sgt. Hwang, who'd had an extramarital affair that resulted in a child. Hwang was conflicted about whether to divorce his wife or not. I encouraged him to research his state's law on divorce and, if he wanted to save his marriage, to consider couple's counseling when he returned home.

There were times when Rob and I had to work hard on our marriage. I remembered when I left the police department, Rob wasn't initially supportive of me returning to school for my master's degree. We had quarreled about this because he worried that I'd like my new circle of friends more than him, but the coursework taught me to be a better communicator and our relationship as husband and wife improved significantly.

This was important because we were unable to conceive a child. Couple's counseling helped me express my hopes and disappointments to Rob. We went through three years of medical tests, which never showed conclusively why we weren't able to have children. After a variety of failed Western and Eastern procedures, we decided not to adopt and to be childfree instead. Our parents were supportive of our decision not to have children, without any pressure. In the years following this decision, however, it was difficult to attend any baby parties. The conversation usually went like this: "Are you married?" "How long?" "Do you have children?" When we replied, "No," an awkward silence followed, because it was too painful for us to explain.

As we have gotten older, it's easier to say we don't have children. The response now goes like this: "No children, no pets, but we have a few plants to care for." Fortunately, Rob and I have many nephews and nieces to indulge and play with, and this satisfies our maternal and paternal needs.

Sgt. Estes had been referred because there was a question of whether he could perform his job as a medic. Estes had had two previous deployments, resulting in severe PTSD that lay dormant until he was assigned tasks that reminded him of past events.

"The work they got me doing, I can't guarantee that I can control my anger. I could hurt somebody."

"Has this happened before?" I asked.

"Yeah...I'm not proud of it. I was confronted, stressed out by this jerk. I told him to stop, but he didn't. So I tried to choke him, but he pulled away."

Because of his history and his admitted overpowering behavior, his command planned to MEDEVAC him home for a medical discharge from the army.

I wasn't thrilled to be going to KAF. Packing, carrying luggage and a rifle, and wearing body armor and the helmet weren't my favorite things to do. I even tried to get out of it, after I realized there was going to be a conference call with the Gray Team at KAF that Friday. If we were having a call, why did I need to go? I could stay at CNS and take part in the conference call, and Reagan could return to KAF, which she wanted to do because she had signed up for a 5K race. Col. Rabb insisted that I go because a live interview was much better than one over the phone. After I hung up, Reagan guessed the colonel wasn't happy (I'd had the speakerphone on). I hoped the colonel wouldn't still be mad at me when I got there.

Tapping for Sleep and Anger

The trip to KAF was a waste because the team meeting ended up being canceled after I got there. Col. Rabb apologized profusely for making me take the trip.

The day after I got back, I was walking near my office when Spc. Safdari from PSS-1 stopped me. Beaming cheerfully, she said, "My unit is getting more time to sleep and a better work schedule, like before."

"I'm glad to hear that," I said.

"Also the guys who got hurt are back, fit and healthy again. We even got stronger T-walls [retaining walls] around our compound. The best thing, we got a new M2 .50-caliber machine gun!"

Soon after getting back into the office, Spc. Pascua was escorted in because he had struck a soldier. With dark thinning hair and a slight scent of musky cologne, Pascua displayed a range of moods.

"Some days, with just a few hours of sleep, I'm energized and nothing bothers me. But other days, even with eight hours of sleep, I'm walking around like a zombie or really pissed off."

He thought this had been on going for the last two years. There was no report of family history of mental health issues. Pascua wanted to stay in theater and he didn't want medication.

So we tapped. "Even though I'm out of control, I forgive myself for punching him. I choose for my mood to be more balanced."

The initial SUD rating was a 9 (out of 10). After one round of tapping, there was a sense of calmness in the room. He reported a SUD rating of 3.

Pascua said, "I can't see me hitting him now...it's hazy."

"You seem less angry," I said.

"Yeah, because you distracted me, right?"

"It could be, but the important thing is that you're feeling better."

He nodded in agreement. We continued to work on other issues, and he said he'd return the next day.

After Pascua, Young came in to follow up on his panic attacks. "I have fewer and less intense attacks, just sporadic now. And I stopped taking protein supplements and drinking coffee. I think it's helping."

"Great news," I said. I encouraged him to tap daily: "Even though I have fewer attacks, I choose it to be fewer and fewer with each passing day."

We also worked on tapping for sleep; he said he tossed and turned for an hour before falling asleep.

"Tap on being pleasantly drowsy, having restful sleep, and being recharged in the morning. Also write down your worries on a piece of paper before going to sleep, so that you don't have to keep them in your head," I suggested.

"Sure, I'll try it," he said.

Later I went to the gym and used the elliptical machine. I shuffled for only a mile and a half. Afterward my legs wobbled for 20 minutes. Boy, was I out of shape! I had been convinced my legs were weak when I had difficulty stepping up into the Chinook helicopter for my trip to KAF. I had needed both hands to hold the railings to pull myself up. So I'd have to do more exercise. Sigh.

On Monday, Reagan returned to KAF and Pascua came back into the office for follow-up. He was doing so much better than the day before and wasn't emotional at all. He described several things that had happened since we had met.

"There's always shit happening, but I was cool...I could easily have lost it, but I didn't. I'm even sleeping better, no racing thoughts, and during the day I'm not so tired."

He admitted to being slightly depressed, though, and I suggested he write down things for which he was grateful. Pascua knew this would help him be more positive. On another note, Pascua had guard duty in a tower for the next six days. I asked if I could come up the tower to gaze outside the camp, and he said I could. Great!

The following day, I cautiously climbed up the uneven rungs of an aged wooden ladder. The inside of the tower was only eight feet by eight feet, with a ceiling and openings on all four sides covered by dull camouflage netting. One side was the entrance to the camp, a checkpoint with high HESCO walls and barbwire. The road had dense cement roadblocks every 15 or 20 meters, which would make it unlikely for any vehicle to ram straight into the camp. Above and facing the road was a mounted M2 .50-caliber machine gun. All these protective measures gave me a sense of safety.

View from a guard tower at CNS.

At dinnertime, I met an army paralegal. I couldn't believe I had been at CNS for two and a half months and never knew there was a JAG (Judge Advocate General) office. The next day, Li and I visited the JAG office and discovered that there were eight attorneys and several paralegals on base. In the coming months, they would move some of their personnel to the Finance office (our old office) so that soldiers would have easier access for power of attorney, divorces, child custody issues, and so on. I traded 10 yellow highlight markers for a ream of paper—a great deal!

That Tuesday was a busy day. I swept and mopped the grimy office floor, saw five clients, and had one command consultation. I also completed a proposal and an Army Risk Assessment for the fencing program for the Mayor Cell. I wouldn't be able to start teaching until I received approval. I was sure it would be fine—just more waiting.

In the evening I worked out on the elliptical again. I went for 30 minutes and traveled 1.92 miles. My goal was three miles in 30 minutes. This was to prepare for my Army Physical Fitness Test (APFT), for which I would need to walk 2.5 miles. Being over 55 years old, I had the option of an alternate aerobic event instead of a two-mile run. The time wasn't a problem, just the effort. I wanted it to be as painless as possible.

The next day, a sergeant dashed into my office and yelled, "You have a shitload of stuff!" We had received 10 boxes in the mail. Many were donations: towels, Xbox games, candies, chewing gum, travel games, Frisbees, baby wipes, combs/brushes, and batteries. From Amazon, I got my broom/dustpan set and an electric kettle. The best gift was a tiny hard drive loaded with movies and television programs from a fencing parent. I was so happy! During the two hours or so of watching a movie, I could forget I was in Afghanistan.

Other than those two-hour respites, it was clear that Camp Nathan Smith was now my home. As time passed, I was forgetting San Francisco and spending time with Rob, forgetting my favorite restaurants, the stores, shopping for groceries, and cleaning the house. In some ways, life on base was easier than civilian life. Three meals a day, wear the same two uniforms, and work. The cycle repeated itself, day in and day out, making it easier to focus. I didn't need to worry about balancing my checkbook, throwing out the garbage, pumping gas in my car, and doing chores. I could see why some soldiers preferred multiple deployments: They had steady income, health benefits, and all-expense-paid "vacations."

Another Friday dinner without lobster tails—they'd had them the previous Friday, when I was at KAF. Li thought the army was trying to save money by serving lobster tails only every other week. I learned the army was downsizing, now that the soldiers would be leaving Iraq by the end of the year. And soldiers deployed to Afghanistan in 2012 would only be in country for nine months, which might sound better, but they wouldn't have R&R. That would save a great deal of money usually spent flying mid-tour soldiers home and then back to the combat zone.

On Saturday the balance of 60 boxes from Staten Island Project Homefront came. What a zoo! There was so much stuff that we invited everyone—soldiers and civilians—into our office. However, some things were taken that weren't meant to leave the office: a pair of scissors, a case of iced coffee, and two bath towels (the towels were in a box under a table hidden by a tablecloth). My home had been burglarized! I definitively wouldn't do that again.

On Sunday we received surprise visitors: our 113th Chaplain Okeze and Spc. Min, the chaplain's assistant. I didn't receive any official notification from HQ, so they were in the midst of the donated boxes in our mess of an office.

My cases were starting to blend together, as they so often combined depression, anxiety, sleep problems, and anger management. I sympathized with the soldiers when they couldn't get enough sleep, worked long hours daily, and had no time to make contact with their family, to work out, to eat a decent meal. When their command refused to consider alternatives to offer relief to their soldiers, the term "toxic leadership" was used.

Soon after breakfast on Monday, September 26, CNS was under attack. "A breach in the west gate, with insurgents coming through…this is [inaudible]…this is a drill," blared over loud speakers. Nevertheless, everyone had to slip into his/her kit, and Li and I reported to the aid station. There were simulated injuries, some ambulatory, many carried on litters to the aid station. Those requiring evacuation by helicopter were carried out of the aid station, placed into vehicles, and driven to the landing zone. This drill lasted about an hour. I was glad we were practicing, as there were complications. I hoped leadership identified them. For instance, I could barely hear the alert over the camp's loudspeakers.

The evening after the drill, I was working late when Sgt. Palmer walked into the office around 1830 hours.

"I need some help to control my temper…every little thing is bothering me…it makes me want to hurt somebody."

This was his second deployment. I asked him to think of an event for which his SUD level was a 7 or 8.

With his face flushed, he said, "Yeah, I have one. Just yesterday my platoon leader gave me a shit detail—to refuel and clean all the trucks. My squad just got back from a mission—we're tired. I don't kiss his ass, so he always gives me the shittiest jobs."

"What are you thinking?" I asked.

"I'm fuckin' mad!"

"What else?"

"He's a fuckin' prick…it isn't fair."

After I explained generally about our body's energy system and gained his willingness to try tapping, I asked Palmer to repeat my words and follow me.

"Even though I'm mad and I hate my platoon leader, I know I'm a good soldier."

"Even though it isn't fair, I know I'm a good soldier."

"Even though he's a prick, I know I'm a good soldier."

Palmer said, "Mad. Prick. Not fair. I'm a good soldier," while tapping on the acupoints on his head, face, and torso.

After one round of tapping, Palmer's face lit up with a charismatic smile and he said, "It doesn't bother me as much…hmm…I feel lighter. I'm trying to be mad at him, and I can't…this is crazy shit."

When the tapping works, it works great.

On Guard, Ready, Fence

On September 27, at about 1745 hours, Capt. Ferrell, of the Mayor Cell, came into the office and told me I had an appointment with Lt. Col. Cook at 2000 hours. It was about approving my fencing program. Ferrell and I went to the 1-10 Calvary office and instead met with Veneklasen, because the lieutenant colonel was running late. Veneklasen reviewed the application and asked about my fencing teaching credential and experiences. Then, without hesitation, he approved the program.

Hooray! I could now start a fencing program at CNS!

Fencing has been a large part of my life. What is fencing like? For me it is like playing chess, but I am all the pieces on the chessboard and I am the player who has to plan and strategize against my opponent. I thrived on the individual competition, the quickness, and the excitement of executing a perfect action. Although there were many moments of frustration and dejection, there was always the curiosity of whether I could push myself a bit more to achieve the next level. By my senior year in high school, I was the girl's team captain and the all-city individual fencing champion.

I didn't compete in fencing during my junior year at Cal, although they had a team. My school medical exam revealed that I had a medical condition that required corrective surgery. So instead, I coached the varsity team. Cal offered fencing classes, but the instructor didn't coach the team. Since I had three years of competitive fencing in high school and two years at City College, the women's intercollegiate director offered me the position of coach. By my senior year, however, I wanted to compete and not coach.

The director asked me to interview a coaching candidate. At a coffeehouse in Berkeley, I met the candidate, a young Jewish man with curly black hair and a goatee who spoke with a strong New York accent.

I thought he was rather overconfident and uncompromising when he insisted on giving only group lessons instead of individual lessons to team members. I reported this to the director and she said to interview him once more, and if things didn't work out, I'd be the coach again. Well, at the second interview, to my surprise, the candidate was now amiable and agreeable to giving individual fencing lessons. And after he gave me a lesson in the presence and quick approval of Cal's fencing instructor, the director hired him. Little did I know that this new fencing coach had trained at the Institut National des Sport in Paris, France. He was one of only three Americans ever to receive a Maitre d'Armes (Master of Arms) from this prestigious fencing institution. In my defense, I would like to plead ignorance. The director didn't give me a copy of his résumé. I'm sure this new coach wondered who this crazy Chinese girl telling him how to teach fencing was. He turned out to be an excellent coach...and husband. Yes, I did meet my husband, Rob, at Cal.

The next day, Chaplain Okeze and his assistant flew out of CNS. Unexpectedly, Col. Rabb and Cpl. Cline had arranged to come in. The colonel's original plan was to travel to an outer FOB, but due to circumstances, it had been canceled. He had tried another FOB, which didn't work out. Finally, he got a flight to CNS. I rushed around trying to get quarters for our two visitors, running back and forth to the landing zone four times trying to meet their "scheduled" flight. From their original arrival time in the morning, they finally arrived at 1915 hours, just in time for dinner and to check out Movie Night.

While waiting for the colonel, Ferrell and I drafted an email to the residents of CNS regarding the start of the fencing program. Within the hour, I had six emails from soldiers expressing interest. That was quick! Fortunately, to help me I had a copy of my fencing book, *Fencing Sabre: A Practical Training Guide for Coaches, Parents and Young Athletes,* by Handelman and Louie. It seemed that I'd forgotten a bit, but I was sure once I got started my fencing mode would return.

It was good to engage with Col. Rabb. We were able to talk about a range of subjects and it was intellectually stimulating. I had missed collegial discussions and sharing, as Li didn't often engage in these types of conversations. In the meantime, I had arranged for the colonel to meet with the 1-10 Cavalry Lt. Col. Cook and Col. Kolesheski. Col. Rabb met with the brigade surgeon, Maj. Stefani, and Chaplain Arguello. Other than that, the colonel and Cline were happy just chilling in our office.

After reading the preferred times of interested students, I decided to hold the fencing class at 1400 hours on Tuesdays, Thursdays, and Saturdays. The allotted space didn't have any lights, so it had to be taught during the day. There was another space the fencing program could move to in the near future that had adequate lighting. I gave a quick lesson to Col. Rabb and Cline in the office on how to hold the sabre, and how to make cuts and parries, so that they could fence the next day on the scoring machine, with red and green lights differentiating which fencer made a touch.

The following morning, Cline and the colonel connected the fencing machine and reels, and they fenced each other. Everything worked out well. I would start the class the next day. According to the number of responses I received, there might be more students than equipment. Rob suggested just giving a group class and then breaking them into smaller groups so that they could get on the machine.

In the evening, Col. Rabb convened with Lt. Col. Cook and Maj. Krattiger. It was a productive meeting to establish more sites for tele–behavioral health systems, which would use Skype-like technology for soldiers in their camp to talk to Combat Stress providers located elsewhere. This would increase the assessment of soldiers and decrease the need to travel. All this was scheduled to happen within the next month. Also during this meeting, Krattiger requested that I travel more outside of CNS, to introduce myself to soldiers and to check on their mental health. Col. Rabb thought it was a good idea. So it looked like I'd be going outside the wire again.

Casualties of War

It was October 2011 and I had been in country for three months, with undoubtedly another seven to eight months to go. Col. Rabb surmised we wouldn't be leaving earlier than May. So much for the promising rumors of leaving in February or March.

The first weekend in October was sunny and warm. I ran my first fencing class. Four students came. Less than I'd expected, but a perfect number, as I only had equipment for four students. We moved from functional warm-up to the on guard position to footwork to cuts and then parries. Then they moved to electronic bouting, hooked up to the machine. They were sweating! The colonel and Cline were my assistants. The colonel even took some pictures of the class. This was special for the soldiers, since many rarely interact with a full bird colonel.

Fencing class at CNS.

Col. Rabb wanted to leave on Sunday because of business in KAF, but there were no flights out. He was hoping for the next day. In the meantime, he was enjoying the quiet time to do his work.

We had only a couple of follow-up clients that day, and so I called my mother to wish her a belated 80th birthday. She was surprised to hear from me. She said I sounded good and had a feeling of a close-by connection. We didn't talk long. She was happy to hear from me, but her voice was edged with concern.

On Monday, Col. Rabb and Cline returned to Kandahar Airfield. Before leaving, the colonel implied that he might move Li out of CNS and into KAF. As always, nothing was for sure until it happened. I had thoroughly learned this by then. The colonel thought a behavioral health specialist with more maturity would be a better match for me. I agreed. But who?

I organized the second fencing class, with just three students—one was new. It was easier with fewer students. The Halberstadt fencing program in San Francisco had offered to fund some equipment.

The 113th CSC executive officer (XO), Capt. Gillespie, called to let me know that behavioral health specialists would move to different sites now that we had been in country for 90 days. The XO said on November 1, Li would go to KAF and Sgt. Lopez would come to CNS. I reminded the XO that my R&R was scheduled for November 4, so that was perhaps not the best timing. Even though Li lacked initiative and was reluctant to run groups, she was easygoing. I hoped that Lopez would be more motivated to help soldiers.

Over the phone, I talked to the Morale, Welfare and Recreation (MWR) manager at KAF, and he said that if soldiers were requesting fencing equipment, he could supply it. I made a form for soldiers to request sabre masks and electric sabres. It would be fantastic to get the funding. In the meantime, Col. Rabb wrote an article about the fencing program at CNS. I edited it a bit and offered it, with photos, to the Mayor Cell to give to the Public Affairs Office for their use.

Earlier that day, a female soldier had come in troubled due to harassment by male soldiers in her platoon. She was the only female; she had been teased and bullied, and she had to arrange her off-duty schedule to avoid them. So Li and I went to find the EO (Equal Opportunity/Sexual Assault) office. I spoke with the brigade's EO and he said he'd advise her to go to his office to file a complaint.

It was Movie Night, but I couldn't go. Staff Sgt. Ramey sprang into the office, complaining about having a short fuse, easily irritated and ready to jump down anyone's throat. He had recently returned from an emergency leave because of the unexpected death of his mother. Prior to her death, he'd been stressed and had problems with an immediate supervisor. I taught him how to tap for anger, stress, and sleep difficulties. This was his third deployment.

Erma from MWR wanted to learn more about my fencing program. I gave her a copy of COL Rabb's article, with photos. I also asked how the equipment would be stored and distributed if I did receive funding from MWR. Each item would be labeled with a number and any soldier could sign out for it. They would also keep the equipment in a safe place, as MWR would be accountable.

I had my fencing students complete the form requesting fencing equipment and I delivered the list to MWR. I hoped this would move through quickly, as I needed that equipment. That day I had five students, and three were brand new. I figured new students would come into class every time; between soldiers' missions, training, sleeping, and eating, getting a consistent core group of students could be difficult. Maybe with time it would happen—and time was one thing that was plentiful.

I couldn't believe I had made it to three months in country. I still had moments when I didn't want to be there, but it was getting easier, as my life on base had become my new "normal." The ever-present dust, the heat, the smells, the unrelenting noise of roaring helicopters and planes flying overhead, vehicle engines, generators, and Muslim calls to prayer weren't normal for me, though. Maybe they were for a "high speed" soldier, but not for me. And I'd never get used to soldiers going out on missions and returning injured or dead.

Despite all this, I enjoyed meeting soldiers and civilians, and I detected they were experiencing similar feelings to my mix of emotions. Some were handling being here well; some were not. I also went back and forth. Thank goodness for fencing. For an hour and a half, three times a week, I was back in San Francisco, back in the fencing club, and hearing Rob's voice giving me pointers on teaching and encouragement with my program. This was a moment of normalcy.

But no matter how I was feeling, I was ready to help, every day, and becoming more confident in my ability to use and teach EFT (tapping). I had so many successes that I rarely experienced the doubts I'd had when I first arrived. I read reports online from other EFT practitioners and continued to hone my skills.

The work eventually seemed rote. The soldiers' problems were almost identical: stressed, irritable, short-fused, and difficulty sleeping. My explanations of how to use tapping and why it works had become clearer. So far, I'd only had one soldier who refused to tap because she felt silly. And on two separate occasions, I had soldiers whose spirituality was Wicca and they weren't receptive to energy psychology. I asked one soldier about the Wicca faith, to learn more about it. And he said, "The Divine is embodied in all matter" (not endorsing Einstein's relationship between mass and energy). With those who didn't want to tap, I used conventional talk therapy instead.

My transition from police officer to psychologist may seem a bit of a stretch. People often ask how this happened. Since I started out as a social worker, I actually just returned to my first interest. The hardest transition was introducing myself to my clients as "Doctor Louie." Initially, I, like many new psychologists, suffered the "Impostor Syndrome." As inexperienced therapists, I think we don't feel as though we know enough to help our clients, and so we feel like imposters, with a title. I knew enough, but the butterflies in my stomach were always there when I met a client for the first time.

At my postdoctoral training at a university counseling center, I had to audiotape my sessions as part of my training so that my supervisor could review my work. In one case, I had established a good therapeutic rapport with the client and was making progress. However, my supervisor said I was just making "girl talk." After spending thousands of dollars and four years earning my degree, it wasn't what I wanted to hear.

My first job after I passed my psychologist licensing exams was as a clinical supervisor at Asian Community Mental Health Services (ACMHS) in Oakland, California. I was one of three staff members that didn't speak another language besides English. But I quickly learned about other Asian cultures—Vietnamese, Laotian, Korean, Japanese, Cambodian, Thai—and the resistance and stigma related to mental health care. Similar to Chinese culture, mental illness was shameful and was kept as a family secret. Many Southeast Asian immigrants suffered from trauma from wars in their home countries or the difficulties endured in refugee camps.

Within a year, I became the clinic director. For the next eight years, I managed the budget, wrote grant proposals, attended management and county meetings, hired and fired staff. The best part, and least stressful, was working with clients.

———————

October 8 was a quiet Saturday, until around ten at night. Li called me on my cell phone, saying something must be happening. Her roommates had been told to get on their kits and report. I went to the aid station to find out what was going on. Apparently, there was word that there was a "green-on-blue" attack (when an Afghan policeman or soldier fires on coalition forces), with at least one soldier killed and two injured in the city at a peace conference. The injured were supposed to come to CNS for treatment, but that changed. I stayed up until midnight but heard no more news.

The following day we learned that two captains—Joshua Lawrence and Drew Russell—had been killed. One soldier had been seriously wounded and flown to Germany. Two others were wounded but expected to return to CNS from KAF after their treatment.

One officer, Lt. Kennedy, walked in heavy-footed. His eyes appeared puffy. He had been at the scene the day before.

"I can't believe it. Everything was going well. Then the shit hit the fan. I've lost two good friends. Maybe I could have done more, to help, I should have known…"

After hearing his story, and prepared with EFT knowledge, I recognized what to tap for. I had the lieutenant follow me and repeat my words.

"Even though I should have known…"

"Even though I should have been there to help…"

"Even though I'll miss my friends…"

After the first round of tapping, he sighed with an emotional release, his shoulders relaxed, and his tone of voice became calmer.

The lieutenant felt an emotional shift, a bodily experience that his mind couldn't explain. I described the body's energy system, and the pairing of energy and thoughts to flush out the negative emotions. Often I do two or three more tapping rounds to bring down the emotional charge to the lowest level. In so doing, the soldier learns how to do the tapping himself. In this case, one round was sufficient. The lieutenant wanted to get a copy of the book on EFT. He said he'd also tell the other soldiers who had been at the scene to come to the office.

I wrote to the executive officer of the 1-10 Calvary, saying that Combat Stress was prepared to conduct debriefings for soldiers at CNS.

Another soldier came in, Staff Sgt. Black, but his visit wasn't related to the previous day's event. He had recently learned that his wife of six years had had an affair. She admitted it after he suspected her and confronted her about it. They agreed to work to save the marriage. Yet the sergeant declared that if she did it again, the marriage would be over. Allowing the sergeant to talk enabled him to come to his own resolution and he left with a future direction.

Monday was supposed to be my day off, but given the recent KIAs and WIAs, my place was in the office. During the day, Maj. Stefani and I were trying to arrange some group debriefings at the brigade and battalion level. Both groups lost their operations and training captains. The memorial services were scheduled for Friday, October 14 at CNS.

Capt. Gillespie called and told Li she was going to FOB Shindand on 26 October. Located in western Afghanistan, Shindand was once the largest Afghan Air Force base. Li's attitude was positive. She was just dreading packing and moving her stuff to a new place. The captain implied that there could be another move in 90 days—maybe not, maybe just a wait and see how well the 113th teams were doing overall. I just hoped I didn't move until it was time to go home.

On Tuesday, October 11, we had three psychological group debriefings at CNS. Two groups were for those who had been on the scene on October 8 providing security and medics who helped treat the wounded. There was obvious sadness but also guilt that maybe they could have done more, as well as disbelief, anger, and mistrust of the Afghan National Army. With the debriefings, the story unfolded.

The event had started in the late evening, at the end of a gathering of nearly 100 Afghan religious and tribal leaders for a peace conference at a nearby palace, when a rocket-propelled grenade aimed toward the medical tent struck the side of the TOC (tactical operations center) tent instead. Then an insurgent dressed in an Afghan National Army uniform opened fire into the TOC with an M16 semiautomatic rifle. Capt. Lawrence, 29 years old and recently married, was killed immediately, and Capt. Russell, 25 years old, was mortally wounded and later died. Three others soldiers were shot. One wounded was MEDEVACed to Germany and would return home. Two others would recover from their injuries and return to CNS.

The third debriefing group was specifically for people who knew the captains, to help them process and cope with the loss. Afterward, a couple more soldiers who had been present that night came in individually for nightmares, guilty feelings, and the loss of a friend.

We planned more group debriefings the next day. It was a long night; Li and I had four TEM debriefings. To be more efficient, we decided to facilitate the meetings separately, two each. I had one with Lt. Col. Cook (commander of the 1-10 Calvary) and nine soldiers who were at the tent during and immediately after the incident. They had a great deal to process.

Lt. Col. Cook shared with the group that it was extremely personal for him to have lost two close friends. But he helped the group see the bigger picture of why the US was in Afghanistan: It was the last chance for the Afghans to secure democracy and life without war. Without the partnership of the Afghans, it wouldn't be possible.

One soldier in the group said, "I noticed that after the attack, many Afghan soldiers were afraid of us, thinking we'd kill them."

Another soldier said, "Although three Afghans attacked us, I don't think all of them believe that we're a bad influence. Some Afghans wanted to turn in their weapons to me. I saw others offer blankets to soldiers suffering from shock and some help wash the blood from their uniforms, body armor, and equipment."

Lastly, one soldier shared that after hours of bringing the aftermath to some semblance of order, they were able to leave and return to CNS. Apparently, the Afghan interpreters at CNS heard the devastating news and silently hugged the returning soldiers.

After seven debriefings, I felt extremely proud to be a US soldier. Overall, each soldier conducted himself professionally, with restraint, with valor, with teamwork. We lost two lives, but without the professionalism shown that night things could easily have gotten worse and could easily have set back the gains made in Afghanistan. There were possible opportunities to fire upon the suspected insurgents, but it was dark and there were soldiers around the insurgents, so firing blindly would've been a mistake. This demanded composed restraint. Yes, there were many statements of "what if," "if only," and "maybe I could have done more," but war is not predictable. It's random, and bad things happen. The memorial service for Lawrence and Russell would be the next day.

Amidst the debriefings, I also saw Pfc. Lewis who Maj. Stefani sent to me for a second opinion regarding the soldier's homicidal ideations toward several people in his platoon. Twenty years old, broad-faced, and heavily built, he had joined the army one year earlier "just for the paycheck," as he said. He had a history of fights in school and in the army. He was conflicted about both staying and leaving. He badly wanted to leave, but finding a job would be difficult. If he was going to stay in the army, however, he wanted others to change. He had no understanding that *he* had to change. By the end of the interview, the soldier realized that leaving was the only choice, which coincided with Maj. Stefani's findings. The soldier was too toxic. The company was spending too much energy trying to "fix him," losing focus on the mission.

I went to fencing class, and when I returned, the Internet and phones weren't working. It was another communication blackout. By now, I knew what must have happened. And I was right. A soldier from the 371st COP Lam died. That unit was far from us, yet within the hour a master sergeant came to the office, requesting that we go. I asked for the grid coordinates so that I could pass it along to my HQ.

We had one more debriefing that night, at 2100 hours—just two soldiers, the ones that called in the 9-Line MEDEVAC request (evacuation of casualties) to transport the wounded to immediate care. With ample time, we were able to talk. This was consoling for the soldiers to process and cope with the loss.

Going to the aid station for a last pee before bed, I was alarmed to see Pascua there. Apparently, he had punched a T-wall with his fists, continuously, until both hands were bloody and swollen, which required medical care.

"My first sergeant lied," said Pascua. "He said a priest was here today, but he left yesterday!"

Pascua wanted to make a confession, hoping it would help him control his moods, but he never received the information. Coincidentally, Chaplain Arguello was also at the aid station and he read passages from the Bible to Pascua. I quietly stepped away and returned to my sleeping quarter.

The following day, Li and I arrived early for the memorial services for Lawrence and Russell; we knew it would be crowded. We sat in the first row behind all the dignitaries, with more dignitaries on either side of us. I was surprised we weren't asked to move back, but Li commented that we were important, too. As I viewed the portraits of the two fallen captains, I sensed some relief that I hadn't met them, feeling it would hurt more if I had. Yet because of all the debriefings, I felt I knew them. As I left the memorial service, there was heaviness in my chest.

When I got back to the office, I called Capt. Gillespie and told him about the request for us to go to the 371st COP Lam because of a KIA. Gillespie knew of the incident and that a psychiatrist and a specialist might be going from KAF, if they could get a flight out. After another hour, we found out they did go and we weren't needed, so one less trip for us.

The day sped by with more clients. Two officers with stress issues didn't want to be seen in the office, so we sat around a table on a balcony. The weather was comfortable, the blue cloudless skies unusually clear. There was a sweeping view of the surrounding jagged mountains. The landscape was dust-colored, reflecting all shades of brown. I was able to help one officer by using tapping. After the first round, he said it was "crazy," but he admitted feeling better. Luckily, the other officer believed in the body's energy and delivered a nod of approval.

The communication blackout didn't lift because there was another KIA, but far away and not related to the camp's brigade area of operation. What a horrific two weeks—four KIAs already! I was really ready for my November R&R.

On Saturday morning, we had two new clients and a follow-up case. I was able to complete my report on the psychological debriefings at CNS and emailed it to my commander. One thing for sure: Due to recent incidents, Combat Stress was now on the brigade and battalion officers' radar.

Stigma of Behavioral Health

Sunday morning began with a client who came in after being medically cleared for "blackouts." Spc. Akers, tall and lanky with an oval face and shiny thick hair, reported a gradual and more noticeable short-term memory problem, to the point that his fellow soldiers didn't trust him on missions. As a driver, Akers had recently "clipped" his ground guide (who walks in front of the truck to guide the driver into the camp). This could result in an Article 15. For two years he had been on Zoloft to contain his anxiety, but it wasn't working.

When I asked Akers to think of an event that was emotionally charged, recent or in the past, he said, "A man and his son were killed after their car hit an IED on the road."

"When was this and where?" I asked.

"2008, in Iraq," he answered. "I think it should have been my truck. Normally, we'd take that road, but on that day my truck commander decided not to."

Akers had seen a therapist twice at his fort in Colorado, but it didn't help. I had him tap.

"Even though I feel guilty for their deaths, I'm a good soldier."

"Even though I'm responsible for their deaths, I'm a good soldier."

"Even though I'm sad for their deaths, I'm a good soldier."

Tapping on the acupoints on his head, face, and torso, Akers said the words, "Guilty. Responsible. Sad."

After the first round, he tilted his head and uttered a long sigh. He said he felt different, that it didn't bother him as much. We tapped another round and he concluded that it wasn't his fault; he could release the guilt.

"I can see the boy in heaven," Akers said.

After catching up on some paperwork, I went to the camp's first Ping-Pong tournament. There were plenty of men, but no females, so

Chaplain Arguello signed me up against a female first lieutenant. He actually strongly convinced us to play. How could I say no to the chaplain? We were evenly matched, but I scraped by and won two games out of three, so I won first place! The men were good, and I watched the chaplain win the tournament. The chaplain really liked his Ping-Pong!

On my day off, the Internet guy came by to drop a cable into my sleeping quarter—and it didn't work. In the meantime, I received seven boxes: four from donors, one from Blue Gauntlet (fencing equipment), one from Rob, and one from Sandra (my sister-in-law). I loved her boxes. They were filled with unexpected stuff, such as Freudian slips (sticky notes), humorous books, and old calendar pages with beautiful scenery that I merrily tacked up in my room.

On Tuesday, I had some follow-up cases in the morning and fencing in the afternoon. In the evening, I received a call on my cell that Capt. Barroso, Public Affairs, had finished the first draft of his article about Combat Stress. Any articles about Combat Stress would only help spread the word that we exist and that we can help.

There were two new cases the following day. Spc. Coughlin came in after a referral from Chaplain Williams. This soldier was extremely frustrated that her sergeant hadn't allowed her to go to the aid station two days earlier.

"I'm being targeted for harassment because my mom wrote a letter to Congress complaining that I wasn't getting medical care."

Coughlin was so distressed that she wanted to strike her sergeant with the butt of her rifle. Her weapon was taken away but was returned two days later. We did one round of tapping, "I'm stressed, angry, he's a jerk, he isn't worth it, I can relax now, I'll be okay." Then she gleefully exclaimed, "Ten times better!"

The second soldier, Pvt. Reynolds, who was wearing black issued BCGs (so-called "birth control glasses" because they are so ugly!), was depressed. As he adjusted his glasses atop his nose, he said, "I've taken Prozac before. It helps, but I don't have any more."

I referred him to Maj. Stefani and he was prescribed Prozac and Ambien for sleep. Reynolds returned to my office and we discussed activities he found fun, how to change his routine and to exercise, and we tapped for sleep problems. I was silently amused when he was yawning after one round of tapping.

That Thursday was a crazy day, the busiest yet. There were four soldiers in the morning: one follow-up, one ANAM test, one referred because of homicidal ideation, and one referred by command because of poor performance. Another came later in the morning, referred by a chaplain, but I couldn't see him until the afternoon. On top of all that, I had to teach fencing. I actually had to place the closed sign on the door so that I could finish seeing one soldier and complete my clinical notes. It was great to be busy—time flew by.

My HQ sent my travel dates for R&R: 29 October to KAF and then out on 4 November. The problem was that my new behavioral health specialist, Sgt. Lopez, was scheduled to come in on the day I was scheduled to leave. How would he know where the office was or where things were located? I wrote back to see if I could go to KAF later, or have him come to CNS earlier. I couldn't believe it, but I actually didn't want to leave. The timing was bad. I preferred having the opportunity to work with Lopez for at least a couple of days.

Out of nowhere, my Internet cable began working in my room! I was finally getting fast connectivity, something for which I'd been paying out of my own pocket for three months and not getting.

Friday began with Staff Sgt. Weil standing by the door. There was a sheen of sweat on his forehead and, with tightness in his throat, he asked, "Can…can I talk to you in confidence?"

I said, "I have limits of confidentiality, which means I'm required to tell your commander if you are a danger to yourself or others. Everything else is private."

He stormed out. I followed him and told him he could talk to a chaplain, who holds complete confidentiality, but he shouted, "No!"

About five hours later, Weil came back and awkwardly said, "I have crazy thoughts to hurt people."

"How would you do it? Do you have a plan?" I asked.

"No, no, just wild thoughts."

"Well, let's go over your options...to talk with me, or go to the aid station for medication and still talk with me. You can give up your weapon so that you can't hurt anyone. But then I'll have to let your command know."

"No, I don't want to do it, to hurt anybody. I've got too much to lose...my marriage, home, my civilian job, and my military benefits."

"What's bothering you?" I asked.

"My job here is meaningless...no one appreciates what I do. It's a waste of time."

We tapped on: "Even though I don't want to be here, my job is meaningless, what a waste of time! I am a good soldier."

At the end, he promised me that he wouldn't hurt anyone, and if he wanted to, he had to call me first. He agreed to return to the office.

After finally getting Internet cable in my room, my service expired. I had a good connection for just one day. I felt cheated and defeated!

Saturday was another busy day, with four cases, three of which were new. It was getting difficult to recall each case, as they blurred with one another. More high-ranking soldiers were coming in, emotional and stressed, not only from deployment but from marital issues as well. I was so busy that I barely squeezed in lunch and made it to the fencing class. After the class, I decided that it would be the last one until I returned from R&R. There was too much to do before I left.

Li returned from KAF after a training class there, and on Wednesday she would leave permanently, not to Shindand as originally thought, but to Masum Ghar, in the Panjwai District of Kandahar province. My first sergeant told me this in the morning. There were many changes and many unhappy behavioral health specialists. Li, on the other hand, thought a change of base assignment was good, to help the time pass faster.

Sunday morning brought four cases: two returned from the day before and two new cases. Of the two new cases, one was a female soldier escorted in for "lack of respect." This Spc. Green had an important task to do, requiring a great deal of focus, and when another soldier interrupted her, she got angry, which was interpreted as being disrespectful.

"To better help you learn tapping," I said, "can you tell me something recent or in the past that was disturbing or emotionally upsetting, something that would be close to an 8 on a scale from 0 to 10, with 10 being the most disturbing?"

Green crossed her arms over her chest. Tears flowed from her eyes. "I was raped when I went home last winter. My friend and I went to a bar to celebrate the New Year," she added, "but that's all I remember, just driving home.

"The next morning, my body was aching and hurting. I didn't understand why. When I wanted to be intimate with my boyfriend, I couldn't because of the pain. I realized what had happened. I went to my doctor."

We tapped on "in the past, this is now," releasing guilt and shame, not to be blamed, not her fault. Afterward, Green felt better, wearing a gentle smile, and as she headed out, she wrapped me in a hug.

The second new case was Sgt. Dunn. Mid-twenties, heavyset, with fair complexion and a chiseled face, he dealt with insurgents on an almost daily basis. His job was to interrogate the detainees.

"What brings you here?" I asked.

"I'm worried. I don't feel good about myself."

"Tell me more."

"My job is to get the insurgents to talk. And sometimes I beat them up."

"And…"

"And...well...I find that I like it...I enjoy hurting them. I know it's wrong, because I'm Christian."

This was Dunn's second deployment in five years. He was on call 24/7, and he was one of six people doing a job that usually requires 20 soldiers. This had become extremely stressful. Also, his platoon was going home early, but he couldn't go. Every morning he thought how it was unfair and about what he could do to go home, too. We discussed things that are in our control and things that are not. Thinking of the past and the future, we forget to enjoy the present. The present is what we have control over, the decisions we make that will affect the future, and our perception of those situations. We can choose to be negative or find the positive, as small as it may be.

After Dunn selected a recent incident of being under a lot of pressure at work, I taught him how to tap to release the stress. After one round of tapping, our eyes met, and he hollered, "It's magic!"

Monday was supposed to be my day off, but as I would be leaving for KAF on Saturday to begin my R&R travel, I thought I better be around the office, given the number of soldiers coming in lately. Sure enough, it was busy.

I had a female soldier who had been sexually assaulted nearly one month earlier. She had been asking to go to Behavioral Health, but due to missions and other excuses she couldn't. It was only after she went to JAG that her command let her go. It's no wonder so few females report sexual assaults or rapes in the military. Once reported, the victim is treated like a leper. Her "friends" won't talk to her anymore. She is shunned. Some say she's making a big thing out of nothing just so that she can go home. On and on, everything except giving her support, giving her help so that she can complete her tour.

Li counseled a soldier, Pvt. Muñoz, from another FOB who was suicidal after being harassed by his squad leader, team leader, and platoon sergeant. Because he told them to take his weapon away from him or he'd use it on himself, he was escorted to CNS. "I've been picked on. I held on as long as I could." Fortunately, the company's first sergeant ordered a stop to the harassment, or so he told me. In the meantime, Muñoz would stay in the camp to "reset" for a couple of days.

Two others came in to report they were doing better: Weil was no longer having thoughts about hurting people, and one soldier was having improved communication with his spouse. This soldier brought in his personal laptop to show me images of his beautiful wife. He thanked me for my advice. It was always fulfilling to hear how well soldiers were doing.

Li and I went to the office of Capt. Ferrell, commander of the Mayor Cell. Li thanked the captain for helping Combat Stress be part of the camp, helping us find a theater for our Movie Night, and publicizing our groups to CNS residents. She handed the captain our unit's coin in appreciation. Since Li was leaving and the captain was scheduled to leave for another FOB, we wanted to acknowledge his support.

The next day there were just a couple of follow-ups, one for Li and one for me. Essentially, both were doing better. It is remarkable how talking to someone who actually listens can help.

I changed my departure date of my R&R from October 29 to November 2. I went to the CNS landing zone and arranged my own flight, with HQ's approval. This would give me time to work with Lopez and for me to stay at CNS instead of hanging around KAF with nothing to do.

On Wednesday, Li went to her new assignment at Masum Ghar and I cleaned and rearranged the office. In the morning, a soldier was escorted in after he received his Article 15 punishment from the night before: rank demoted to E-1 and 45 days of extra duty. This soldier struck his sergeant when the sergeant tried to wake him up. He admitted that he was wrong. The soldier had a long history of anger issues, having learned it from his family. He joined the army to prove to his family that he wasn't a "beast." I taught him to tap: "Even though I can easily be angry, I can choose peace, joy, and calmness."

A sergeant was "voluntold" by his senior NCO to come into Combat Stress because of anger issues. The sergeant admitted a problem with his first sergeant when he was accused of having chow at the DFAC while others were working. He claimed this wasn't true. I suggested he go to the DFAC and obtain records showing that he didn't get a meal on that day in question. (Before getting any meals, everyone must show their ID card and sign their name with the last four digits of their Social Security number.)

The next morning was easy, with just two follow-ups: Pfc. Jones, who came in sunny and smiling, saying that she'd grown calmer, watching others get mad. She had tapped at least four times since we met. She found it rewarding that she was no longer quick to anger.

The other soldier, Sgt. Samuels, had also been using tapping for stress, and especially on this day for "emotional pain" related to his ex-wife. He had dreamt about her the night before, waking up in a state of panic. As he wanted to get rid of his emotional ties with his ex-wife, I asked to see how he would tap it away. He tapped, but it was different from the way I taught him, tapping on the inside of his wrist instead of the side of the hand area. Yet he said the way he tapped had worked with other issues before. EFT is an amazing technique—it works even when you don't do it "right"!

Attack on Camp Nathan Smith

It was quiet after lunch on October 27, so I decided to watch a movie on my laptop. The movie was *Cloudy with a Chance of Meatballs*, and I was enjoying it when there was a loud explosion in the camp. I quickly removed my one earplug and when the second blast occurred, I kissed the floor. I could feel my face tense up and my heart beat faster. By the third louder and nearer explosion, I had thrown on my Kevlar and body armor. Clutching my rifle, I went outside.

People were rushing to the closest bunker. I did the same. I checked my watch. It was 1416 hours. For the next hour and a half, I listened to intermittent rocket-propelled grenades (RPGs) and small arms fire. With each nearby explosion, the ground shook and my ears rang. There was a nervous energy in us and around us, emptiness in everyone's eyes, and a feeling of unspoken fear. I kept telling myself that it would be over soon, but the gunfire continued.

Finally, there was enough of a break that leaders told soldiers to report quickly to their units for accountability. As I was the only one in my unit, I reported to the aid station, where I saw a couple of soldiers hurt during the initial attack—shrapnel and concussions. Soon after, three more wounded returned to the aid station; the helicopter couldn't MEDEVAC these patients because the landing zone hadn't been secured yet. While I rotated to the aid station and provided security at a nearby gate, there were reverberations of intermittent small-arms fire, volleys of RPGs, and two car bombs. (Luckily, I never had to discharge my weapon or feel bullets or rockets zipping by me.)

As the K9 team made their sweeps around the camp, the soldier handling the dog found an interpreter dead in his tent, where an RPG had exploded. Around 2000 hours, the army dropped a Hellfire precision missile onto the nearby house (about 150 yards away) from which the insurgents had conducted their assaults, followed by 30-mm machine gun fire from an Apache helicopter to finish the job. By the time the camp received the all-clear signal, it was 0200 hours.

The final tally was one KIA, six seriously wounded MEDEVACed to KAF, and 24 treated for injuries at the aid station. I was tired, after wearing my kit and having my adrenaline run most of the day. I went to sleep around 2300 hours, three hours before the all-clear signal. I needed my rest so that I could help the next day. The multiple blasts were strong enough that in my sleeping quarter and office, debris fell from the ceiling and walls. Exhausted as I was, I had to clean my bed before going to sleep.

The next morning, I hiked around the camp and saw high walls peppered with shells and bullet holes. Rocket-propelled grenades had ripped through tents and contorted metal bunk beds.

Attack on Camp Nathan Smith.

Two soldiers came in first thing when the office opened. Pvt. Harper had been in Tower 7 when the initial mortars came in.

"I was so scared," she said. "The tower was filled with smoke. I couldn't see, couldn't breathe, my wrist was hurting, bleeding. I ducked down in the corner and called in the attack."

Harper had only been in the army for eight months and at CNS for only one month. Her sergeant escorted her into Combat Stress because she hadn't slept the night before. In addition, the private suspected she could be in trouble, since she forgot to grab her weapon when members of Special Forces helped her down and out of the tower. Since she had only recently joined the army, I hoped her command would be sympathetic. I had Harper tap for doing the best she could, given the time she had to react, and to forgive herself for any embarrassment, guilt, and shame.

The second person that came in was with the navy, Petty Officer Davies.

"The attack didn't bother me. I've had worse attacks when I was in Iraq," he said, then frowning, complained of his command firing him from his position because of "disrespect" and poor performance. He admitted stress from home as well. He had a 6-year-old autistic son, and he badly wanted to communicate with him. When asked if he felt some guilt, he said yes, as there was another family member with autism. We discussed childhood vaccines and Jenny McCarthy's book *Louder Than Words: A Mother's Journey in Healing Autism*. McCarthy's son "recovered" from autism with a gluten-free, casein-free diet, vitamin supplements, and heavy metal detoxification. McCarthy believed that childhood vaccines should be reduced and certain toxic ingredients eliminated. I had him tap for guilt and forgiveness, and the possibility of finding a way to communicate with his son. He stood up and, during our handshake, said, "I've never shared about my son with anyone before."

In the afternoon, I met with Capt. Conant to arrange some debriefings for the camp regarding the previous day's attack. There were multiple groups to identify, times and dates to schedule. My new behavioral health specialist, Sgt. Lopez, was going to walk into a firestorm.

I woke up early on Saturday because Lopez was supposed to arrive at 0700 hours. Due to the recent threat level, however, no flights were coming to CNS, so no Lopez. I hoped he would arrive before I left on my R&R.

I counseled six soldiers throughout the day. All but one was because of the recent attack. All were edgy, nervous, and jumpy.

Davies with the autistic son returned. He had lightness in his heart, saying he was much better. A warm feeling swept through me. Such news is forever rewarding to hear.

Capt. Conant would arrange four debriefings the following day for the camp residents traumatized by the attack.

On Sunday, Harper returned. She had gone back to her tower that day, for her guard-duty shift, and she wasn't emotionally ready. She was afraid and had an empty feeling in her stomach. Worse, her unit scrutinized everything she did, inspecting for faults. Because of what she went through in the attack, she might receive the Purple Heart and Combat Action Badge and an Article 15 for neglecting her weapon. Others were feeling envious of her awards, since she had only been in the army nine months. It was petty and childish, but real and sad.

Harper's sergeant and lieutenant came in for an update.

"How's Harper doing?" the lieutenant asked.

"Well, I want to keep her in the fight. I think going back to guard duty, to the same tower, is too soon for her," I said. "I'd like her to be off today and reevaluate her tomorrow."

When the lieutenant walked away, the sergeant remained.

"I'm embarrassed that many aren't supporting Harper," she said. "They're acting with meanness and hatred toward her. I don't know how to protect her."

With an understanding nod, I said, "You're in a difficult situation, Sarge. Unfortunately, I'm guessing, this isn't the first time you've seen this."

"No..."

"What have you done before?"

"I usually wait it out...do what I can."

"Good for you."

I conducted three group critical stress debriefings for the camp that day. Many voiced vulnerability, uncontrollable angst, hypervigilance, loss of appetite, and poor sleep. It was a rough week.

The last day of October was another busy Monday, with three new cases and two follow-ups. I needed to refer two of the new cases to the aid station for medication evaluation. Both of these soldiers needed something to settle down, one because of the October 27 attack and one because he was fed up with his unit and said he might do something he'd regret.

Harper returned, perky and ecstatic since she would work in the Mayor Cell for the next month. I didn't understand how that had happened, but I was glad for her.

I counseled two other soldiers, off the books—a lieutenant and sergeant complaining of toxic leadership. We discussed the options of going to the inspector general and chaplain to find some remedy, and I taught them tapping to let go of anger, frustration, and helplessness and to choose joy and calmness.

I caught up with reports and charting only because I closed the office at 1600 hours. I'd arranged a teeth cleaning with the aid station's dental hygienist for the next day, and then I had one follow-up case. After that, I planned to close the office so that I could finish packing and do some laundry before leaving for KAF and my R&R.

I saw Davies and he reported no incidents in the previous three days. He planned to apologize to his colleagues for being "a jerk" the past month. I had him practice his apology, using assertive communication with "I" statements.

"I've been under a lot of stress. I've been a jerk, and I would like to say I'm sorry."

By starting his sentence with "I," Davies was able to express his opinions and feelings without hurting the feelings of others.

Next was a new case in which the soldier reported poor sleep since the attack, overwhelming fear, and frustration. She was also questioning why she had joined the army. Spc. Cruz, of medium height and slim build, with dark hair slicked back in a bun, apparently had the opportunity to fire upon the house that was attacking CNS. Cruz was a gunner on patrol during the attack, but her immediate chain of command ordered her not to fire. We tapped on being scared, irritated, and frustrated. Finally, we tapped that she could grow from the experience, by following orders, and that she could finish the tour with pride.

Even though I wanted to close the office at noon, I met with two more soldiers after lunch. One was an R&R briefing and then Staff Sgt. Deleon, who had been experiencing a recurring dream since he was a child. I taught him tapping to stop the dreams, with the images fading away. He didn't think it would work but was willing to try tapping before he went to sleep that night.

I finally closed the office, completed some reports, finished my packing, and took a shower. Lopez was still not at CNS. Earlier I had gone to the landing zone, and the flight that he was scheduled on had been canceled. There was hope that he would arrive around 1700 hours. But alas, he did not.

R&R and "Home" Again

On Wednesday, November 2, I got a flight to KAF. Two days later, I would fly from Kandahar to Kuwait. There was nothing for me to do while waiting, except hang around the HQ office and socialize. But I did see Lopez and gave him a verbal orientation to the office at CNS. Being at KAF was also an opportunity for me to unwind after a demanding October.

On Friday, I leaped into a C-17 military plane and had about a three-hour flight to Kuwait. In less than 24 hours, I had my itinerary and was on my way to Genoa, Italy. I had emailed Rob my arrival time and he met me at the airport. I was thrilled to see him again. We hugged silently, for a long time. Rob appeared a bit thin, and I had warned him that I was thin as well. So we had a common mission—to eat, eat, and eat some more. A perfect mission for Italy!

I filled Rob in on my missions outside the wire, but I didn't tell him of the recent attack on CNS. He was already worried about my safety; there was no need for him to be more concerned.

I had a great R&R with Rob, going to Genoa, Portofino, Cinque Terra, the Tower of Pisa, and Florence. I had to constantly remind myself where I was, no longer in a combat zone, no need to wear boots and carry a rifle. Yet it was difficult to relax. I couldn't switch off. To conserve my mental energy, to lower my stress, I trusted Rob to make the decisions of where to visit and what to see. But I decided on the restaurants for our meals!

Rob flew back to the US on November 21. I departed Genoa the next day, flying to Munich, Frankfurt, and then Kuwait. I stayed on the Ali Al Salem Air Base, approximately 23 miles from the Iraqi border, for two days, spending Thanksgiving Day there. The dining facility was decorated with large pumpkins and black-and-white pilgrim figurines. I sat down with a paper plate of dried sliced turkey, soggy bread stuffing, and canned cranberry sauce. I already missed the scrumptious Italian cuisine with Rob.

On November 25, I flew to KAF, and back to Camp Nathan Smith two days later. The many travel transitions were hectic, but it had been well worth it to be with Rob again. I was rested, recharged, and ready for the second half of the tour. I'd even gained a few pounds.

By chance, I flew from KAF to CNS with Lopez, who was returning from a mission at Frontenac. We spent the day cleaning the office and opening and sorting donation care packages, and I evaluated one soldier for recruitment school. As I walked around the camp, several soldiers respectfully saluted and said, "Welcome back." I didn't realize I had been missed. It felt nice.

Five soldiers came in the next day, three follow-ups and two new cases. As usual, the majority of the problems were dealing with stress and anxiety, so tapping was the treatment of choice. I enjoyed watching the reaction of each soldier after completing the first round of tapping. When I had soldiers revisit the initial disturbing thought, they would laugh or shake their heads in disbelief, or both. They had just experienced relief, a weight lifted, and a calming effect. It was visibly apparent how well the technique worked.

Lopez and I spent the evening in the office talking, getting acquainted with each other. I told him about my upbringing, jobs, fencing, and my relationship with Rob. Then I asked about his life, interests, and goals. This was Lopez's second deployment and he was thinking he might not reenlist when his term of service expired. He wanted to return to school, complete his college degree, and work as a health care administrator.

On November 29, I had just one official follow-up case, but two unofficial cases I decided not to document. One of the unofficial cases was Deleon, who I had seen the day before I went on my R&R, the one with the recurring dream.

"I had the dream that night after tapping, but it was slightly different, and I haven't had it since," he said.

As I'd suggested, he'd also written the dream on a piece of paper and burned it. He said that if he had the dream again, he'd "come right back and ask for a refund."

Ha, ha.

After the soldier left, I went to Maj. Stefani's office to catch up on the cases and general events that had occurred at CNS while I was away. I also checked out a new place to restart the fencing program. This was the room with the overhead lights and where I could leave the fencing equipment out, since the room was lockable. This would be so much better than to unpack and repack the fencing machine each class. Lopez wanted to learn to fence and he tried on the new, larger metallic scoring jacket donated by Blue Gauntlet Fencing.

I had one new case the next morning, referred by his command because of home-front issues, a pending messy divorce due to his wife's adulterous behavior. Apparently, it was her second extramarital affair.

Another new case was escorted in because of her threat to harm another soldier. Staff Sgt. Tyler admitted being stressed and that she could get to the point where she was unable to control what she said and did.

"I'm mad and loud, I'll explode," she said. As I taught her tapping, I asked her to think of an event, past or present that was emotionally disturbing.

She hesitated slightly, glanced at Lopez, and returned her gaze at me. "Can the sergeant leave?" she asked softly. Without hesitation, Lopez stood up and left the room.

Once he was gone, Tyler flexed her fingers and was quiet for a moment. Her eyebrows drawing together, she said, "My father raped me...since I was eleven. It lasted awhile. I finally told my mom a few years ago. The police came. He has to stay away now...a restraining order."

We did several rounds of tapping, for helplessness, feeling sick, dizzy, tense, and not telling anyone. I was proud of her courage and openness.

After she left, Cpl. Landis came in, still feeling the loss of his friend and fellow soldier on October 8. He had been unable to focus on his work, performing below his ability. We discussed the five stages of grief and tapped on his poor concentration and on choosing clarity and concentration one task at a time.

After Landis, another soldier walked in, asking to begin therapy for anxiety. He'd had therapy for a year before his deployment and found it helpful.

From Stars and Stripes, we received 20 boxes of beautiful handmade Christmas stockings, filled with snacks and personal hygiene items, like lotions, toothpaste, and toothbrushes. Each box contained 20 stockings. It was a gratifying feeling to distribute them to smiling, thankful soldiers.

December 2011

Another month was gone. The first day of December brought three follow-up cases: marital issues, depression, and depression/anxiety. One new case had multiple issues: childhood physical and sexual abuse, witnessing parental domestic violence, the death of his mother a month earlier, displacing his anger on his pet dog, stuffing down his feelings, and "numbing." He was neither suicidal nor homicidal, however. Two rounds of tapping on his mother's death, frozen in grief, had no improvement. I suggested he consider medication to curb his anxiety. The soldier agreed and went to see Maj. Stefani.

Upon returning to the office after dinner, we discovered the phone and Internet weren't working. Oh, no...my thoughts immediately assumed more KIAs and wounded soldiers.

There wasn't a KIA. I learned at the aid station the next day that the Internet apparently had been off and on for the previous few days. Whew!

December 2 was another busy day at the office: six soldiers, all follow-ups, all doing better than their initial visit.

Well, actually, Spc. Logan came in and, in mid-stride, stated in a droning voice, "I dropped all of my medications in my mouth but spit them out."

Was this a serious suicide attempt? I wasn't sure.

"Do you want to die?" I asked.

Shifting in his chair, Logan shrugged his shoulders.

"Do you want to stay in theater or do you want to leave, go home and be chaptered out of the Army?"

"I'm not sure."

"Why don't you think about it? Let me hold onto your rifle and come back in half an hour and let me know your decision."

About 30 minutes later, Logan came back in.

"I want to go home."

I escorted him to the aid station, where he was placed on an intensive buddy watch while the paperwork was done and an escort was found to travel with him to KAF. Logan took off within three hours.

Pascua came in later. Although still angry with some of his higher-ups, saying, "It's bullshit," he was handling the stress better. "Every day I'm choosing peace." He was getting ready to go home in two months.

Saturday was quieter, with just a couple of soldiers. Although both were follow-ups, one case was new to me. Lopez had seen Sgt. 1st Class Frankel while I was on R&R. He thought Frankel was overemphasizing psychological symptoms, perhaps feigning illness for some benefit of attention or sympathy. Lopez had a behavioral health provider from another base meet with Frankel via tele–behavioral health. The provider thought the same and told the sergeant this. Frankel was extremely angry that after 15 years of service and achieving the rank of a senior noncommissioned officer, he would be accused of lying.

Frankel didn't return to Combat Stress after the initial assessment but continued talking with Chaplain Williams. The chaplain encouraged him to see me. We talked and at no time did he even claim symptoms of PTSD, depression, or anything. He did have "what if…" concerns. What if he had died on October 27? Who would have taken care of his family? He had some guilt related to being away for so long—19 months—and missing his children's major milestones. He was also having sleep disturbances and physical pain from the October attack. He agreed to continue working with me.

I had my first fencing class after returning from R&R. It was fun to teach again, even though the new space was smaller and the floor a bit slippery. Lopez gladly participated in the class, and he was quick for a big guy.

Sunday was a quiet day, with just one follow-up. I spent the time updating some forms and records, sorting and giving away donated items to the chaplain's annex and to the landing zone office. Slowly, but surely,

I would give out all the care packages in my office before the next batch came in.

Lopez and I played Ping-Pong after dinner. I couldn't buy a win. He won every game. By then I knew that Lopez—hardworking, professional, and with an easygoing attitude—was a positive addition to the Combat Stress Control team.

The weather remained cool and breezy in the mornings and evenings, but sunny and pleasant during the day. I hoped it would stay that way throughout the winter.

Maj. Stefani told me that Logan, who on December 2 had put all of his medications in his mouth but spit them out, would be going home after seeing two psychiatrists at KAF. Perhaps his suicide attempt was a cry for help. He lacked coping skills and wanted to be with his wife. They couldn't guarantee that the soldier wouldn't hurt himself, and his symptoms would probably escalate until he got what he wanted.

On Monday, December 5, I had one follow-up, Spc. Stahl. She had been at PSS-1 on August 27 when the VBIED exploded, killing a friend and fellow soldier. She still suffered physical and emotional pain. She glanced away when she talked, but behind her eyes I sensed a deep and distant sadness.

"I got caught drinking alcohol. My brother sent it to me. I asked him to."

"What's going to happen now?" I asked.

"I think I'm going to lose rank, maybe lose my top-secret clearance, too."

Stahl knew that alcohol had a numbing effect on her emotions, but that it was only temporary at best.

I spent part of the day doing my laundry, cleaning my room, and sorting out some clothes. I needed to "destroy" my first two sets of multi-cam uniform and wear the remaining two sets. Why not use them? I wouldn't be able to wear them when I returned to the States, and I didn't want to carry or send them back.

That evening, Lopez and I met with Vernes, a Bosnian former physical education instructor who was at CNS as a civilian contractor. He was an excellent Ping-Pong player, and I had asked if he could teach us. He agreed and soon he had us doing certain exercises: striking the ball slowly, only forehand, only backhand, alternating sides, and then two times on each side. This was helpful for me, as I had a weak forehand. Eventually, he had us rally faster and added the spike as well. It was fun, and I could see the improvement. I'd soon beat that Lopez!

Tuesday brought only two soldiers. Both were follow-ups, one that I hadn't seen since October. His words tumbled out, as he reported doing extremely well, enjoying his new job, and preparing for his promotion board. He had only come in because the aid station wanted him to see me, since he wanted to refill his Zoloft.

Later that day I learned that Mail Rodeo (traveling postal service) would be on base for only a couple of days—a wonderful surprise. I planned to send home a box of items I didn't need.

Wednesday, December 7 was my 59th birthday—although I'd like to believe I'm 29 years old. I need to think I'm young so that my body believes it. It helps to be youthful in deployment, so I needed all the help I could get.

Unfortunately, being older meant I had to go to the bathroom during the night, at least once. If I didn't, I'd have relentless dreams where I'm in distress, searching place to place for a bathroom and never finding one. Eventually, with the persistent discomfort in my bladder (and the fear of peeing in my bed), I'd rouse from my sleep. I'd have to dress warmly, slip on my running shoes, and sneak out of my building into the dark cold night—"sneak" because I went without my weapon and eye protection, which were required when venturing outdoors. Once inside the aid station, I'd be blinded for a few seconds by the bright lights. Squinting, I hoped no one else was in line for the toilet. With my hair tousled and mouth dry, I was in no mood to chat with anyone. Finally, relieved, I'd need to scramble back to my room without being caught. This, sadly, was a nightly affair.

It was a busy day, with six soldiers and one command consultation. There were three new cases: depression, depression, and marital issues—wife posting nude pictures of herself over the Internet to another soldier, a friend of the husband here at CNS. Tough situation, but the soldier was willing to save his marriage of two years and his wife felt the same.

Lopez and I went to the Mail Rodeo and mailed our boxes to the States. I was glad to clear some things out of my small room.

We had just one new case the next day, Staff Sgt. Shelton, with a history of familial problems (schizophrenic mother), foster care placements, and sexual and emotional abuse. She was referred because her first sergeant learned her "boyfriend" had struck her six months earlier. In fact, he had stuck a gun to her head. We tapped for this and guilt, shame, responsibility, things that happened in the past, lessons learned, and taking care of herself. She cried intensely during the first round of tapping. She conceded that she rarely shows her emotions, and that she felt relief.

Friday brought four cases: one command consultation, one Recruitment/Retention evaluation, and two soldier follow-up cases. One specialist I hadn't seen since September had just returned from R&R that morning and was ordered into her commander's office. She was told there was a "no-contact order" in place with a male soldier at CNS. The male soldier's wife was claiming her husband and the specialist were committing adultery. The specialist claimed this wasn't true. She said she was offering support and advice to the soldier, as he was preparing to divorce his wife and wanted sole custody of his two children. The specialist felt some responsibility for the soldier having to pack up his belongings to move out of CNS.

I received some care packages and brought a blanket back to my room. I now had five layers of blankets on my bed. The temperature had dropped considerably, especially in the early mornings. When it was extremely cold outside, the wind tried, rather insistently, to get into my quarter.

Eric from Edge City Internet services surprised me with a simple plywood table he had built for me—so thoughtful of him. He remembered that I didn't have a table in my room, as I had my personal items strewed on the floor. He noticed this when he had checked to see if he could drop a cable from the ceiling. Now my room was getting too comfortable. I might not want to leave—NOT!

I wore my crisp new uniform that day, after "destroying" my first two multi-cam uniforms. Our old uniforms must be witnessed and signed off when they are placed in a locked box to be destroyed, preventing the possibility of insurgents getting them.

Sgt. Tyler, who had revealed the abuse by her father, returned, saying that she felt much better, with more energy. Her movements were more fluid and relaxed.

"I grew up needing to please people, to be perfect. If I wasn't, no one would love me."

We tapped for that. We also tapped for confidence and practiced assertive communication skills.

"I want to come in every other day. I like talking to you," she said. "Maybe if I'd had someone like you in Korea and Iraq, I wouldn't have had any problems."

I felt a flush across my cheeks. It was a kind, heartfelt compliment.

I decided to buy a space heater for my room. In checking the weather, I discovered that it would get down into the 20s at night and reach only into the 50s during the day. Sleeping with five thin blankets, wearing socks, a fleece hat, PT pants, and four shirts was getting ridiculous!

The next day one soldier, a follow-up case, said with a slow smile, "I had a vivid dream about my mother…She's dead…she died two years ago. But in the dream, we had a long conversation and she told me she loved me." The soldier now had some closure.

After the office closed, we met with Vernes for our weekly Ping-Pong lesson. I was getting better, but I still couldn't beat Lopez. One day…

On Tuesday, it was sunny and cold. No rain that day. I went to the Mayor Cell's weekly meeting and found out there was a food shortage.

No wonder the food had been terrible! But two truckloads of food were supposedly coming that day.

Lopez and I played Ping-Pong after dinner. We practiced the fore-hand, backhand, serving and spiking, and then we played a game. I won! But I suspected that the next time Lopez would get me.

Happy Holidays

Although I kept a daily journal, it was getting skimpy, as work was the same most days. Even the cases we saw were the same: depression, stress, toxic leadership, and home-front issues (marital, financial, children). So there wasn't much to write about, which was a good thing. The aid station and chaplains also reported a slowdown. Maybe it was true that there was a break in the fighting.

With the holiday season, the camp became more festive, with bright, colorful lights strung up on the dining facility walls and a few artificial Christmas trees placed in the corners of the room. More care packages were coming in, which meant sorting and giving them out as quickly as possible. The number of organizations that support deployed military personnel always impressed me. Each box represented time, effort, and money from a volunteer or groups of volunteers. And all of this was done with love and gratitude for soldiers' collective sacrifices in service. More important, each box meant the soldiers' service wasn't forgotten or taken for granted. The care packages provided a reminder of the tastes and comforts of the US...and for a moment, we were home.

The 113th Combat Stress Control Unit was scheduled to remain in Afghanistan until the end of May 2012. I told myself the second half of the deployment would be easier. No more 120-degree weather (I hoped). I'd adapted to the living conditions, I had a spacious and comfortable office, and I'd built professional relationships with the camp's command staff, the aid station's brigade surgeon, the chaplains, and the Mayor Cell. Now it was just a matter of continuing to work with soldiers, and to pass the time.

When I wasn't in my office, I read thrillers and watched movies and old television shows on my laptop. And since returning from my R&R, I'd continued fencing classes three times a week. Plus there was Ping-Pong. I now really appreciated the game; it was a quick workout with no need to change into my PT uniform, and no need to shower right after play. It was more physically challenging than walking or running, and it required a minimal amount of equipment. I especially enjoyed the competitiveness and speed involved.

In the next few days, USO would be sending me a USO2GO kit for the camp. On larger bases, the USO offers a little fun to relieve the harshness and boredom of deployment. At CNS, USO didn't exist, so I applied to receive furniture, games (Nintendo Wii, PlayStation 3, Xbox360), leisure kits, and edible enjoyments. The kit was more than I could handle, so I'd made arrangements with the camp's MWR to take over the responsibility and distribution of the USO equipment.

On Friday, December 16, there was the unit's biweekly conference call. I actually dreaded these, as there were never adequate details of what would happen and when. From time to time, I caught myself holding my breath, my body tense, waiting for the bad news. For example, there was a plan to move personnel around because of the overall needs of the mission. That's it: no specifics, no timeline. It just made me clench my teeth. But as the army sayings go: "It is what it is," or you just have to "Embrace the suck."

On December 20, Lopez taught a suicide prevention class to 60 soldiers. He was covering for Chaplain Arguello, who went on his R&R in the morning. It was a 30-minute presentation, with a television game theme where the group was divided into two teams to see who knew more about suicide: myths versus facts.

For example, "Asking someone about suicidal thoughts may trigger the act" is a myth. Talking about suicide with a suicidal person doesn't give him or her the idea. In fact, talking openly about suicidal thoughts is one way to approach the topic. The army has each soldier carry an ACE Suicide Intervention card (playing-card size), to Ask, Care, and Escort a buddy who may be thinking of suicide.

After the presentation, I had two new clients: one a referral from Maj. Stefani because the soldier was on Zoloft, and the other wanted to leave the army and return home so he could get custody of his two teen children from his ex-wife. He was concerned that his children weren't well cared for and might be abused.

December 22 was another cold, gray winter day, and the bleakness only added to the monotony. Lopez and I decided to drop off some holiday chocolates for Lt. Col. Cook, Maj. Krattiger, and Command Sgt. Maj. Veneklasen. These and other treats had come in the care packages we'd just received. Then we picked up some old magazines to recover our office wall. The plaster behind the pictures was cracking and falling, so we removed the old pictures, scraped off the loose plaster, and sprayed the wall with Lysol (there was mold). Lopez and I selected photos from *Travel* and *National Geographic* and covered the wall. No one appeared to notice the new décor.

For fencing that night, I had five students; two were females!

On Christmas Eve day, two soldiers came in for smoking cessation class. I introduced tapping for cravings, but they sat with arms crossed and glanced around uneasily. Both soldiers just wanted medication, a patch, or gum to stop the cravings. I referred them to the aid station. Another soldier came in for anger management and effective communication.

The local Afghan repairmen fixed our heaters in our office. One was leaking oil and one was just barely blowing out heat. I also had them fix the broken noisy heater in my sleeping quarter. Of course, in the evening when we picked up our mail, my quiet space heater from Amazon had arrived. Now I could enjoy plenty of warmth at work and in my room.

I attended the Christmas service, and then played Monopoly with the aid station staff. I enjoyed the silly, friendly razzing of players with unlucky throws of the dice, but I strained not to yawn. When the game ended, I went to bed at 0030 hours—way past my bedtime.

It was Christmas morning. I only knew that because it was on the calendar. No presents to give, no presents to open, and no special breakfast—another holiday without fanfare. Three soldiers came in for R&R briefs. One was a new case of PTSD, but he didn't want a paper trail, and one was an old case with a fear of flying who was leaving on R&R the next day.

We had our Christmas dinner. As I had suspected, the food tasted the same, but the DFAC was unusually spirited, with smiling civilian staff dressed in Santa hats. Then Lopez and I played in the Ping-Pong tournament. I was the only female, so I played against the men. In my first and only round, I faced a seriously skilled player, who reached the semis. Lopez also played only one round, losing to a finalist. The MWR was talking about running a Ping-Pong league. I didn't understand what that meant, but if I could develop more skills, I knew it would be awesome to be part of it.

I woke up early the next morning so I could call home and wish my family a Merry Christmas. As Rob was hosting the family festivities, I had a chance to talk to everyone. My 88-year-old father even got on the phone and told me what was on the mouth-watering dinner menu. I'd hoped that hearing my voice would offer my parents and siblings some comfort, making them feel that I was safe and doing reasonably well.

After that, since it was Monday and my day off, I stayed in my room in the morning, watched two episodes of *Deadwood,* and then went to the office and did the usual daily routine. Going to the office was more stimulating than staring at the walls of my small room.

On Tuesday, I had one official follow-up case, a female who was dealing with depression, and she was doing well. Of two unofficial cases, one session lasted two hours and focused on the soldier's marital problems.

In the evening mail, I received a new Ping-Pong paddle and six 3-star Halex balls I had ordered. I could hardly wait to try them out the next day. While at the DFAC for dinner, Lt. Col. Cook thanked me for dropping off his Christmas gift. This provided me a chance to introduce him to Lopez.

On December 29, there was a follow-up on the soldier who wanted to return home to fight for child custody.

After meeting with four soldiers for their R&R briefing, I went off to practice Ping-Pong. I used my new paddle and it was great for the first hour. I had more control and made fewer errors. But when it came to game time, I played as badly as before, not handling the pressure well. I needed to tap for this—use a bit of my own medicine!

There were two new cases the next day. First was Spc. Moul, who expressed suicidal ideation because his girlfriend, Pfc. Hall, wouldn't quit smoking (both were at Camp Nathan Smith). He wanted her to quit because his grandmother had died from lung cancer.

Soon after, Pfc. Hall came in. Taking deep breaths in an effort to calm herself, she said, "I'm concerned about my boyfriend, Spc. Moul. He was just here. He texted me…he said Combat Stress should have taken his weapon from him…I think he's going to hurt himself."

I advised Hall to notify her boyfriend's immediate command and to return to the office. She did so, calmer now. Then we focused on the depression she'd suffered when she was in her teens.

Capt. Gillespie scheduled me to go to KAF for two weeks in March, for what he named "Operation Slingshot." Apparently there weren't sufficient numbers of behavioral health providers in Role III (the NATO hospital). So certain 113th CSC behavioral health providers would rotate into KAF to dispense counseling services to military and civilian contractors. Everything was subject to change, so I hoped I wouldn't need to go—traveling in Afghanistan sucks!

On the last day of December, as the weather was somewhat mild and warm, Lopez and I walked around the camp, visited two guard towers, and talked to soldiers. Actually, the visit to the towers was an excuse to look outside the camp. Unless we were on a mission, we were basically imprisoned. We scanned some boys playing in the street and watched a small herd of goats trot by.

Later we played Ping-Pong, picked up some mail, and in our office watched *Ip Man*, a Chinese Wing Chun movie. After some reading, I went to sleep around 2215 hours. I just couldn't make it to midnight to welcome the New Year.

Welcome to 2012

"I'm going home this year!" It sounded so close, but I had another five months. At least I could now say I was part of Operation Enduring Freedom 2011–2012. OEF is the official name used by the US government for the Global War on Terrorism in Afghanistan.

I counseled three soldiers on New Year's Day, two follow-ups and one new, a soldier who had depression, despised Afghanistan, and worried about her loved ones at home.

In the course of the deployment, I was extremely grateful for everyone's letters, emails, and care packages. Every item I received lifted my spirits and generated more motivation. Now that I was halfway through the deployment, though, I was in the process of reducing or sending things home that I didn't need. Care packages were no longer necessary, unless I could eat or share the contents within the next couple of months. Because when it was time to go home, I wanted to carry the least amount of gear possible!

There were five cases on January 5, when only two were scheduled. Three soldiers came in because of pending Article 15 UCMJ actions: drinking and fighting. Staff Sgt. Patel came in with nightmares due to PTSD from three deployments. His emotional scars ran deep. There were beads of sweat on his upper lip, he clenched his fists, knuckles going white, and, from time to time, he would look toward the door, as if wanting to escape.

"I see the body on the ground.

"He was my best friend…

"It wasn't pretty…he was shot in the head.

"I wanted to be with my friend…to hold him, but we were told to keep moving.

"Gotta keep moving… suck it up…keep moving.

"I can hear the screams…the shooting…the shouting…

"How, how did I survive this?

"Lucky, I guess…"

We tapped on all these past sights and sounds, and how it wasn't his time to die. With each round, I could see that Patel was less disturbed, more calm and relaxed.

This busy day served as a good reminder of what our job is—helping soldiers. We had gotten complacent over the previous couple of calm weeks.

After fencing in the evening, I picked up the mail. I received a beautiful wall mural hand-drawn and colored by a fencing parent and fencing students that I gladly hung up in my office. And I tacked up a scenic poster (a family gift) in my sleeping quarter—at last, some beautiful things in Afghanistan.

The next day, Friday, the Internet and a phone line went down around 1040 hours because of four KIAs near FOB Frontenac. An armored route clearance truck struck a roadside IED, which was so powerful it killed four soldiers in the vehicle.

I thought that we would be required to go, as Frontenac was in our area of operation. But 113th HQ decided to send a team out of KAF instead. I was relieved, but Lopez was disappointed. He wanted to go.

The temperatures remained frigid, hovering around 41 degrees Fahrenheit.

Saturday brought three more groups for R&R briefs and three follow-up cases. It was always heartwarming when a soldier acknowledged, "I've never said this to anyone before…" before revealing a traumatic childhood event during the session. One round of tapping usually breaks down some protective barrier, and once the soldier can openly talk about the event, healing starts.

In one follow-up case, a soldier who had cut his thigh with a razor blade to release his anger and stress reported that he was self-cutting less often. He used tapping when he was feeling good, but would forget to

use it when he was angry, instead resorting to his usual self-inflicted painful release of emotions.

Toward the end of Monday, January 9, a soldier was escorted in
because of marital problems—possible adultery. He was only 21 years
old, married to a 22-year-old with four children, none of which were his.
While in the session, he unintentionally told us that his tent mate, Pfc.
Ross, tried to kill himself by placing his gun in his mouth.

Lopez and I hurriedly ran to Ross's HQ and notified his command.
Eventually, they found Ross and brought him over to our office. A stocky
soldier of medium height, he'd had a difficult childhood, which had
affected his self-esteem and self-worth.

"I heard that you wanted to eat your gun...is this right?"

Looking down, clearing his throat, Ross answered, "No...just foolin'
around with the guys."

"How's deployment going for you?" I asked patiently.

He kept looking down.

"Deployment...it's okay," he said in a quiet voice, not smiling.

"What's the worst part? Everyone doesn't like something about this
place."

He crossed his arms. "I'm not...a...good soldier...everyone...every-
one says I suck."

"Everyone?"

"I screw up all the time!"

Ross believed he wasn't capable of being a good soldier, and if he
couldn't be a good soldier, then maybe all the negative comments people
had made when he was growing up were true. But he hadn't gotten in
trouble during the previous four months while at CNS. I emphasized
this, and then we tapped to release the negativity and past issues. His
SUD level went from a 10 to a 2 in one round of tapping. Ross promised
not to hurt himself, and I suggested he come in the next day. After the
session, he was released to his commander.

Ross returned the following day.

"Hey, Doc, I fell asleep early, for the first time!"

"Feel rested?"

"Yeah, but..." Ross was rubbing his lips. "I feel like shit...the guys know that I tried to kill myself."

"I think the guys care about you."

"No one cares about me. They talk behind my back all the time, saying I'm a bad soldier."

We tapped for his anger, as he had confessed that he didn't like feeling angry.

"How about making a list right now of who you really are, not what people think you are?"

"Well, I'm likeable, sensitive. I like to laugh..."

To help him remember tasks to do, I offered him a small notebook to keep in his pocket and record things.

A couple of hours later, when Lopez and I were walking to the gym, we saw Ross with his battle buddy.

"Ma'am...Sarge...I feel much better!" Ross said with an enthusiastic wave and lightness in his steps.

I was thrilled. Lopez said the soldier's remark was worth more than any Bronze Star. I agreed that moments like this gave me great satisfaction for the work I was doing and affirmed my reasons for being in Afghanistan.

(Unfortunately, about a month later, Ross came back in, complaining bitterly about unfair treatment by his section leader, to whom he had therefore talked back in a disrespectful way. As a result of this outburst, he was facing an Article 15.)

Meanwhile, I spoke with Maj. Stefani. "Sir, Sgt. Lopez is going on R&R soon. I won't have any accountability. I'd like to check in with you daily," I said.

"You can, but I can send a 68X (behavioral health specialist) to CNS from FOB Walton to help you," he said.

Splendid!

"By the way," Maj. Stefani said. "There was a green-on-blue attack, a suicide bomber, at PHQ (Provincial Headquarters). No KIAs and a couple of soldiers slightly injured. I think PHQ is going to request your team to conduct a Critical Stress Incident Debriefing."

Sure enough, later in the afternoon, PHQ made the request. After informing 113th HQ, we were set to go the next day at 1300 hours. Lopez was thrilled that we were going out on a convoy.

On Friday, January 13, we had one follow-up case, Hall, for smoking cessation.

She was blushing. "I'm sorry...I'm still smoking two to three cigarettes a day."

As we talked more, she said, "I was anorexic when I was in high school. My grandmother helped me get healthy."

"Since your grandmother is an important person in your life, would you like to attach your grandmother's photo to your lighter, as a reminder to be healthy?"

Wholeheartedly, Hall said, "Yes."

In the afternoon, Lopez and I went outside the wire to PHQ (10 minutes away), where the suicide bomber had charged into the compound on January 11. We traveled in an MRAP vehicle and, like tourists, we had our small point-and-shoot cameras out, trying to take pictures of the people and the city. We got terrible shots, as the windows were filthy and spotted from an earlier rainfall.

We conducted two TEMs for 21 soldiers. The soldiers shared what they heard, saw, and did after the explosion. Many expressed their fear, anger, and how things could have been worse. We were able to return to CNS within three hours.

Transported through the streets of Kandahar.

On my day off, I vacuumed the enduring fine layer of dust in my room, and then went into the office around 1000 hours, as I had a soldier scheduled at 1030 hours. Whether it was my day off or not, my priority was always to work with soldiers—it wasn't as if they could arrange their schedule to fit my office hours.

I found out that Spc. Villar, the behavioral health specialist from FOB Walton, was in the office. He was there to help me while Lopez was away. A friendly, self-assured young man from the Dominican Republic who grew up in New Jersey, Villar had been in the army two and a half years. The best part was that he played Ping-Pong, too!

While the three of us were playing, Capt. Ferrell called my cell phone because he had a soldier he wanted me to evaluate for homicidal ideation. We quickly returned to the office and chatted with the soldier, who had been in the army 16 years. In my opinion, he wasn't homicidal. The soldier denied that he was, and he understood the magnitude if he were to kill someone—court-martial—and the effect on his wife and child.

Early in the morning on January 17, Lopez traveled to KAF to begin his R&R. Calvin, a civilian contractor who worked in IT, came in for counseling because he was having flashbacks of the October 27 attack.

His tent was near where most of the rocket-propelled grenades had come in. I taught him EFT.

"Even though I was scared, I deeply and completely accept myself."

"Even though I thought I was going to die, I deeply and completely accept myself."

"Even though it was crazy, it wasn't my time."

His SUD score went from an 8 to a 2. We did one more round and it went to 0.

Feeling an urge to play more Ping-Pong, I went to the gym after dinner, and with luck, there were two civilian contractors playing, both quite good. I played three games, and lost every one. But I got close in two of them. I needed to play more under pressure so that I wouldn't choke as much. My goal was to get better and beat Lopez when he returned from R&R.

As I was leaving the gym, Hall, whom I had seen for smoking cessation, stopped me. A big smile took over her glowing face as she said, "I haven't smoked since we last met." I was genuinely pleased to hear it.

The next day I had my first Chapter 13 evaluation, a separation from the army, for a soldier who had been in for six years. I thought this was for unsatisfactory performance, but it wasn't that. The soldier wanted a transgender operation—male to female. Transgender troops are not allowed to serve openly in the military. As required, he came in for formal counseling to review his separation action. He said he understood the ramification: a possible discharge with Other Than Honorable Condition. Although he would prefer an Honorable Discharge, he wanted more to be a female. He conveyed a sense of composure and contentment with his decision to leave the army.

I was watching a movie in my room when I heard, "INCOMING!" over the camp loudspeakers. Oh, no! I hurriedly laced my boots and grabbed my rifle. But within two minutes, the all-clear signal was given. Whew! It must have been a mistake. At least the loudspeakers were working now.

The following day I had another session with Hall, who quit smoking. We used the session to talk about her relationship with her boyfriend. Next, another female soldier, Spc. Logan, came in because of bad news from home: Her 11-year-old son was depressed and suicidal. Her chin trembling, she sobbed, feeling helpless being so far away.

Computer problems continued. Microsoft Outlook still wasn't working—for the third day in a row—so I couldn't receive or send out any work-related emails. Villar helped me pick up some donated care packages from the mailroom. It was still nice to receive boxes. In December, there had been so many donations from generous and caring people in the States that there were still many unopened boxes around the camp.

On January 21, the sky turned black, dropping heavy rain, which then turned to snow. It was freezing cold!

We had two follow-up cases: anxiety attacks and anger management.

In the evening, around 2000 hours, I met with three soldiers for a Critical Stress Debriefing. They had been involved in a vehicle accident, striking an elderly Afghan. The medic had treated the man before he was transported to the hospital. This happened earlier in the day. Perhaps due to the rainy weather and a blind spot on the right side of the vehicle, the truck commander only saw the man just as he was struck. It wasn't clear whether the man didn't hear and see the truck, or whether he wanted to be hurt to collect some compensation.

January 23 was Chinese New Year's day, the Year of the Dragon. I counseled one follow-up case for anger management. The soldier hadn't had any incidents in a week. He was doing fine and thought he didn't need to continue with sessions. I agreed.

Soon after, a soldier quietly knocked on the door and walked in.

Pointing to a metal folding chair, I said, "Have a seat. What brings you here?"

He sat down slowly, his shoulders curling. There was a pained look in his eyes. I waited, but he didn't say anything. I waited. Soon I noticed his eyes turning red, and then he began to tear up.

I said, "You don't need to say anything. Even though we just met, can you just tap on your hand along with me?"

He looked up and nodded.

Tapping on the side of the hand, I said:

"All this emotional pain.

"I can't talk.

"I have all this anger...all this sadness.

"I choose to relax and feel safe now.

"I don't want to be doing this tapping...I feel silly.

"All this emotional pain..."

Then we tapped on the points on the top of our heads, face, and torsos, as I said, "All this emotional pain."

After completing one round, the soldier took a few deep breaths, and stared at me. Looking calmer, the soldier said, "It's creepy...but it's okay... I don't have to talk." Grabbing a tissue, the soldier blew his nose and laughingly said, "I hope I don't have any boogers hanging out!" I cracked a smile and assured him he didn't.

In the afternoon, I played Ping-Pong with a man from Bhutan named Shyam, a civilian contractor working in the dining facility. He was a really good player and beat me easily.

The weather remained quite cold, so I decided to stay in my room after work, lying under my warm blankets, watching movies.

It snowed again the next day. Some local Afghans said that the last snowfall in Kandahar City had been 10 years ago, and now it had snowed twice in the last four days. The snow wasn't deep, barely an inch or two covering the ground.

Villar finally got a new case to do an intake. Sgt. Anton had one more month to go before returning home and he was afraid of doing something "wrong."

Wrinkling his brow, fidgeting in his chair, Anton took a deep breath and with a raised voice said, "I worry all the time, you know what I mean, like a ticking bomb, can't relax, can't breathe, feels like I'm suffocating all the time, can't screw up...can't even eat, when I eat, bad heartburn... you know what I mean...feel like takin' someone's fricking head—"

"Whoa," I said. "When was the last time you felt like this?"

"My job...I'm a correctional officer at home. It was messed up. This crazy inmate cut himself really bad, on both wrists. There was blood everywhere...he put it in two Styrofoam cups!"

"And..."

"I had to go in the cell, to take him down, so I could get him to medical. We're wrestling. I got blood everywhere. I'm soaked with the guy's blood."

We did one round of tapping regarding his job as a civilian correctional officer, seeing, feeling, and even smelling blood. After one round of tapping, his SUD level went down from a 10 to a 3. With a slight smile and flushed cheeks, the sergeant felt funny doing the tapping, but he admitted improvement. The "3" was his fear of returning to work, and after another round of tapping for the dread, he was feeling less afraid and ready for work.

Anton returned on January 27. He didn't complain about his fear of making mistakes but of not being able to sleep.

"I just lie on my bunk for hours," he said.

"Let's examine your routine before sleep," I said.

"Well, I eat protein bars, drink water, and listen to music before sleep."

After a discussion, he planned to change things: Before going to sleep he would eat carbohydrates, avoid water, and listen to one piece of relaxing music that he could associate with sleep.

One new case that Villar took dealt with abusive leadership and another case was an Article 15, sleeping in the guard tower.

On Sunday, January 29, Chaplain Arguello returned from his R&R. He visited our office and ended up sharing the story of his conversion to religion. He had spent 11 rebellious years before finding his calling. As his father was a veteran and his brother was still in the army, it was a natural transition for him to join the army's chaplaincy.

At 1830 hours, my cell phone rang. The aid station passed along a message from a Combat Operating Base that Spc. Blake had been sexually assaulted. Her commander was hoping that a female victim's advocate could talk to her over the phone. I called and spoke with Blake for nearly an hour. At the end, she agreed to come to CNS for a session. I was deeply concerned for her, as this was the third time she had been assaulted in her young life of 20 years.

Later that evening I received Ping-Pong instruction from Wayne, a civilian contractor. He had played against the chaplain one day and beat him in two straight games. Lopez and I happened to witness this. Wayne was truly an excellent player. I took a chance and had asked if he would teach me. He agreed to give me lessons once a week. Wonderful!

Counting the Days

Life is forever controlled by linear time. But in deployment, time passes either very quickly or very slowly; and sometimes it feels like time is standing still. It is never steady. For many soldiers, the days crawl painfully by, as they live the same routine day after day: guard duty, missions, a few hours of sleep, and the same food. Every soldier can hardly wait to go on R&R; then every soldier can hardly wait to go home.

The brigade that I was supporting at Camp Nathan Smith was more than halfway through its deployment. So the question on everyone's mind was "When are we going home?" Rumors were abundant. Moreover, with President Obama's mandate to downsize troops in Afghanistan, some units were going home early.

When I thought about how long I had been in country, I couldn't believe that I'd made it seven months already. I must confess, there were times that I didn't think I could keep going. I'd sent soldiers home because deployment was mentally too demanding.

Looking ahead, I had four more months. It would be a long time before I could return to my family, my home, and my bed. Yet there were moments when I believed that time was passing too quickly, that my experience in Afghanistan was coming to an end too soon. Had I accomplished what I sought to do? Were there things I needed to see, do, and learn before I headed out? Every morning when I went into my office, I wondered who would come in and what problems they would bring. In recent weeks, the cases had been eating disorders, critical debriefings, sexual assaults, pending divorce, and a suicide attempt. There were, of course, many cases involving soldiers' irritability and frustration, as they had been living and working together for so many months. It doesn't take much to get angry on base.

In March I was scheduled to work two weeks at the NATO Multinational Medical Center at Kandahar Airfield, to provide crisis-intervention psychological services to service members and government civilians. The change of venue would help pass the time. As much as I complained about the slowness of time, I did prefer the sluggish days rather than being busy, because if I was busy, that meant soldiers were in crisis. So when the office was quiet, I used the time to read, write, or just chill. In addition, I continued to teach fencing and play Ping-Pong to vary the tedium and maintain a healthy, physical outlet.

On Wednesday, February 1, Spc. Ford came in. He was waiting for UCMJ action for drinking alcohol and spraying a fire extinguisher at soldiers in his tent. He said he didn't remember using the fire extinguisher—he was too drunk. He and his wife were also divorcing, after he discovered she was having an affair with another married soldier in garrison. I offered him a rubber band to wear on his wrist to snap as a distraction, for "thought-stopping," as he worried constantly, and also encouraged him to tap for calmness.

I had three cases just on Friday morning: two follow-ups that were doing well, and Blake, with whom I had spoken on the phone about the sexual assault. Her sergeant had sexually assaulted her twice, using his rank as coercion.

With deep anger, Blake said, "I thought I gave the wrong signal, mad at myself...I thought it was me. Why? He was looking down at me...I felt horrible, felt something was wrong with me...I'm powerless, trapped."

She continued, "He did it. Why? I didn't have a choice..."

After the session, the sexual assault team spoke with Blake, and one member of the team accompanied her to KAF for a CID (Criminal Investigation Command) interview.

On Saturday, Sgt. Nguyễn strolled in. His jet black hair was cut short, barely an inch long. I had seen him in December, and this time he wanted a refill of his anti-anxiety medication. He admitted that three days earlier he had thought of hurting others and himself because of constant hazing. Looking younger than his stated age of 24, this soldier had a history of behavioral health issues and two hospitalizations, and was on many medications. Yet Nguyễn had good insight and acknowledged that his coping skills worked better with medication, which he, unfortunately, had run out of. Maj. Stefani interviewed him (I sat in), and after the interview we both agreed Nguyễn could return to duty as long as he came in weekly.

That night at Ping-Pong league, I won my first match—by default—as my opponent didn't show. Well, a win is a win.

Around 2030 hours, I got a call on my cell phone. A soldier at the aid station wanted Combat Stress. I went there and escorted her to my office.

Spc. Gondela's eyes were puffy. Wiping her nose, she said flatly, "My ex-husband abandoned our two young children at my mom's house. He was supposed to pick them up after the weekend, but he never showed…"

Gondela's mother couldn't care for the children because she had just started a new job.

"I want an emergency leave to go home and get my kids resettled. And I'm going to bring charges against him for abandonment."

After examining some options, Gondela said she had an aunt who lived 40 minutes away and could temporarily care for the children.

The next afternoon Gondela came in to say she hadn't seen the brigade commander (BC) yet because the BC was away on a mission. In the meantime, Chaplain Arguello was tracking Gondela's request. Around 2000 hours, my cell phone rang. The chaplain requested that I meet with Gondela, who had just met with the BC.

"The commander refused my request to go home," she said.

"I'm sorry to hear that. Perhaps you'll want to let your mother know that you can't go home now and maybe contact Child Protective Services for assistance."

Gondela fell silent, covering her face with her hands. Seconds later, she put her hands down and, with a slight headshake, said, "I want to turn in my weapon."

Gondela's commander placed her under buddy watch.

The next day brought Spc. Nadal, tall, easygoing, with short blond hair. She revealed a history of eating disorder (bingeing and purging). We discussed writing and posting the list of things she wants to be: confident, healthy, fit, with a good sense of humor.

On Monday, Sgt. Masters walked in with a confused expression on his face. "Am I crazy?" he asked.

"What makes you think that?" I inquired.

"I had a girlfriend and a wife that cheated on me before. I'm good now. I've been married for three years and she's not cheating. But when she goes out with her girlfriend, I worry."

"Worried that she may be cheating?"

"Yeah. My wife says I don't trust her."

So I had him tap for a "7 or 8" event (meaning the disturbed feelings about that event were at a 7 or 8 on the SUD scale). As it turned out, his "8" wasn't his wife going out, but that the court had judged him an unfit father and he had lost custody of his daughter. After one round, he said tapping was "ridiculous" but also that he felt calmer. We did two rounds, for his wife going out and trusting her. His tight face had loosened and his eyes softened by the time he walked out of the office.

On Monday, February 6, I conducted another fencing class. Just two classes remained, as I'd decided to end the program before going to KAF for Operation Slingshot at the NATO Multinational Medical Center.

Two new cases on Saturday: both dropped in. The first soldier fumed that his wife was cheating on him and the second seethed about "toxic leadership." We also had two follow-up cases: depression and PTSD.

On Sunday, the air was crisp with a gentle breeze. Nadal returned and was doing better.

"I only wanted to binge once, but I tapped it away," she announced.

She had also created a list of who she is (wants to be), placed it by her bed, and read it daily. We talked about her anxiety about returning home on R&R, and bingeing and purging. And we discussed her ability to make nutritious choices, and generally to see herself as a confident, healthy person.

Monday, February 13 brought four cases: three new cases and one follow-up (anger management). One new one was a civilian contractor, Ahmad, an interpreter, who was depressed over the upcoming third anniversary of his mother's death.

"My mother suffered a massive stroke and couldn't speak for the last 28 days of her life. I stayed in the hospital, not showering, not shaving, and barely eating, so that I could be with her."

"Would you like to write on a piece of paper things you wanted her to know that you didn't tell her three years earlier? Once you've done that, you can burn the paper so that she can receive it."

With his eyes wide and shining, he said, "I'd like to do that."

Later, Staff Sgt. Cokin came in on the strong urging of his command. Cokin had suffered an anxiety attack a few days earlier after he and fellow soldiers exchanged stories of their tour in Iraq. During that tour, he had suffered PTSD symptoms and, after returning home, received behavioral health and medication support. He responded well and thought he had dealt with his problem, but apparently not. I taught him tapping to manage his anxiety attacks and referred him to the aid station for a medication evaluation.

Pfc. Lynch cleaned my rifle that evening. I paid cash for his expert service, in anticipation of Sgt. Maj. Schumacher's visit that week. Schumacher was recently promoted from first sergeant and was making his rounds to different FOBs to check on his soldiers (and perhaps their weapons). I'd never seen my rifle so clean!

My brother Gary's care box arrived. It was like Christmas morning again, opening up presents and seeing all my favorite snacks.

On Tuesday, February 14, I noticed that Rob had sent me a Valentine e-card, but I couldn't get it to open. Oh, well. It's the thought that counts.

We had one case scheduled, but he was a no-show. That was all right, as this soldier's issue wasn't bad—a complaint that his platoon was treating him too seriously and he couldn't fool around like he did with his old platoon.

Later we saw three drop-in soldiers: two follow-ups (anger management and an old back injury, which might cause the soldier to redeploy earlier). In one new case, the soldier was so angry he destroyed his guitar. This soldier had been in theater eight months.

On Thursday we had two follow-up cases. One was dealing with anger management and reported doing better since using EFT, once we were able to identify specifically what was upsetting him. The other soldier finally understood the charges against him in a general court-martial. He was fine about it, having already anticipated the worst-case scenario and accepting that he had never meant to harm anyone. He had also signed his divorce papers and sent them off a couple of days before—another failed marriage because of spousal cheating and multiple deployments.

Sgt. 1st Class Reyes walked in after his father encouraged him to seek help. He was on his fifth deployment in 11 years in the army. His five-year marriage had come to an official end two weeks earlier, probably because she was dreading having him come home with unresolved PTSD, mTBI, irritability, isolation, and excessive drinking. He spoke in a low tone, with a sense of loneliness and fear, revealing some horrific incidents from his time in Iraq.

"Yeah, I lost a lot of friends. I had to pick up the body parts…put them in plastic bags, but I couldn't let anyone know it bothered me. It is what it is. I had to be strong, to help others." He was composed as he spoke, but there was strain in his voice. "I can't sleep and I'm angry a lot," he added.

After two rounds of tapping for his anger and one round to teach him about sleeping, I asked him to come back the next day.

He did but reported no change. He had reviewed EFT on YouTube and had done some tapping, without relief. I was disheartened that I couldn't make a dent in his problems, asking myself: Had I spent enough time? Had I gathered enough details to tap on? I referred him to Maj. Stefani for a medication evaluation.

It was raining all day, so there weren't any flights from KAF. This meant no Schumacher and no inspection of my spotless weapon.

Cokin returned to the clinic on Saturday. He reported feeling better, with less anxiety, and had realized more things he could do to help release his stress. He didn't need to make another appointment but planned to drop by before I headed off to KAF in March.

On Sunday, February 19, the rain stopped, leaving a brown haze in the afternoon. It was a quiet day, with just one soldier coming in for drill sergeant school evaluation.

Later in the evening, however, around 1945 hours, the camp's loudspeakers announced the need for litter bearers, Gator drivers, and medics because of casualties coming in from PSS-4. Four soldiers had been peppered with shrapnel after insurgents threw grenades from their motorcycles into the soldiers' trucks. Mercifully, none of the wounded was seriously hurt, but all were flown to KAF for treatment and observation.

LOSS

On the morning of Monday, February 20, Chaplain Arguello escorted Spc. Arada in for counseling.

"I can't control my anger." As he looked down at his hands and fingered his wedding band, his eyes welled up with tears.

"Things got really rough in Iraq..."

"When were you there?" I asked softly.

"In 2006. That was my second deployment there. You figured I'd be used to it, the IEDs, taking fire, the killings, my friends dead, being scared shitless..."

Taking a deep breath, he wiped his eyes with his sleeve. "I don't understand why I feel this way..."

He had been trying to cope with his flashbacks, anger, and sadness by ignoring them, setting them aside, and drinking alcohol to numb them.

I presented EFT. We tapped on:

"Even though I don't understand why I still feel so bad about Iraq, it was so long ago, I want to get better."

"Even though I still cry over my fallen buddies, I want to be better."

"Even though I was really scared, I am a good soldier."

After tapping on the top of the head, face, and torso points, Arada said, "I feel better... because I can...talk about it."

I said, "Do you want to go to the aid station to see if medication can be of help?"

"No, I don't want to take anything."

When the chaplain returned to my office, Arada was poised and confident.

With the chaplain observing closely, I asked, "Do you have thoughts of hurting yourself or others? If so, we can let command know and they can assign you a battle—"

"No, I'm good. I don't want command to know. Really, I'm good."

Arada was scheduled to return in a few days for a follow-up.

While I was in session, a car bomb exploded nearby, hurting five soldiers who were then treated at the aid station. The fighting season had begun.

The next day, as I was heading to the showers across the camp, Chaplain Arguello walked rapidly by, calling to me, "Suicide ideation." I wasn't sure who or what the chaplain was referring to, but I knew he could handle it. As I was toweling off, the camp's loudspeakers called for soldiers and civilians to report to their unit for accountability. I immediately went to the aid station, where a medic told me there had been a suicide. As I went to my room to dress in my uniform, I was wondering if it was one of my clients or someone I hadn't seen. Just as I was ready to leave my room, the chaplain called my cell phone and asked to meet at my office.

When I arrived, the chaplain asked, "What was the name of the soldier we met yesterday?"

I replied, "Spc. Arada."

"Arada just shot himself with his own rifle. His body was found around 0715 hours in the latrine."

I couldn't believe it! I was angry and sad at the same time. I mentally flashed back and reexamined our session. I berated myself for missing something, but what? Arada had left my office more contained and feeling better.

The chaplain and I went and spoke to Lt. Col. Winton, letting him know that we had seen Arada individually the day before. After my talk with the lieutenant colonel, I realized that, in nearly 16 years of practice, this was the first client I had lost. Walking away, with a need to be alone, I burst into tears.

When I returned to my office, I forlornly called my clinical director, Maj. Diaz.

"Sir, I have some bad news. A soldier I saw yesterday committed suicide this morning."

"Oh, I'm sorry to hear this."

"I want to know how much of my case notes I can release to CID?"

The major had Capt. Gillespie call me back and authorized me to release everything. Gillespie also wanted me to talk to Col. Rabb. The colonel told me it wasn't my fault, and he planned to come to CNS the next day.

Soon after that, Chaplain Arguello and I were requested to be present when the dead soldier's commanding officer assembled his company to announce the death. I then conducted two debriefings for 60 soldiers. During the meetings, many were puzzled. They hadn't seen it coming. Some were angry, some sad, numbed, confused, and shocked. One called the suicide "selfish." Arada was married, with young children, and many plans for the future.

Maj. Way, brigade chaplain, arrived at CNS to debrief Chaplain Arguello and me. We met in my office. Maj. Way offered us time to talk about the unexpected death, our sadness, and "what ifs." Even though my heart was aching, I did my best not to cry, to be professional.

But when I was alone, I wept a few more times. I couldn't attend the fallen soldier's flight out of CNS because I had a new soldier come in (for anxiety attacks). I called Rob that night and told him what had happened. Rob was quiet as he listened. He gently said it wasn't my fault.

On my second call with Col. Rabb, he told me he wanted me to go to KAF.

"I think there might be some finger-pointing at you, and I want the unit to accept the hit," he said.

"Sir, I respectfully do not want go to KAF. If anything, soldiers and command here have been extremely kind and understanding. I feel that my support system is here, and I want to help the other soldiers on my caseload." I added, "I need to be available for CID, and if I went to KAF it would appear I did something wrong and ran off." Lastly, I said, "Sir, I want to attend the memorial service."

Col. Rabb was in agreement; I would remain at CNS.

On Wednesday at 1130 hours, Chaplain Arguello, Maj. Way, and I conducted a debriefing for the aid station staff who processed the remains. All these debriefings helped fellow soldiers deal with the loss. They helped me, too.

Col. Rabb and Sgt. Ramirez arrived at CNS during lunchtime. It was good to see them again and I appreciated their support. I released a copy of the soldier's BH records to CID. They interviewed me and I provided a written statement. At the end of the interview, the CID agent hadn't yet found any obvious reason why the soldier would kill himself. Prior to his death, Arada had emailed his wife. The company's leadership in the States received a message from his wife, via the Red Cross, that she was worried about her husband. Unfortunately, the phone message arrived an hour after he had killed himself. When CID and Maj. Stefani checked the soldier's pockets, they found my business card. They also found a sheet of paper I had given him. The soldier had underlined these words: *Control your temper. He who angers you controls you. He who is slow to anger has great understanding. – Proverbs 14:29.* Apparently he was trying to work through his anger.

We had two new cases on Friday. There was no time for me to be lost in my thoughts; I needed to focus on my clients. One vented about how the company's leadership didn't care about soldiers after the suicide case. The other felt out of control, striking another soldier. This soldier was escorted in, and the escort stayed in the room because the soldier wanted him there.

Afterward I met with Arada's company commander, as he wanted me to read what he'd say at the memorial ceremony the next day. This commander was also going through a possible divorce. There were a lot of problems on his plate.

Arada's memorial ceremony was held on the morning of Saturday, February 25. For the first time, the chaplain was emotional as he began the service. It is never easy to lose a soldier. I think it's even worse when that soldier believed there was no other solution but to kill himself. It's a permanent solution to a temporary problem. Was it preventable? Was it predictable? Why? And many more questions that were unanswerable.

From this painful experience, I realized that many people at CNS—from noncommissioned officers to the highest ranked commander (Lt. Col. Cook)—offered their gentle and comforting support to me, checking on my well-being. I also realized that command staffs are appreciative of the role Combat Stress plays in a combat zone. Not all commanders, of course, but those that had limited knowledge or some doubts now understood the usefulness of critical stress debriefings to help soldiers process their losses and begin healing. I think acknowledging the anger, pain, and crying is helpful, so that soldiers can focus on the mission. The reality is that we are still in a combat zone, at war, and every leader wants to bring their soldiers home.

Chaplain Arguello referred one new case for anger management. Lopez was back from his R&R, and he started the interview. But after realizing that tapping would be most helpful, I took over. The soldier was angry about the October 27 attack because at the time he had anticipated wishing happy birthday to his mother. He thought how unfair it would have been if he had been killed. His mother wouldn't have been able to cope with the loss. We tapped on being scared, angry, and that he's a survivor. We also tapped for better sleep.

I enjoyed my last fencing class, being in the moment. Teaching and judging the bouts was a welcome relief after the last few days.

Moving On

Sunday was a day off for both Villar and Lopez. Even though Lopez was back from R&R, Villar's commander allowed him to stay at CNS for the rest of the tour—fortunate for me. When we decided the days off, I wanted both of them to be off on the same day, so that I could have one day in the office to myself. Alone, I caught up on peer reviews and required online trainings, and met with two clients.

The next day I counseled Sgt. Milford, who was overcome with emotions.

"My ex-husband just got released from prison…" She had a watery gaze, sniffling from time to time. "He killed our 6-month-old daughter 20 years ago." This triggered an old painful belief: "I'm a terrible mother. I couldn't protect my baby."

We tapped on "Being a terrible mother. Couldn't protect my daughter. Doing the best I could at that time."

We talked about grief, forgiveness of her ex-husband and of herself. Her eyes tearing up, Milford said, "Thank you."

Later I played Ping-Pong with Wayne and introduced Lopez to him. After playing with Wayne for nearly an hour, my left knee buckled, giving me a scare. I'd had multiple surgeries on that knee, so I stopped playing. I decided to start wearing my knee brace from then on.

I packed up all the fencing equipment in a large box to send home. At the same time, I had to start packing my army personal footlocker, as that needed to get to KAF by March 15. I couldn't believe that I was finally at the stage of planning to go home.

As each day passed, I enjoyed being in Afghanistan more and more. I hadn't imagined that I would ever feel this way. For so many months, I'd wanted to go home—seriously. But as the end of my tour approached, I was going to miss the people I'd befriended: colleagues, clients, Ping-Pong opponents, local nationals, dining facility workers, and MWR staff. It was a difficult situation, many miles away from home, with many sacrifices, and everyone making the best of the situation. People on base were kindly and approachable, with a small-town feel, and supposedly, the best food on any FOB. Perhaps when the weather got back up to 120 degrees, I'd be ready to leave.

On Tuesday, Vasquez, who had come in for anxiety attacks, returned to say he was doing better. The combination of talking, tapping, and medication had worked, resulting in less frequent and less intense anxiety attacks.

An officer investigating the suicide of Arada came in to talk with me. It was a short interview, but he wanted me to make a written statement, followed by written questions and answers. Unfortunately, I couldn't get a copy of the one I had done for CID, so I had to write another one. I wasn't happy that I had to relive my emotions, but I did it anyway.

February 29, the last day of the month in that leap year, was a quiet day, so I completed my Request for Extension packet. Somewhere along the way, my two-year contract, which would expire in March 2012, had disappeared...*poof!* (The army is notorious for misplacing documents.) So now I needed to extend my Mandatory Removal Date (MRD) on December 31, 2012, for another two years in the Army Reserves in San Pablo, California. Along with completing required forms, I wrote this:

> Dear Sir/Ma'am:
>
> I am requesting an extension of my mandatory removal date so that I can continue my duty to help combat veterans. As I am writing this request, I am deployed in Kandahar Province as an OIC of Combat Stress Control at Camp Nathan Smith. With my knowledge and experience, I would like to provide follow-up care for soldiers returning home.

Generally, MRDs are for soldiers reaching their 60th birthday. Rob agreed with me that I would extend, as this would help with our health insurance costs. More important, I wanted to stay in the army.

The next day brought just one client in the morning, Ford, the one who had been drunk and used a fire extinguisher to hose some soldiers.

After talking to his defense attorney, Ford had decided to plead guilty to all charges, as the prosecutor was offering a lesser process, a special court-martial instead of a general one. Ford admitted to the act, so he didn't want to fight the charges. He had a good attitude about it.

There was a Ping-Pong tournament that day. I won the first match by default/no-show. Then I played a soldier who won the first game, but I won the next two. Boy, I was nervous. (I should have been tapping!) I think I gave away five points per game with bad serves. Next I had to play the winner between Lopez and Chaplain Arguello. Of course, the chaplain won and, of course, I lost to the chaplain. Wayne ended up winning the tournament.

On Saturday, we had two morning walk-ins, both long sessions. One was the coworker who was the last person to see Arada before he committed suicide. He admitted to some numbing, guilt, and sadness.

"I don't understand why Arada didn't talk to me. Maybe I could have helped."

The other soldier, 2nd Lt. Heid, remembered when she was 14 years old and her mother's boyfriend had abused her.

"My mom didn't believe me when I told her. Now I find out that Mom wants to be a part of my sister's life and her grandchildren. I need to protect my sister, her children. I can't...I feel helpless being so far away."

"Are you willing to tell your sister what happened to you?" I asked.

"Yeah, I'll have to...maybe she'll believe me."

We talked more and role-played what Heid would say to her sister.

The next day, Sgt. 1st Class Moriz, an EOD (Explosive Ordnance Disposal) specialist came in so angry he was ready to feel the "breaking of someone's bones."

"I ran for an hour on the treadmill, but it didn't help," he said. "This isn't like me," he continued. "I'm usually a funny, easygoing guy, but this morning I woke up and really wanted to bust someone's ass."

This was his second deployment and he had been in theater for nine months. I felt this was a typical case of unresolved issues from the first deployment and now months of stress. After the first round of tapping, he joked it was "weird and retarded" but beamed calmness. Halfway through the second round, his left leg stopped shaking. After more talking and a third round of tapping, he looked at me with wide eyes, laughed, and said, "I'm ready to eat chocolates and take a nap."

Later a soldier came in, a follow-up, now reporting getting along with his sergeant, making wedding plans with his fiancée, and discovering he had an older sister that his mother had given away for adoption at birth. All exciting, happy news.

In the evening, I met with a captain and a second lieutenant, roommates having difficulty living together. Although similar in age, they had nothing else in common. I couldn't get them to agree or compromise on any issues, so one officer would ask the Mayor Cell for another sleeping quarter.

On Monday, March 5, a lieutenant and her commander talked to me about one of their soldiers, Nguyễn, whom I had seen after he had thoughts of hurting others and himself due to the hazing he was enduring. They said he had made a suicide gesture of pointing his gun at his head. Neither Maj. Stefani nor I recalled Nguyễn telling us he had used his weapon. Nonetheless, an evaluation was necessary, since he was assigned to a combat outpost without any oversight. Stefani and I agreed that Capt. Gerould at FOB Walton would conduct the evaluation, as he hadn't met the soldier before. Wanting to complete his tour, Nguyễn came up with an action plan to reassure his command that he would comply with an intervention by specific individuals if he presented signs of depression or suicidal/homicidal ideation.

In the evening, I did lots of packing to get my footlocker and boxes ready for a flight to KAF, so that our supply sergeant could ship them home for me. I also packed for my two weeks of Operation Slingshot at KAF, which would begin the next day.

Operation Slingshot

On Wednesday, March 7, I began my rotation at Role III (the NATO hospital) as part of Operation Slingshot, which consisted of 113th CSC behavioral health providers taking turns going in to help out the understaffed hospital team.

After a three-hour delay from my scheduled flight, I made it to KAF around 1400 hours. Staff Sgt. Diaz picked me up and drove me to the Warrior Recovery Center (WRC), where Col. Rabb met me and showed me around. It was a beautiful place: spacious, relatively free of dust, with new furniture. The task of opening the WRC had been assigned to the 113th unit, and it hadn't been finished the last time I was at KAF. It was a comprehensive clinic that performed case management for TBI, wound and injury care, nonemergency care, behavioral health care, and chaplain services. The purpose was to provide the necessary treatment in Afghanistan, instead of Germany, so military personnel could return to duty with the fewest adjustments.

Next I went to Role III, the NATO Medical Center, where Maj. De la Cancela gave me the right seat/left seat training (a turnover process of observing the more experienced person and, about halfway, switching places for some last-minute mentoring before leaving). The major was hugely helpful. Finally, off I went to my room, which I'd be sharing with a member of my unit, and no one else. Plenty of space, and showers and flush toilets just down the hall!

Throughout my 10 days at Role III, I saw scheduled or drop-in clients, a steady stream of four or five a day, busier than at Camp Nathan Smith. I also had to do the patient movement request (PMR) paperwork, whereas at CNS the brigade surgeon did this. I asked if I was going to have a day off and I was told no, as I wasn't on call. In other words, evenings were my day off.

The counseling cases were similar to those I saw at Camp Nathan Smith, except most individuals were members of the air force, navy, or marine corps. Usual issues related to combat stress, lack of sleep, anxiety, depression, sexual assault, marital problems, infidelity, and wanting to go home before the completion of the tour.

There were two noteworthy events that happened while I was at KAF, however. One evening during dinner with Lt. Col. Goodwin and Navy Lt. Commander Cunha at the Cambridge DFAC, there was a rocket attack and everyone quickly ducked under the tables. After a few minutes, people returned to their seats and continued eating, as did I, taking my cue from those around me. A short minute later, another attack siren went off. At that time, the lieutenant colonel adamantly insisted that we go to the nearest bunker. Off we went, leaving our uneaten desserts (bummer). About 45 minutes later, we were able to leave the steamy bunker. I returned to my sleeping quarter and took a shower, hoping that the siren wouldn't go off again.

The second event started on a Sunday morning with: "Did you hear what happened? A US sergeant left COP Tarakan with rifles and ammunition, walked about eight kilometers into Panjwai, went into several homes, and shot and killed approximately 16 people." Some of the injured were children, and they were brought to Role III for medical care. Apparently, the sergeant had acted alone and later surrendered.

With the recent burnings of the Quran in Kabul by Americans, and US Marines urinating on dead militants, and now this, Americans were now more in harm's way. I wondered whether President Obama was going to pull everyone out of Afghanistan, as the mission of winning the Afghans' hearts and minds was undoubtedly lost.

After eight months in country, I now believed that everyone should go home. It's a war that cannot be won.

Saturday, March 17, was my last day at Role III. I met with Maj. Reagan, delivered her a tour of Role III, and passed along the right seat/ left seat training.

At 0545 hours on Sunday, March 18, Ramirez drove me to the Stallion Ramp, but my bird didn't take off until 0815. After three other stops, I finally arrived at CNS at 0850 hours. I was so glad to be back—to something familiar, and fewer rocket attacks!

CNS landing zone.

We had three clients on my first day back. The weather was shifting from warm to sticky to unbearably hot. We had to turn on the air conditioner in the office. The nights featured strong, howling gusts of wind. The dust was so powdery that I could smell it in my sleeping quarter.

Monday morning I went into the office early, and there was Spc. Darby with his escort waiting for me. The escort, his commanding officer, didn't understand why his soldier was shouting and being irritable to others, since the soldier had been able to cope for the previous nine months. After holding in his pent-up combat stresses, the soldier could no longer suppress his anger and frustration.

After I taught Darby how to tap to manage and minimize his anger, I talked to his CO.

"Lieutenant, Darby's behavior isn't unusual. All soldiers have different capacities for handling stress in country, and after nine months, I think it doesn't take much to lose control. I'm sure Darby is a capable solider."

Tuesday brought just one new case, the chief warrant officer who had discovered Spc. Arada's body in the latrine. Holding his stomach and rocking slightly, he said, "I can't get the image out of my head." The chief was disturbed by the recurring, intense image, and for a month now he had been more stressed and hypervigilant. "I can still see his slumped body, blood everywhere, his rifle."

"Chief, copy me and tap on your hand and repeat after me," I said. "Even though I can still see the scene in color, I choose to switch it from color to black and white, and then have the image grow progressively smaller and blurrier to the point where I can't see it anymore."

We repeated this three times. Then we tapped on the acupoints on the top of the head, face, and torso. After completing the process, the chief exhaled and, with raised brow, said, "That helped."

About 1600 hours, a loud explosion rattled our nerves. A VBIED exploded at PSS-10. One Afghan National Police hurt, no deaths.

In the evening, I met with a commander that wanted one of his soldiers to go home early as a BH case. I explained to him I could only send a soldier home if he or she was suicidal or homicidal. If the commander wanted a Command Directed Evaluation, the soldier had to have 48 hours to go to the inspector general, JAG, and the chaplain. I wasn't sure if the commander planned to follow through or not.

Lopez and I played Ping-Pong during the lunch hour. I played again with Vernes after work. The MWR was starting another Ping-Pong league, and I wanted to play as much as possible.

On Friday, March 23, I had a new case: Spc. Griffin, a gunner who had shot and killed an insurgent dressed in an ANP uniform. This insurgent, a Pakistani, had been involved in the previous day's PSS-10 attack.

The gunner was quite impressive: a 19-year-old soldier whose flushed round face reflected a quiet confidence.

"My sergeant told me to talk to you," she said. "I'm confused. I thought I did the right thing. People were yelling at me to kill the insurgent, but I wasn't sure."

"What were they saying?" I asked.

"My truck commander told me not to shoot. But the ANPs were yelling and gesturing me to shoot. I don't really understand them. The ANPs were pointing in a panic at the insurgent. Eventually, my truck commander gave me the order to shoot."

She continued, "I thought I did the right thing, but later an officer came to investigate and said it was a bad kill. I thought I was going to get an Article 15 for wrongful death."

Griffin said there were many eyewitnesses to back her up. She had justly killed the insurgent. Through an interpreter, the ANPs confirmed they didn't know the attacker. Her action prevented the insurgent from hurting others.

"Specialist, can you follow me? Just tap on your hand, and say, 'Even though I was afraid, people yelling at me, I didn't know what to do, I did the right thing. I am a good soldier.'"

After saying it three times, Griffin quietly exhaled. Biting her lower lip to keep from smiling, she said, "It's weird, but I feel better."

Of Sunday's five cases, all follow-ups, only one was scheduled. There was a communication blackout because an IED had injured a soldier and killed another during the night. I would probably not be scheduled to conduct the TEM, since it was about an hour drive from CNS—too far and too dangerous.

The next day, Chaplain Williams wanted me to see Pvt. Foxx, who had come in because of many losses in her extended family. Her grandfather had died the day before. The army wouldn't give her a compassionate leave, so I asked what she would need to help her grieve, to find closure.

"I want to go home to support my family, for them to support me…"

Quickly thinking of what she could do from here, I asked, "Do you want to write a letter to your grandfather, and perhaps have your letter read at the memorial service?"

She said yes.

I added, "Ask your family members to take video or still photos to share with you via Skype and/or Facebook."

That brought a smile to her face.

The last day of the month—just one more full month to go! I had a couple of follow-up cases and Ping-Pong practice with Lopez. He kept winning, but I was gaining on him.

April 2012

On Sunday, April 1, I had just one safety check (check on the well-being of the soldier) and he was doing well. I received a call from Capt. Gillespie about going on a mission to Terra Nova and Kuhak, but as Kuhak had no facilities for females, I sent Villar and Lopez. They would leave on Wednesday and be gone for four or five days.

Monday I had two follow-up cases and an old case. Spc. Stahl was having stress reactions and nightmares about the attack on PSS-1 and the death of Spc. Roberts on August 27. She had been injured that day. She was escorted in, having refused to come to Combat Stress because she didn't want to be seen as "weak." But her work and relationships with other soldiers were noticeably deteriorating.

After I explained about EFT, and she was willing to do it, we tapped.

"Even though I was scared, I deeply and completely accept myself."

"Even though I can still feel the blast and headaches, I deeply and completely accept myself."

"Even though I miss my friend, I deeply and completely accept myself."

Then we tapped on the top of the head, face, and torso points while repeating "scared, headaches, I missed my friend."

When we finished the tapping, her eyes lit up. She marveled and called it "freaky."

On Tuesday, Stahl returned, rested and with a brighter affect. We worked on assertiveness skills. Then two other soldiers came in. The first was Staff Sgt. Hargis, for marital issues. He was surprised that his wife wasn't happy after nearly 10 years of marriage. He believed everything he had done had been for his wife and children. Hargis wanted to talk more and made another appointment.

The other soldier, Pfc. Lowe, revealed that his mother had died when he was 10 years old, and he realized that he still had a lot of anger surrounding old abandonment issues. "She never got to know how I turned out," he whispered. I listened while he sadly expressed missed opportunities of sharing with his mother.

The next day, Lopez and Villar went to KAF for the mission to Kuhak and Terra Nova.

Stahl came in, fit and ready to return to duty. This would be her last session. Three other follow-up cases were military operational stress, anger management, and Mayer, who had been trying to go home for months because of a back injury he sustained in a firefight the previous August. Mayer had also been advocating, without success, for a Purple Heart.

April 5 brought in Lowe, with the old issues about his mother's death. He started to write a letter to her, telling her things that he hadn't had the chance to say when she was alive.

Hargis also came in for a follow-up for marital issues, most likely a pending divorce. He talked about his concerns and annoyances and being unable to convince his wife to reconsider. He thought he didn't need medication but was considering it because he couldn't shake the continuous loop of anger. I taught him tapping for the first time.

"Even though my wife doesn't appreciate all my sacrifices, I am a good husband. I am a good father." After one round he felt better. He was less emotional, and had less pain and sadness. He decided not to start medication at that time.

At Ping-Pong league, I won my match against Lopez—because he hadn't returned from his mission. Then I gave Wayne the new paddle that Lopez and I bought, to thank him for teaching us. He was pleasantly surprised, appreciative, and used it right away.

On April 7, Mayer returned, still angry that his commander wouldn't send him home. Every day he was getting more frustrated and angry. He even mentioned thoughts of hurting himself. I sought consultation from Maj. Stefani and Capt. Gerould, the behavioral health officer of the area. I had Mayer complete the Beck's Anxiety and Depression Inventory, which indicated clinical symptoms. Gerould would speak with Mayer's brigade commander and ask that he be released from theater administratively.

Lowe came in for follow-up in the afternoon, further discussing his mother's death.

Sunday, April 8 was Easter, and only Mayer came by. I told him that he should be going to Kandahar Airfield for a WRC assessment. The next day, I learned that Mayer was scheduled for an interview at the WRC for the following Saturday. I hoped he could be PMR (patient movement request).

On April 10, I had one follow-up visit, Lowe. He had written more of what he wanted to say to his mother, about his difficulties and achievements in school.

Hargis dropped by to say, "I wanted you to know I'm one thousand times better. Considering where I was, you practically saved my life, really."

What music to my ears!

Mayer's commander came in and told me he was reluctant to send Mayer for the assessment with WRC. It wasn't clear to me if the commander thought Mayer was feigning illness. It was unlikely that Mayer would be accepted to the WRC, however, as the purpose of the center was to provide the necessary treatment so military personnel could return to duty. After months of pain, anxiety, and depression, Mayer wanted to be sent home. This would require the unit to assign an escort to go with Mayer back to the US. Later that day, I found out Mayer did travel to KAF for his assessment.

I heard Lopez and Villar had completed their mission to Kuhak and Terra Nova and landed in KAF. They were waiting for a flight back to CNS.

On Thursday, April 12, I had one new case, for military operational stress. One follow-up was the soldier from the previous October, concerned about his wife's health, and another was Nguyễn, who had just returned from R&R and was doing well—considering his suicide gesture with his handgun several months before.

Afterward I spoke with Spc. Alba. With deep-set, teary gray eyes, she cringed with embarrassment and said, "I'm pregnant." She was stressed and terrified about having to return to her COP and be ridiculed for having an affair with a married soldier.

Chaplain Williams, Maj. Stefani, and I recommended that Alba stay at CNS until her packet to leave theater was complete. That way she had daily access to Combat Stress. After speaking to the soldier's first sergeant, it was decided that Alba would return to her COP only for two days, to teach her replacement and pick up her gear.

I also met again with Lowe about his mother's death. By now he had written several pages. He hadn't decided what he wanted to do with them, bury the pages at her grave or save them.

On Saturday, as scheduled, Mayer was interviewed at WRC. He was deemed an increased risk of self-harm, and would be PMR from KAF as soon as possible. Later in the day, I received a surprise call on my cell phone from Mayer, thanking me for helping him get home.

Spc. Logan came in on Sunday. Her last visit had been a few months earlier, when she was worried about her son who was depressed and suicidal. This day she was emotionally distraught and had a quick thought of hurting herself, but she said she wouldn't. "Here, take my firing pin," she offered. I walked her over to the aid station. Maj. Stefani decided to MEDEVAC her to Role III.

Villar returned. Lopez would be back the next day—maybe.

On Monday I had three follow-ups (all for anger management) and one new one for marital issues. Sgt. James suspected that his wife, of barely one year, was cheating on him. He was 33 years old and she 22. Both were on their second marriages and both were in the army.

"I'll admit…I have thoughts, bad thoughts of hurting ANPs, cause they kill us, and they don't respect our help."

Frowning and rubbing the back of his neck, he moaned, "This deployment is ruining my perfect marriage."

I notified his commander of his homicidal ideation.

One soldier returned for anger management. He told me he was leaving the camp. His case had been ongoing since August 2011. A couple of hours later this soldier was MEDEVACed to KAF for a psychiatric evaluation because Maj. Stefani was leaving theater the next day and wouldn't be able to follow the case. Stefani's replacement, Col. Wash, was an OB/GYN, and was uncomfortable prescribing anti-anxiety and antidepressant medications. I hadn't realized how good I had it working with Stefani.

Alba would be leaving her combat outpost the next day, moving to FOB Walton instead of CNS as originally planned, since the alleged father of her baby was at CNS. Her unit was conducting an Article 134 investigation of adultery on the male soldier, which "prohibits conduct of a nature to bring discredit or conduct that is prejudicial to good order and discipline."

On the morning of April 18, Villar and I waited for two soldiers, both no-shows. So we brought our stuff to the Postal Rodeo to send things home. I wanted to send clients' records to Garden Grove, California, as requested by HQ, but this postal service couldn't process registered mail. So I instead had to load the box of records onto a helicopter heading for KAF to be picked up by HQ. I was glad when the entire running around was over, as the weather was unpleasantly hot and windless.

Around 2100 hours, while I was at the aid station, I received a call to see Pvt. Weston in my office. There I met a young man barely old enough to shave, who was afraid he might act impulsively to harm himself and others. He was suffering from military operational stress. His weapon had been taken away and he had been assigned a battle buddy. Weston had been in theater for two months and had a history of depression. I escorted him back to the aid station to begin the process of sending him home.

226 The Hidden War

The next day, Hargis called and asked to see me. He came in at 1100 hours. He'd had violent thoughts of hurting himself. Hargis handed me his dog-eared journal.

"Look, I wrote a suicide letter for my wife, and here's a map showing exactly how to get to her place."

No matter what rational explanation I offered, that suicide wasn't the answer, that things weren't as dire as he believed, Hargis countered it with his determined, depressed point of view. Apparently, he'd had a huge argument with his wife on April 16. This was the day he had written the suicide note to his wife. I had no choice but to take his side arm and notify his commander. The commander came to my office.

"Come on, Hargis, finish the tour," he urged. "We're just a few weeks out. You're going to leave the unit short-handed."

The persuasion was unsuccessful, however, so Hargis, his escort, and I went to the aid station. He was immediately MEDEVACed to KAF.

I guess I did save his life, after all.

It was Friday morning when Sgt. O'Reilly came in, seen once before for surviving an abusive childhood. She stood before me, lean and fit, with short brown bangs.

"I need to talk to someone. I'm on edge all the time…I need some space to myself…or…or…I'll crack."

Her recent attitude had been quiet, not the usually motivated soldier. We talked and reviewed tapping. She'd stay overnight at CNS for a bit of R&R and would be back in the clinic the following morning.

One new case was a soldier reporting nightmares and walking in his sleep, probably due to the attack at his PSS last August. After one round of tapping for his anxiety, he called it "super dope," feeling an emotional discharge.

On Saturday, O'Reilly came back and said, "Since I've been away from unit, where I help others, I realized that I have my own problems."

Tearful, with a quaking voice, she continued, "I think it's time for me to get some help."

"How would you like to go to WRC?" I explained that WRC was a one-stop center at KAF that focused on soldiers' physical, mental, and spiritual care so that they could return to duty and finish their tour.

With strong eye contact, she agreed to go.

Sunday, April 22 brought new faces to the camp—a welcome sight. The new arrivals were the replacements of units "ripping out." I was feeling melancholy, however. People that I'd come to appreciate and built a working relationship with since summer were now leaving or had already left. New relationships needed to form again, even as I prepared to leave theater in three weeks.

Lopez finally made it back to CNS.

O'Reilly came by on Monday, still wondering what it would be like at WRC. I reassured her about the WRC goals. She was scheduled to go to KAF that day.

"I told my family that I was finally getting help," she said.

I sensed a feeling of peace in her. The worst part was over: telling someone about her abuse for the first time.

"I didn't think those words would ever pass through my lips," she said.

From then on, she felt it would be easier.

HQ told us that we had to take our Army Physical Fitness Test (APFT) at CNS rather than at KAF as planned, as the completed records were required before flights were set to Manas. I was ready, but Lopez wanted a few more days to prepare.

On Tuesday, Lt. Col. Guilmartin, commanding officer of the 385th Military Police Battalion, came by our office and presented Lopez and me with a framed Certificate of Appreciation—nice!

The days were passing slowly. As it got closer to leaving, time seemed to stand still. I was more than ready to go home.

I had to squeeze in my APFT test on Thursday, April 26, because the office was busy. We had five cases, three of which were new. The first soldier came in anxious about flying home. The second soldier had just found out that his wife had had a miscarriage. He was troubled and unable to focus on his job. Although he had only been at CNS for nine days, it would be a long nine-month deployment. So I suggested that he go home on an emergency leave, once his wife's doctor could provide documentation to his command. The third new case was an evaluation as to whether the soldier was fit enough to go to another FOB, after the PSS-1 attack. Although receiving support from the chaplain, the soldier wasn't mission capable, dealing with depression and chain-of-command issues. Two follow-up cases were for sleep hygiene and for an Article 15 (late for guard duty).

No soldiers came in on Friday, so we watched a movie, *Ninja Assassin*. My APFT walk had made me more tired than I had expected. My left knee wasn't feeling strong either; it had buckled on me a couple of times. But I wore my knee brace and won my Ping-Pong match.

On Saturday, there were again no soldiers, but there was an attack nearby in which Col. Hicks was shot in the arm. Apparently, he was the liaison for the Kandahar Governor and the assassins were aiming at the governor. Fortunately, no soldiers were killed.

Lopez decided to take his APFT test and, naturally, he passed. In the evening, there was an attack at a nearby police substation, which was within earshot of CNS. No one was hurt.

Sunday saw just one soldier for sleep issues, referred by Col. Wash at the aid station, who also had a problem with sleep. I taught the colonel tapping.

"Even though my mind is racing, I choose to stop it. I choose to be pleasantly drowsy, to have pleasant dreams, to sleep throughout the night, to be recharged, and be ready for the day's challenge."

He was skeptical, but the following day he said he'd had a good night's sleep.

On the last day of the month, with only two more Mondays in country (I hoped), HQ emailed us the dates that our replacements would arrive at CNS, when we would travel to KAF, and, finally, when we would return to the States. So close to the end of the tour, each day was dragging by.

In the office, I had one last follow-up case for anger management and two new cases: anger, and a female soldier concerned about going home because her husband had suffered from PTSD for the previous six years. She didn't understand how to deal with his invisible wounds. Her husband believed talking to a counselor was a waste of time.

Wayne couldn't give us Ping-Pong instruction that night. He just found out that his mother had died suddenly, and he would be leaving for home immediately. We offered our condolences.

The Handoff

On May 1, Lopez and I mailed the last few boxes home. It had been a challenge to figure out what we wouldn't need, so that we could carry the lightest and the fewest bags when we redeployed.

I completed the last peer review for Maj. Diaz and prepared hand receipts for office equipment, M-16 ammo, and magazine clips from HQ to CNS to 1972nd. The 1972nd was our replacement team from Joint Base Lewis-McChord, Washington.

I also had two follow-up cases: one last session with Lowe, and Nguyễn, who came in for his weekly safety check. I discussed with him his possible diagnosis of bipolar disorder, being on the right medication, and staying on it. Unfortunately, if he did have bipolar disorder, he wouldn't be deployable in the future.

When I checked my email on May 3, I was shocked to read that Sgt. Major Schumacher, of 113th CSC, had had a heart attack the night before. He was in the ICU and awaiting a flight to a higher level of care. Schumacher was just two weeks shy of completing his mission—getting everyone in our unit home.

After work, Lopez and I played Ping-Pong as usual, to get ready for the next day's tournament. Between games, while I was resting, a soldier walked up to me and said he wanted to give me a hug. He had met with me about four months earlier and I had taught him tapping. He said that since then, due to using it from time to time, he was "smooth and calm." The soldier didn't embrace me, since he was sweaty from working out with weights, but we shook hands warmly. This was an unexpected and gratifying moment.

Lopez and I started to clean the office on Friday, May 4. Our replacement team had arrived in KAF. They would stay there two to three days for mandatory briefings before heading to CNS.

Lopez and I had only one follow-up case that day, Spc. Mark. He shared that he had been angry for the previous six years, since his father had died unexpectedly, perhaps from a heart attack. They'd had a close relationship.

In the Ping-Pong tournament, I made it to the third round: a bye in the first, a win in the second, and two close games in the third. But then I lost. I stayed and watched the rest of the matches.

The camp scheduled a battle drill on Saturday. We settled into our IOTV and helmet, and reported to the aid station. Then we stood around for an hour until the all-clear signal.

Our BH replacement team—1st Lt. Busse and Cpl. Thompson—arrived at 0700 hours on May 7. This was the corporal's second deployment, so she was confident and knowledgeable. The lieutenant had only been in the army for a year and half, but he was an experienced psychologist. The team was energetic and motivated.

Of two new cases that day (for sleep and stress), the second was much more serious. Spc. Ramon was very angry and scared.

"I thought I was dreaming about shooting my sergeant, but I wasn't dreaming. I found myself in his tent... a gun in my hand. I ran out before anything happened."

This was actually a dissociative episode. There was no option but to send him home.

PSS-10 called requesting Combat Stress Control (CSC) to come there for unresolved issues from an attack approximately one month earlier. Maybe the replacement team would go instead.

With just seven more days at CNS, I felt a sense of relief. The end of the tour had almost arrived. I was practiced, confident, and knowledgeable about what to do around the camp, and familiar with many people and their jobs. At the same time, I had to introduce myself to the new soldiers and leaders in the camp, to let them know that Combat Stress Control exists. But I was also sad, realizing that I'd never again see so many people I had met: civilians, soldiers, merchants, and local Afghans.

Lopez and I spent the bulk of the day with the replacement team. We began the right seat/left seat (LS/RS) training and helped set up their computer accounts. The new team's commander was aware of the PSS-10 request for a CSC team. Lopez and I wouldn't be going outside the wire so close to going home.

On Wednesday, May 9, we completed the LS/RS training with the replacement team and accompanied them to the chapel, MWRs, EO/Sexual Assault office, and the Postal Rodeo. The mission to PSS-10 was approved, but the team was awaiting information required by the 1972nd colonel before they could push out.

I had only one follow-up case: Spc. Mark. With a satisfied smile, he told me he did write a letter to his late father, sharing thoughts and feelings he had embraced for a long time.

At 2000 hours, the new CSC team, Lopez, and I met with Lt. Col. Cook and Veneklasen. We introduced the new team, and the lieutenant colonel and command sergeant major awarded Lopez and me the brigade and battalion coins. They acknowledged and appreciated CSC's service during the deployment.

On Thursday, a new case came in, Sgt. Rosen. He asked for me, but I referred the case to the new team. Cpl. Thompson did the initial intake. The soldier shared that for the last 10 months his job had been dealing with dead detainees, obtaining their DNA. This job had been difficult, but he didn't want to complain. Now that he was days from going home, he wanted to document his experience. Lt. Busse discussed sleep hygiene and encouraged the soldier to go to the VA for follow-up care. My original intent wasn't to get involved, but as the sergeant wasn't staying in theater, I didn't want him to go home with the thoughts and smell of death.

"What else is on your mind, Sergeant?" I asked.

"It's been awhile. It's far back in my mind, but I was bullied when I was a kid because I had crooked teeth. It bothers me still." So I taught him tapping. We tapped for "Death. Poor sleep. Bullied."

Later, Col. Wash asked if I had seen Sgt. Rosen. I hadn't known he had referred the soldier, so I was glad I did work with him.

Everyone (the 1972nd and the 113th) was present for a combined conference call on Friday. The new team's mission to PSS-10 was postponed until Saturday. There were no clients all day, so time seemed to stand still.

There were no clients on Saturday either. The soldiers redeploying didn't need to come in, and the new soldiers didn't even know there was a Combat Stress Control office at CNS.

Lopez and I used the time to clean our rifles, as there would be an inspection when we got to KAF. It was strange, looking around the camp and recognizing only a few faces. The majority were new soldiers who would be there for the following nine months.

Vernes, the Bosnian Ping-Pong instructor, came by our office and presented Lopez and me each a farewell gift, black and brown-checkered headscarves—so thoughtful of him.

On Sunday morning the new team went off to PSS-10, and probably wouldn't return until Monday. It was another quiet day in the office. Some officers came in to show the Combat Stress Control office to their replacements.

The camp ran another battle drill: the third one within two weeks. Lopez and I hid in our office for an hour until the all-clear sign.

The new team returned from their mission at 0500 hours on Monday.

It was the last full day for me—I couldn't believe it!

The 113th CSC HQ forwarded our statistics for the previous 11 months:

- Contacts outside office: 1,295 soldiers
- New clients: 199 soldiers
- Follow-ups: 375 soldiers
- Traumatic Event Management: 48 groups
- Prevention classes: 39

I hoped that my team had made an impact in easing soldiers' emotional pain. If so, it was well worth our many sacrifices. My service had given me a sense of purpose and fulfillment.

I went up to the balcony to take one last look at the towering coarse mountains. They were difficult to see; the brown sky was already hazy with the heat of the day.

I was ready to leave the balcony when a tall, tired-looking soldier approached me. I recognized him, Spc. Allen, a medic.

"Ma'am, do you have a minute?"

"Of course. Let's sit down."

We pulled out two wooden chairs and sat around the table.

"I'm going home soon…really happy to see my wife and kids again… but I'm not looking forward to seeing the family members of the soldiers I've lost…"

"What do you mean?"

"Before we left for Afghanistan, I promised the family members that I'd bring everyone home…but I failed."

"How many died?"

"Two…"

"Did you to talk to the brigade surgeon about the losses?"

"Yeah. He said, 'One third we treat would make it, but one third we treat would die. And the other third would die because medical care cannot be given.'"

"How did the soldiers die?"

"Umm…one was shot in the head, and the other died from an IED."

"Where you there?"

"Only one…the one that was shot in the head. When I got to him…I knew he was dead. The other one died instantly when he stepped on a buried roadside bomb. I heard the confirmation over the radio. I cried, I cried a lot."

"You feel responsible?"

"Yeah, I failed...I can't be forgiven..."

He was looking down at his empty hands.

"You mentioned that one third would die because medical care cannot be given. Could you have provided life-saving procedures to these soldiers?"

"No...no...I know logically I didn't do anything wrong. They were mortal injuries. I couldn't do anything."

"But you feel you can't be forgiven?"

"Yeah."

"That's a heavy burden you're carrying. You're angry with yourself, you're sad. You have 'what ifs'...if only they didn't go out on their missions. But they were doing their jobs, and unfortunately, war is unpredictable."

"Yeah, it sucks."

He looked down at the weather-aged wood table and with his fingers traced the grain pattern.

"Maybe one day you'll forgive yourself, unload the weight, when you're ready, so that you can move forward. For now, maybe not forgiving yourself allows you to focus on being a better medic, perhaps even pursue a medical degree, so that you can help people."

"Maybe..."

"When you get back home, get some counseling to help sort out your feelings. I'm sure you want to enjoy your time with your family, friends, and this burden will interfere with that. There was nothing you could have done."

"Yeah...I know...thank you for your time, Ma'am."

"Be well and safe travels."

I spent the rest of the day packing and throwing things away. I brought useful items to the women's latrine, where other women could take them. Show time was the next morning at 0540 hours. The bird wouldn't arrive until 0710 hours and wouldn't get to KAF until 0805, making several stops before KAF. As it would be an early start the next day, I dragged my bursting duffle bag to the office after dinner, because it was closer to the landing zone. To my surprise, when I picked up my bag in my room, I caught sight of some rather fresh mouse droppings on the carpet. I guessed my mouse had visited me often, after all.

Full Circle at KAF

On Tuesday, May 15, Lopez and I got out of CNS as scheduled. Vernes saw us off at the landing zone. Ramirez met us at KAF and drove us to the transient tents. The place was crammed with military personnel coming in or waiting to go out of KAF. I saw some 113th women and went to breakfast with them, and then off to Role II, 113th HQ, where we had our daily unit debriefings. I returned to shower. It was 110 degrees.

In the evening, I attended the end of the tour awards for five members of my unit who were leaving theater early to Conus Replacement Center at Fort Benning, Georgia. The rest of us were scheduled to stay until May 19.

We had weapon inspection that afternoon. I had to go back four times before mine was deemed clean enough. It was strange to see so many soldiers from Camp Nathan Smith there, like seeing old friends. Many had departed days before I had, but they were still at KAF. We were scheduled to leave in three days. I was keeping my fingers crossed.

I slept 11 hours that night, even with jets roaring overhead. It was finally sinking in that I was no longer responsible for running a CSC office and caring for soldiers. I'd worked every day since coming into theater, at times taking a few hours off, but always feeling the need to be in the office. I realized that I was exhausted.

Thursday was the TOA (Transfer of Authority) ceremony rehearsal, then the official TOA ceremony to the 1972nd CSC, and the End of Tour award. At last, we were officially done! I was awarded the NATO medal, the Afghanistan Campaign medal, and the Bronze Star for Meritorious Service medal. Our replacement company now controlled the WRC. My unit was relieved of that responsibility—thank goodness. I hated the long, hot, dusty walk from the transient tent. My uniform blouse constantly clung to my damp back.

I'd come full circle at KAF. When I first arrived at the base, I was nervous, unsure, and hated the blinding heat. And now I was tired, but confident in my abilities as an army psychologist, and relieved that my job was done, though I still hated the desert.

Sunset at KAF.

We had a meeting on Friday afternoon, regarding what to pack and to carry to Manas the next day. But a few hours after the meeting, we found out we wouldn't leave until Monday. Another three nights at KAF—yuck! The good news was that now we'd stop in Qatar and not Manas. Qatar was rumored to be quite plush. And, supposedly, this wouldn't change our arrival time to Fort Dix, New Jersey. But we'd see.

On Saturday, I played Ping-Pong with the guys from 113th. I stood my own. I was just glad to do something physical. I could only do so much reading and watching movies on my computer. Later, I went to dinner with Staff Sgt. Diaz, Sgt. Lopez, Sgt. Ramirez, and Capt. Gillespie. I was comfortable with these guys—they were like brothers to me.

Though we were scheduled to leave KAF Monday, we didn't. We boarded a bus and went to the air terminal but were told our flight was canceled. Soaked with sweat, I was fuming, as I had to carry and drag everything back to the tent and remake my bunk bed.

Three days later, on Thursday, May 24, on our fifth attempt to get out of KAF, we finally succeeded. While waiting at the terminal, there was a massive explosion within 25 yards of us. I ducked down and felt the aftershocks. Looking up through the window, I saw a cloud of dust and debris swirling high in the air. What a send-off! We had to move from the second floor to the ground floor, where we waited for the all-clear, which came about 45 minutes later.

I thought the blast would cancel our flight. But, with relief, we flew out on a jam-packed C-130 plane. Once the pilot said we were out of Afghanistan air space, everyone loudly cheered and clapped. I took a big breath, noticing an unexpected release of tension. Lurking in the background daily had always been the imminent threat of death. I had survived.

Four and an half hours later, we arrived in Qatar.

Back in the US

After six hours in Qatar, we were able to fly to Aviano Air Force Base in Italy (on a Boeing 747 Atlas Airline), then to Ramstein Air Base in Germany, and then finally to Baltimore-Washington International Airport, an approximately eight-hour flight. After a three-hour bus ride, we arrived at last at Fort Dix in New Jersey.

I was glad to see a healthy looking Sgt. Maj. Schumacher standing to welcome us off the bus. I didn't go to sleep until 0330 hours, after we turned in our weapons and gas masks and sat through a welcome briefing. Then I had to wake up at 0600 hours for the first of our many mandatory meetings. No rest for the weary!

Friday was a full day at Fort Dix, with lots of assemblies for medical, financial, dental, legal, chaplaincy, Veterans Affairs, and reintegration.

Col. Bluett, Lt. Col. Urbanec, Command Sgt. Maj. Word, and Capt. Moore from 2D MED Brigade came to speak to us on Saturday, congratulating us on a successful mission. We had another full day of gatherings similar to the day before, adding TriCare information. I could see why soldiers were in a hurry to leave. As important as the briefings were, they were repetitive and some were extremely boring. But this afforded us time to sit and exchange our deployment experiences, everyone with a different story.

On Sunday, the 113th CSC was treated to a barbecue. Even with an hour-long thunderstorm, it was an enjoyable time: volleyball, horseshoes, swimming, basketball, and a dunking tank—normal American activities to ease us back into our lives. As I scanned the members of 113th, I realized each one had been involved in challenging, uplifting, and difficult phases in deployment. I hoped each of us could process the negative experiences, take the lessons learned, and move through them.

On Monday, a one-star general came to welcome us home. The rest of the day was free time. In the evening, I played Ping-Pong with some of the guys.

Tuesday was our first full day of going through Solider Readiness Processing Center. I had my blood drawn for HIV and cholesterol, and an examination for dental, vision, and hearing. Without my uniform and boots, my weight was 100 pounds. I also had a medical appointment for having been exposed to mold. I wanted this documented in case I had problems with my lungs down the road. I scheduled a behavioral health appointment for the next day. This time, I would be the client.

The following day, I went to Dr. Steel's office. A psychologist, she was friendly, but there was so much required documentation. She was focused on her computer screen more than on me, but at least I had a chance to talk about the attack and suicide on base before going home. My stay in Afghanistan had created a time stamp that would never be erased—physiologically and psychologically.

On the last day of May, we finally turned in our IOTV (body armor) and ceramic plates, and three-day multi-cam assault pack. I wanted to keep mine, as a keepsake, but instead I had to buy a backpack for the trip home. Most everything else was sent home or to the 113th unit in Garden Grove, California. We did our finance paperwork for accrued and transitional leave. My end of active duty was now July 10, 2012.

We completed the DD214, discharge paper from active duty, checked our end of the tour awards, and received our Veterans Affairs card, entitling us to medical care for service-related injuries for the next five years. Now it was just waiting to receive our flight time to go home, which for me turned out to be the following day.

Home

On Saturday, June 2, after a one-hour bus ride to Philadelphia Airport, and waiting for five hours for my flight, I boarded my flight to SFO. Five and a half hours later, I landed in San Francisco. I couldn't believe that this moment had finally arrived. I was home!

Rob picked me up. We kissed and shared a long heartfelt hug. The first thing I wanted was Chinese food. Unfortunately, there wasn't any parking near the restaurant, so we ordered to go. At last, arriving home and eating some long-awaited delicious food, I was truly happy!

My adjustment to being back lasted a long time, however. In mid-July, I was still feeling like a stranger in my own home. While I was away, Rob, with contractors' assistance, had remodeled the kitchen and built an entertainment center. I didn't understand how to use the new microwave oven or dishwasher or even turn on the flat screen television. All the clothes in my closet overwhelmed me. It took me nearly five minutes to select a hand towel from the linen closet. This reminded me of the movie *The Hurt Locker* when the soldier played by Jeremy Renner returned from deployment and couldn't decide what box of cereal to buy at the supermarket.

I enjoyed seeing my family and friends.

I enjoyed the cool, crisp, foggy air against my skin.

I enjoyed eating my favorite foods again. The first few bites were an endorphin rush, with all my taste buds awakened and eager for more flavors.

I enjoyed sniffing different fragrances of freshly cut lawns, flowers, soaps, body lotions, and shampoos.

I enjoyed wearing vibrant new clothes and shoes.

I listened to and soaked up the quietness.

I especially enjoyed, in the middle of the night, the clean bathroom just seven steps from by bed!

I was concerned the first time I got behind the wheel of my car, as I hadn't driven in so long, but it came back easily. What was scary was my fast and reckless driving! I'd changed. I had always been a considerate and careful driver. I'd gleaned that many redeploying soldiers seek out activities that are daring and filled with adrenaline. Perhaps being on constant edge when in country, in an environment of prolonged unknown danger, with the muscles primed for flight or fight, the body develops a need for the adrenaline rush. I'd also noticed that I was easily startled by loud and unexpected noises. I was especially triggered by the thumping sound of traffic and news helicopters flying over the city. I was alarmed when people were behind me, impatient in grocery store lines. And, at times, without reason, I was irritable.

I tapped to ease my anxiety and, though it was helpful, my jumpiness didn't stay away. Perhaps I was too close and couldn't see my problem objectively. Perhaps I couldn't or wouldn't allow myself to delve into the specific details. Perhaps I didn't tap enough. Was I suffering from PTSD? How could I be when others soldiers had it much worse? How could I have it when I provided care for others? Did hearing their horrendous experiences cause my PTSD?

After two and a half years of denial, I finally admitted to myself that I couldn't control my angst, hypervigilance, and tearfulness. It was affecting my work. I sought treatment, and was diagnosed with PTSD. I don't believe one incident caused my PTSD, but the constant fear and frequent attacks in Afghanistan as well as listening in my office to veterans' combat experiences triggered flashbacks.

Eventually, with the passage of many more months in the safety of familiar surroundings, my uneasiness lessened. During my adjustment, I was grateful for Rob's patience, support, and understanding.

Sometimes it felt as though I had just woken up from a coma, or recently recovered my memory after a period of amnesia. Many things were familiar, though, in fact as if nothing had changed, like my desk, items in my drawers, people in my neighborhood. I'd returned to helping with the youth fencing program. Many of the younger students I'd never seen. The older students had grown; some were now taller than I. Rob's lessons had changed while I continued to teach the old stuff.

My 11 months in Afghanistan gradually became a distant memory, a dream. I had to remind myself that I had been there, where I believed time stood still. Nevertheless, all the experiences and memories of deployment were timeless. On the other hand, the time since arriving home was flying by. I find the experience of time and the perception of time a conundrum.

After several months at home, I returned to my Army Reserve unit, 2D Medical Brigade, in San Pablo, California. There were many new faces, and a few I recognized. I had to admit I walked around proudly, with my combat badge on my uniform. I was no longer just a reservist, but a combat veteran. I had learned a great deal about how to run a combat operational stress control office and how to manage the many issues that soldiers face.

My Mandatory Retirement Date had been approved and extended for two more years with the Army Reserve, which would require one weekend drill a month, two weeks of annual training a year, and the possibility of deployment again until December 31, 2014. With my retention bonus, I bought an army dress-blue uniform, not realizing how seldom I'd need to wear it.

I applied for unemployment insurance benefits with the Employment Development Department (EDD). With the benefits, I had to report that I was actively seeking work. I updated my résumé and went to the Human Resource department of the San Francisco Veterans Affairs Medical Center. Although I didn't receive a call from them, I did meet with a clinical social worker employed there, a referral from Col. Rabb.

I discovered that the VA only authorizes two therapeutic techniques to deal with PTSD: prolonged exposure (PE) and cognitive processing. Though familiar with both, I would use neither, since both require the veteran to reexperience the trauma(s) again and again. This is extremely painful. One veteran gave a telling summary of how he and others experienced PE: "It tore off my scab, but the wound was still there, rotting, and then the sessions were over. I was told I was better, but I wasn't."

I wouldn't have fared well at the San Francisco VA Medical Center. The previous year had convinced me more than ever that I would primarily use EFT (tapping) with veterans.

After just one round of tapping, soldiers were noticeably relieved and calmer. Soon thereafter, soldiers added more details about their problems or expressed issues that they had kept to themselves for years. Feeling the positive profound result, it was then easy to encourage soldiers to learn how to tap, something they could do on their own in a matter of minutes in order to release the past, current, or anticipated problems— "preemptive tapping," as one soldier called it. The ease of learning and applying the tapping technique was an important element of EFT, because I often met with a soldier just once.

A week after a mandatory meeting with a job service representative at the EDD, I walked over to the nearby SF Vet Center. I handed my résumé to the office manager and asked who would be reviewing it. The team leader, Lance, spoke to me and said apologetically that there was no opening. I told him I understood, but added that I hoped I would be considered if a position opened up.

Within a week, Lance called me saying that vet centers had a new program to hire OEF (Operation Enduring Freedom) veterans, and asked if I was interested in interviewing for a position as a readjustment counselor. I enthusiastically said yes. I went back to the Vet Center and met with Lance and a clinical psychologist. Soon after the interview, I was offered the position. And I was welcome to use EFT.

After waiting six months to clear all the hiring requirements, I started my job at the center in March 2013. My experiences in Afghanistan gave me credibility: a personal understanding of tragic deaths, physical and psychological injuries due to war, and the constant angst soldiers must shove aside in order to complete the mission.

The San Francisco County Veterans Service Office refers veterans to the center for PTSD evaluations and possible treatment. These veterans are in the process of submitting a service-connected disability claim with the Department of Veterans Affairs. The disability claim is for injuries that were incurred in or aggravated during their military service, such as physical conditions and/or mental health conditions.

I saw few veterans from Iraq and Afghanistan. More Vietnam veterans than those from the current wars are referred. They were in an unpopular war, often hiding their involvement, feeling proud of their service yet feeling they had done something wrong. Mental health services hardly existed when they returned home. They are now in their late 60s and early 70s. Since they were combat veterans, the counseling services are free, for individual and group sessions. I can meet with them as often as they find it helpful.

Since returning home, many Vietnam veterans have silently suffered from PTSD, depression, or anxiety disorders resulting in years of alcohol/drug abuse, failed marriages, and terminations of employment. This is the first time they're seeking help since education, jobs, and relationships are no longer a distraction for them. What has surfaced is their short-tempered, isolating behaviors, and nightmares.

Vietnam veterans often declare: "I was fine all these years. Shit! Why am I so angry all the time? I don't like family gatherings. I cry easily now when I think back on the war. Why am I so weak? How could it be from Vietnam? It was 45 years ago!"

As I work with Vietnam veterans, my treatment of choice continues to be EFT. Once there is a rapport, I provide veterans an introduction to the technique. Sometimes I focus on their physical pain. This is less threatening for them than to confess their emotional distress. Relief is often rapid. Veterans are in disbelief, but this gives them hope after years of pain. They return for more sessions.

For others, I have them tap on specific events, memories that continue to haunt them: their first kill, dreaded missions, or their helplessness in watching their battle buddies die.

I prefer EFT because once they've used this simple technique they can use it anywhere, anytime. For example, they can tap in their car while stuck in traffic, or they can tap while in a noisy, crowded shopping mall. They notice an immediate quietness in their mind and body. Whether they believe in the technique or not, they often feel a lowering of stress and an increase in calmness—enough to take the edge off. Enough to walk away, to take a few deep breaths, to realize getting into an altercation isn't worth it.

My hope when working with Vietnam veterans is for them to encourage veterans from Iraq and Afghanistan to seek help sooner rather than later. Many younger veterans are busy getting a degree, finding the perfect job and the perfect mate. In the meantime, they are ignoring or locking away their emotional pain, just as the Vietnam vets once did. But PTSD continues to fester in the mind and body. And when the body's energy can no longer contain it, symptoms will erupt and there follows a realization that something is wrong.

Researcher Bessel van der Kolk, MD, explains the mechanisms of trauma in his book *The Body Keeps the Score: Brain, Mind, and Body in the Healing of Trauma*. Van der Kolk asserts that trauma literally rearranges the brain's wiring. Most important, the book presents innovative techniques such as neurofeedback and EFT as methods for reprogramming the brain and reclaiming lives in the process.

I appreciate the opportunity to help heal the lives of the combat veterans I work with: veterans from World War II, the Korean War, the Vietnam War, the Gulf War, Iraq, and Afghanistan. For years, many of these veterans have suffered traumas that have been frozen in time. They suffered silently, unable to share with anyone who wasn't there. It remained frozen until their health started to deteriorate, or alcohol or drugs no longer numbed their feelings or erased their horrid memories. Traumas are not just hardships to overcome, however. They can be transformative. There is no doubt that soldiers are different after a war. Initially, the changes are reflected in negative symptoms of rage, nightmares, hypervigilance, anxiousness, or depression. They struggle, and after enduring the struggle, many start to heal. They learn to integrate the past with their new life, which gives them strength, wisdom, and joy. This resilience gives a new purpose of who they want to be, what they want to fight for, and the pursuit of a meaningful career. This is called posttraumatic growth.

———————

On November 2, 2014, at 1725 hours, I stood at attention for my last formation as a member of the US Army Reserve. Although I was interested in continuing my service, the army was unwilling to offer me, at 62 years old, another extension, feeling it was time for me to go. I saluted and watched the lowering of the US flag. I was called up by the first sergeant, who announced to 2D Medical Brigade that I was leaving after nearly five years of service.

In a relatively short amount of time, I'd gained an important perspective on the army and I'd met many selfless, exceptionally brave men and women. I am honored to have served them and to have served with them.

EFT at the SF Vet Center

As of October 2017, I've seen approximately 782 clients at the SF Vet Center (since March 2013) in more than 3,076 visits that include individual, couple, and group sessions.

Life is difficult after deployment. The Vet Center Program was established by Congress in 1979 out of the recognition that a significant number of Vietnam era vets were still experiencing readjustment problems. Currently, there are 300 Vet Centers across the country, all community based and part of the US Department of Veterans Affairs. Vet Centers provide a broad range of counseling, outreach, and referral services to combat veterans and their families. Services for a veteran may include individual and group counseling in areas such as major depression, anxiety, and PTSD, alcohol and drug assessment, and suicide prevention referrals. All services are free of cost.

Approximately 80% of the combat veterans I see at the SF Vet Center suffer from Complex PTSD due to repetitive and prolonged trauma in a war zone. After completing the initial assessment, military history, cooperative treatment planning, and providing education and information about psychological trauma, I use EFT, about 90% of the time. Tailored to veterans' needs, EFT is a safe, less intrusive technique than the standard prolonged and cognitive processing exposure methods. Veterans do not need to say much when they tap, as their body is emotionally charged with certain images, smells, sounds, and feelings—all aspects of their stored trauma. Tapping for one or two minutes on acupoints allows negative sensations to be released, to be processed out of the body. From my experience, 80% to 90% of the time, veterans will experience some relief after the initial EFT session. Most veterans are in disbelief, curious, and willing to use tapping between sessions for self-care. I validate their courage to use an unfamiliar but quick and effective technique.

As sessions continue, veterans disclose more traumatic events, some from the war, some from their childhood. Along with trauma education, I also teach EFT to the veteran's spouse or partner. Often the partner feels it is his/her responsibility to "fix" the veteran. But I would like veterans to take ownership and do the work: to use tapping to alleviate their anxiety, to manage their stress. Partners are advised to say, "Tap," when veterans are getting annoyed or angry.

No one technique is successful for everyone; often it's a combination of techniques. Along with EFT, I use mindfulness and grounding techniques (50% to 70% of the time) to help veterans be more in the present. I may also use EMDR (10% to 20% of the time) for trauma work. Not having conducted a research study, of all the veterans I've treated, I estimate that 60% to 80% of the issues are resolved within six to 10 sessions. Their past traumas are no longer their center of focus. Instead I have conversations about their new hobbies, new friends, going to school, or starting a new job. There is a sense of recovery and return to balance of the mind, body, and spirit.

Case Study: Iraq Combat Veteran

Tony, a veteran of three deployments, came in with issues of hypervigilance, nightmares, anger, and loss of closeness to family and friends. As an officer, he blamed himself for the deaths of two civilian interpreters when his six-truck convoy was ambushed in Iraq. Ultimately, he was able to direct the rest of his team out of the kill zone and return safely to a nearby base.

Tony chose to use EFT to release his second-guessing, guilt, and anger. His SUD score was a 10 of 10. During the first round, he was angry, questioning every decisive action he made. "Even though everything happened so fast, I am a good solider."

After tapping on the acupoints, saying, "Did I make the right decision?" his SUD score was a 7.

We continued: "Even though I'm not sure I did everything I could, I am a good soldier." After the second round, he offered more descriptions of his surroundings, the directions of the attacking insurgents, and the urgency to return fire.

After tapping on the acupoints, saying, "I'm not sure. Too much to consider," his SUD score was a 4.

We continued: "Even though I shouldn't have lost any lives under my command, I did the best I could." We tapped on the acupoints, saying, "Lost lives. Did the best I could."

After the third round, Tony took a deep breath and was able to analyze calmly his decisions made during and after the attack. With visible relief, he said, "It wasn't my fault. My actions were correct. I followed the operating procedures. It could have been worse." Unfortunately, the interpreters had panicked and run from the truck's protective cover. At the end, Tony's SUD score was a 0.

Months later, he returned to school. He made friends with his classmates, went out to dinner with them, and gladly shared a few of his amusing military stories with them. At his last session, he said, "I have a new feeling. I'm more grounded and not as distracted."

Case Study: Wife of a Veteran

Madeline came in because she was arguing frequently with her husband of nine years. She had a history of drug abuse, starting in her teen years. She tearfully reported a trauma when she was 6 years old: She witnessed her father firing a handgun that wounded her mother.

She was willing to try EFT and acknowledged her sadness, helplessness, and fearfulness. Her SUD score was a 10 of 10.

"Even though I knew what my father was going to do, I was only a child."

"Even though I should have yelled so my mother was warned, I was only a child."

"Even though I did nothing, I was so scared, I was only a child."

Tapping on the acupoints on the top of her head, face, and torso, she said the words "Helpless. Responsible. Scared."

After crying and releasing her guilt, she said, "I was only 6 years old. They were the adults." She added that although her mother was injured, she was able to grab Madeline and run to the neighbor's home for help.

Wiping away her tears, she said, "I can't believe it. I've been carrying this burden around for years, and now it's gone!"

Two weeks later, Madeline came in and said, "Since we last met, we are arguing less. In fact, my husband and I are spending more time together, going for walks, and babysitting our nieces and nephews. We're just happier."

———————

For many veterans, the SF Vet Center has become a safe place for them to talk. Previously, they hadn't been able to share their disturbing memories with anyone, not wanting to concede to any "mental problems." Moreover, specifically for Vietnam veterans, a group session that I facilitate two times a month has become their family. They have a place to express their horror, anger, guilt, sadness, and even funny moments to a fellowship of "brothers." I am always in awe at how supportive each member is to the others, even in silence, just to be present and witness a "brother's" healing journey.

About the Author

Connie Louie-Handelman worked for the Department of Veterans Affairs at the San Francisco Vet Center as a readjustment psychologist from March 2013 to March 2018. Connie served in the US Army Reserve from March 12, 2010, to February 1, 2015. She was on active duty from May 29, 2011, to July 10, 2012. She is the coauthor of two fencing books with her husband, Rob Handelman, DC, Maître d'Armes.

Acknowledgments

First and foremost, I want to thank my husband, Rob, for his constant support in all my endeavors.

I am so grateful to family and friends who sent letters and delectable and delightful care packages.

I want to thank Harriett Jernigan, PhD, Sandra Wortzel, and Randy Rosenthal for their excellent feedback in early stages of this project, and Stephanie Marohn, my editor, for her helpful, thoughtful suggestions and meticulous copyediting.

I want to extend a special thank you to the many kindhearted professional soldiers and civilians I met at Camp Nathan Smith. You significantly eased my time in Afghanistan.

An enormous thank you goes to Col. David Rabb, 113th CSC commander, for your leadership, spirit, and positive can-do attitude.

My gratitude goes to Gary Craig, EFT founder, and Dawson Church, PhD, for being my teachers, helping me mend soldiers' lives.

Finally, my heartfelt appreciation to all you courageous and resilient veterans who allowed me into your lives and taught me to be a better therapist.